AMERICA'S ROLE IN NATION-BUILDING

FROM GERMANY TO IRAQ

James Dobbins, John G. McGinn, Keith Crane
Seth G. Jones, Rollie Lal, Andrew Rathmell
Rachel Swanger, and Anga Timilsina

RAND

This research in the public interest was supported by RAND, using discretionary funds made possible by the generosity of RAND's donors, the fees earned on client-funded research, and independent research and development (IR&D) funds provided by the Department of Defense.

Library of Congress Cataloging-in-Publication Data

America's role in nation-building : from Germany to Iraq /
   James Dobbins ... [et at.].
      p. cm.
   Includes bibliographical references.
   "MR-1753."
   ISBN 0-8330-3460-X
   1. United States—Foreign relations—1945–1989—Case studies.
   2. United States—Foreign relations—1989—Case studies. 3. United
   States—Military policy—Case studies. 4. Intervention (International
   law)—Case studies. I. Dobbins, James, 1942–

E840.A6215 2003
327.73'009'045—dc21

                                                         2003014127

Cover photographs: U.S. Navy (left), Goran Tomasevic/Reuters (right)

RAND is a nonprofit institution that helps improve policy and decisionmaking through research and analysis. RAND® is a registered trademark. RAND's publications do not necessarily reflect the opinions or policies of its research sponsors.

Cover design by Stephen Bloodsworth

Published 2003 by RAND
1700 Main Street, P.O. Box 2138, Santa Monica, CA 90407-2138
1200 South Hayes Street, Arlington, VA 22202-5050
201 North Craig Street, Suite 202, Pittsburgh, PA 15213-1516
RAND URL: http://www.rand.org/
To order RAND documents or to obtain additional information,
contact Distribution Services: Telephone: (310) 451-7002;
Fax: (310) 451-6915; Email: order@rand.org

PREFACE

This report contains the results of a study on best practices in nation-building. Its purpose is to analyze U.S. and international military, political, and economic activities in postconflict situations since World War II, determine key principles for success, and draw implications for future U.S. military operations. This report contains the lessons learned from each of these operations, then applies them to the case of Iraq.

The preponderance of this research was conducted prior to the March 19, 2003, commencement of Operation Iraqi Freedom, but the project team focused on the near-term implications of our effort throughout the course of this work. To that end, this study served as the point of departure for a RAND conference on nation-building and the future of Iraq that was held in Arlington, Virginia, on May 6–7, 2003. The results of that conference were factored into the final version of this study. (The appendix lists the conference attendees.)

This report is a result of RAND's continuing program of self-sponsored independent research. Support for such research is provided, in part, by donors and by the independent research and development provisions of RAND's contracts for the operation of its U.S. Department of Defense federally funded research and development centers. This report should be of interest to defense and foreign policy decisionmakers, practitioners, analysts, and others concerned with the roles of the United States, other nations, and international and nongovernmental organizations in postconflict situations. Comments are welcome and should be addressed to James Dobbins or Seth Jones.

This research was overseen by RAND's National Security Research Division (NSRD). NSRD conducts research and analysis for the Office of the Secretary of Defense, the Joint Staff, the unified commands, the defense agencies, the Department of the Navy, the U.S. intelligence community, allied foreign governments, and foundations.

CONTENTS

FIGURES AND TABLE

Figures

Table

The goal of the work documented here was to analyze and extract the best practices in nation-building from the post–World War II experiences of the United States. To do this, we examined U.S. and international military, political, and economic activities in postconflict situations since World War II, identified the key determinants of the success of these operations in terms of democratization and the creation of vibrant economies, and drew implications for future U.S. nation-building operations.

This report includes seven case studies: Germany, Japan, Somalia, Haiti, Bosnia, Kosovo, and Afghanistan. The final chapter examines the challenge ahead of building a democratic, economically vibrant Iraq and recommends best-practice policies for achieving these goals based on the lessons learned from the case studies.

FROM GERMANY TO AFGHANISTAN

The post–World War II occupations of Germany and Japan were America's first experiences with the use of military force in the aftermath of a conflict to underpin rapid and fundamental societal transformation. Both were comprehensive efforts that aimed to engineer major social, political, and economic reconstruction. The success of these endeavors demonstrated that democracy was transferable; that societies could, under certain circumstances, be encouraged to transform themselves; and that major transformations could endure. The cases of Germany and Japan set a standard for postconflict nation-building that has not since been matched.

For the next 40 years, there were few attempts to replicate these early successes. During the Cold War, U.S. policy emphasized containment, deterrence, and maintenance of the status quo. Efforts were made to promote democratic and free-market values, but generally without the element of compulsion. American military power was employed to preserve the status quo, not to alter it; to manage crises, not to resolve the underlying problems. Germany, Korea, Vietnam, China, Cyprus, and Palestine were divided. U.S. and international forces were used to maintain these and other divisions, not to compel resolution of the underlying disputes. U.S. interventions in such places as the Dominican Republic, Lebanon, Grenada, and Panama were undertaken to overthrow unfriendly regimes and reinstall friendly ones, rather than bring about fundamental societal transformations.

The end of the Cold War created new problems for the United States and opened new possibilities. Prominent among the problems was a rash of state failures. During the Cold War, the United States and the Soviet Union each—and, in some cases, both—propped up a number of weak states for geopolitical reasons. For instance, Yugoslavia and Afghanistan were regarded as important geostrategic pieces on the Cold War chessboard, and their respective regimes received extensive external support. With the disappearance of the Soviet Union, Moscow lost its capability and Washington its geopolitical rationale for sustaining such regimes. Denied such support, these and other states disintegrated.

After 1989, a balance of terror no longer impelled the United States to preserve the status quo. Washington was free to ignore regional instability when it did not threaten U.S. interests. The United States also had the option of using its unrivaled power to resolve, rather than simply to manage or contain, international problems of strategic importance. Since the end of the Cold War, the United States has felt free to intervene not simply to police cease-fires or restore the status quo but to try to bring about the more-fundamental transformation of war-torn societies, much as it had assisted in transforming those of Germany and Japan four decades earlier. The United States was also able to secure broad international support for such efforts when it chose to mount them. The rest of the international community has also become more interventionist. Of the 55 peace operations the United Nations (UN) has mounted since 1945, 41 (or nearly 80 percent) began after 1989. Fifteen of these were still under way in 2003.

Despite a more-supportive international environment, the costs and risks associated with nation-building have remained high. Consequently, the United States has not embarked on such endeavors lightly. It withdrew from Somalia in 1993 at the first serious resistance. It opted out of international efforts to stem genocide in Rwanda in 1994. It resisted European efforts to entangle it in Balkan peace enforcement through four years of bloody civil war. After intervening in Bosnia, it spent another three years pursuing a non-military solution to ethnic repression in Kosovo.

In spite of this reticence, each successive post–Cold War U.S.-led intervention has generally been wider in scope and more ambitious in intent than its predecessor. In Somalia, the original objective was purely humanitarian but subsequently expanded to democratization. In Haiti, the objective was to reinstall a president and conduct elections according to an existing constitution. In Bosnia, it was to create a multiethnic state. In Kosovo, it was to establish a democratic polity and market economy virtually from scratch. During his presidential campaign in 2000, George W. Bush criticized the Clinton administration for this expansive agenda of nation-building. As President, Bush adopted a more-modest set of objectives when faced with a comparable challenge in Afghanistan. The current administration's efforts to reverse the trend toward ever larger and more ambitious U.S.-led nation-building operations have proven short lived, however. In Iraq, the United States has taken on a task with a scope comparable to the transformational attempts still under way in Bosnia and Kosovo and a scale comparable only to the earlier U.S. occupations of Germany and Japan. Nation-building, it appears, is the inescapable responsibility of the world's only superpower.

COMPARISONS ACROSS CASES

Following the elaboration of the seven case studies, we compared quantitative data on inputs of nation-building and progress toward democracy and the creation of a vibrant economy. On the input side, we collected and compared statistics on

- military presence
- police presence

- total external assistance in constant 2001 dollars
- per capita external assistance in constant 2001 dollars
- external assistance as a percentage of gross domestic product (GDP).

On the output side, we looked at statistics on

- postconflict combat deaths
- timing of elections
- changes in the number of refugees and internally displaced persons (IDPs) over time
- changes in per capita GDP over time.

Although each case is unique, we attempted to find areas in which comparisons might be useful. In particular, we attempted to quantify and compare measures of nation-building input (troops, time, and economic assistance) and output (democratic elections and increases in per capita GDP).

Military force levels varied significantly across the cases. They ranged from the 1.6 million U.S. forces in the European theater of operations at the end of the World War II to approximately 14,000 U.S. and international troops in Afghanistan currently. Gross numbers, however, are not always useful for making comparisons across the cases because the sizes and populations of the countries are so disparate. For purposes of comparison, we chose to calculate the numbers of foreign and U.S. soldiers per thousand inhabitants for each country. We used these numbers to compare force levels at specified times after the end of the conflict or after U.S. operation began.

As Figures S.1 and S.2 illustrate, force levels varied widely across these operations. Bosnia; Kosovo; and, particularly, Germany started with substantial numbers of military forces, while the initial levels in Japan; Somalia; Haiti; and, especially, Afghanistan were much more modest. These levels all decreased over time by varying degrees, then rose in the case of Germany for external reasons. Overall, the differences across the cases had significant implications for other aspects of the postconflict operation.

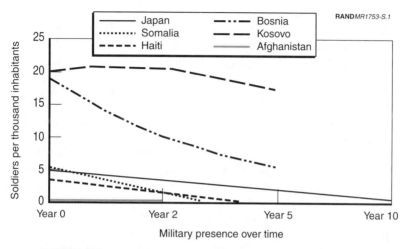

NOTE: Year 0 represents the end of the conflict.

Figure S.1—Military Presence over Time, Excluding Germany

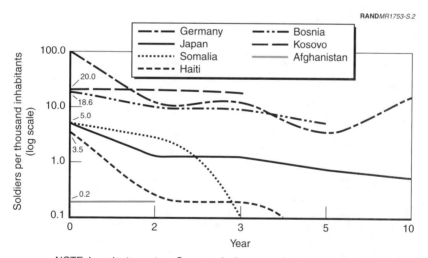

NOTE: In order to capture Germany in the same chart, we used a logarithmic scale because Germany started with a much higher troops-to-population ratio than all the other cases. The figures for Germany represent the level of U.S. troops at the end of the war as a proportion of the population in the U.S. sector.

Figure S.2—Military Presence over Time, Including Germany

We conducted a similar analysis of external assistance for the seven cases. Cumulative figures are useful to some degree, but to assess the true impact of assistance on individuals in postconflict situations, it is important to look at how much assistance was provided per capita. Figure S.3 captures the amount of assistance per person during the first two years in the various cases in constant 2001 U.S. dollars.

Germany, which received the most assistance in aggregate terms ($12 billion) after the first two years of conflict, does not rank very high. Per capita assistance ran a little over $200. Kosovo, which ranked fourth in terms of total assistance, received over $800 per resident. Levels of per capita assistance have had some bearing on the speed of economic recovery. Kosovo, with the second-highest level of assistance on a per capita basis, enjoyed the most rapid recovery in levels of per capita GDP following the conflict. In contrast, Haiti, which received much less on a per capita basis than did Kosovo, has experienced little growth in per capita GDP since the end of the conflict.

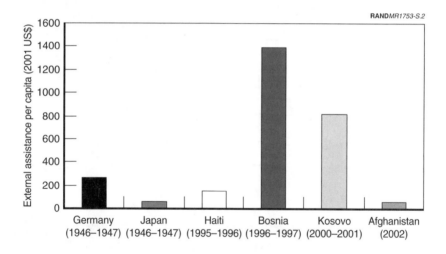

Figure S.3—Per Capita External Assistance

CRITERIA FOR SUCCESS

The German and Japanese occupations set standards for postconflict transformation that have not since been equaled. One of the most important questions an inquiry such as this must address, therefore, is why those two operations succeeded so well while all subsequent efforts have fallen short to one degree or another. The easiest answer is that Germany and Japan were already highly developed, economically advanced societies. This certainly explains why it was easier to reconstruct the German and Japanese economies than it was to make fundamental reforms to the economies in the other five case studies. However, economics is not a sufficient answer. Nation-building is not principally about economic reconstruction; rather, it is about political transformation. The spread of democracy in Latin America, Asia, and parts of Africa suggests that this form of government is not unique to Western culture or to advanced industrial economies: Democracy can, indeed, take root in circumstances where neither exists.

No postconflict program of reconstruction could turn Somalia, Haiti, or Afghanistan into thriving centers of prosperity. But the failure of U.S.-led interventions to install viable democracies in these countries has more than purely economic explanations. All three societies are divided ethnically, socioeconomically, or tribally in ways that Germany and Japan were not. Thus, homogeneity helps. But it is not a necessary condition. The kind of communal hatreds that mark Somalia, Haiti, and Afghanistan are even more marked in Bosnia and Kosovo, where the process of democratization has nevertheless made some progress.

As Table S.1 summarizes, what principally distinguishes Germany, Japan, Bosnia, and Kosovo from Somalia, Haiti, and Afghanistan are not their levels of Western culture, economic development, or cultural homogeneity. Rather it is the level of effort the United States and the international community put into their democratic transformations. Nation-building, as this study illustrates, is a time- and resource-consuming effort. The United States and its allies have put 25 times more money and 50 times more troops, on a per capita basis, into postconflict Kosovo than into postconflict Afghanistan. This higher level of input accounts in significant measure for the higher level of output measured in the development of democratic institutions and economic growth.

Table S.1

America's History of Nation-Building

Country	Years	Peak U.S. Troops	International Cooperation	Assessment	Lessons Learned
West Germany	1945–1952	1.6 million	Joint project with Britain and France; and, eventually, NATO	Very successful; an economically stable democracy and NATO member within 10 years.	Democracy can be transferred. Military forces can underpin democratic transformation.
Japan	1945–1952	350,000	None	Very successful; economically stable democracy and a regional security anchor within 10 years.	Democracy can be exported to non-Western societies. Unilateral nation-building can be simpler (but more expensive) than multilateral efforts.
Somalia	1992–1994	28,000	UN humanitarian oversight	Not successful; little was accomplished other than some humanitarian aid delivered in Mogadishu and other cities.	Unity of command can be as essential in peace as in combat operations. Nation-building objectives need to be scaled to available resources.

Table S.1—Continued

Country	Years	Peak U.S. Troops	International Cooperation	Assessment	Lessons Learned
Haiti	1994–1996	21,000[a]	UN help in policing	Not successful; U.S. forces restored democratically elected president but left before democratic institutions took hold.	Exit deadlines can be counterproductive. Building competent administrations and democratic institutions takes time.
Bosnia	1995–present	20,000	Joint NATO, UN, and OSCE effort	Mixed success; democratic elections occurred within 2 years, but government is constitutionally weak.	Nexus between organized crime and political extremism can be a serious challenge to enduring democratic reforms.
Kosovo	1999–present	15,000[b]	NATO military action and UN support	Modest success; elections occurred within 3 years, and economic growth is strong. But there has been no final resolution of Kosovo's status.	Broad participation and extensive burden-sharing can be compatible with unity of command and U.S. leadership.
Afghanistan	2001–present	10,000	Modest contribution from UN and NGOs	Too early to tell; no longer a launch pad for global terrorism, but there is little democratic structure, and there is no real governmental authority beyond Kabul.	A low initial input of money and troops yields a low output of security, democratization, and economic growth.

[a]Plus 1,000 international police.
[b]Plus 4,600 international police.

Japan, one of the two undoubted successes, fully meets these criteria, at least in terms of the amount of time spent on its transformation. On the other hand, Japan received considerably less external economic assistance per capita than did Germany, Bosnia, or Kosovo. Indeed, it received less than Haiti and about the same as Afghanistan. Japan's postconflict economic growth rate was correspondingly low. U.S. spending on the Korean War, however, spurred Japan's economic growth during the 1950s, which subsequently helped consolidate public support for the democratic reforms that had been instituted soon after the war. As with the German economic miracle of the 1950s, this experience suggests that rising economic prosperity is not so much a necessary precursor for political reform as a highly desirable follow-up and legitimizer.

The stabilization (or, as it was then termed, occupation) force in Japan was also smaller in proportion to population than those in Germany, Bosnia, or Kosovo, although it was larger than those in Haiti and Afghanistan. The willing collaboration of the existing power structures and the homogeneity of the population undoubtedly enhanced the ability to secure Japan with a comparatively small force. But the very scale of Japan's defeat was also important: Years of total war had wrought devastation, including the firebombing of Japanese cities and, finally, two nuclear attacks. As a result, the surviving population was weary of conflict and disinclined to contest defeat. When conflicts have ended less conclusively and destructively (or not terminated at all)—as in Somalia; Afghanistan; and, most recently, Iraq—the postconflict security challenges are more difficult. Indeed, it seems that the more swift and bloodless the military victory, the more difficult postconflict stabilization can be.

Unity of Command Versus Multinational Participation

When it was shouldering the burden of Japan's transformation and most of that for West Germany, the United States generated some 50 percent of the world's GDP. By the 1990s, that share had dropped to 22 percent. The decline in the United States' share of global GDP and the concomitant rise in output and incomes elsewhere have made international burden-sharing both politically more important for the United States and more affordable for other countries.

Throughout the 1990s, the United States wrestled with the problem of how to achieve wider participation in its nation-building endeavors while also preserving adequate unity of command. In Somalia and Haiti, the United States experimented with sequential arrangements in which it organized, led, and largely manned and funded the initial phase of each operation but then quickly turned responsibility over to a more broadly representative and more widely funded UN-led force. These efforts were not successful, although the operation in Haiti was better organized than that in Somalia. In Bosnia, the United States succeeded in achieving unity of command and broad participation on the military side of the operation through the North Atlantic Treaty Organization (NATO) but resisted the logic of achieving a comparable and cohesive arrangement on the civil side. In Kosovo, the United States achieved unity of command and broad participation on both the military and civil sides through NATO and the UN, respectively. While the military and civil aspects of the Kosovo operation remained under different management, the United States ensured that the mandates and capabilities of the two functional entities, the Kosovo Force (KFOR) and the UN Interim Administration in Kosovo (UNMIK), overlapped sufficiently to prevent a gap from opening between them.

None of these models proved entirely satisfactory. Arrangements in Kosovo, however, do seem to have provided the best amalgam to date of U.S. leadership, European participation, broad financial burden-sharing, and strong unity of command. Every international official in Kosovo works ultimately for either the NATO commander or the Special Representative of the Secretary General. Neither of these is an American, but by virtue of the United States' credibility in the region and its influence in NATO and the UN Security Council, the United States has been able to maintain a satisfactory leadership role while paying only 16 percent of the reconstruction costs and fielding only 16 percent of the peacekeeping troops.

The efficacy of the Kosovo and Bosnian models for managing a large-scale nation-building operation depends heavily on the ability of the United States and its principal allies to attain a common vision of the enterprise's objectives and then to shape the response of the relevant institutions—principally NATO, the European Union, and the UN—to the agreed purposes. When the principal participants in a nation-building exercise have such a common vision, the Balkan models offer a viable amalgam of burden-sharing and unity of command.

In Afghanistan, the United States opted for parallel arrangements on the military side and even greater variety on the civil side. An international force, with no U.S. participation, operates in Kabul, while a national, mostly U.S. force, operates everywhere else. The UN is responsible for promoting political transformation, while individual donors coordinate economic reconstruction—or, more often, fail to do so. This arrangement is a marginal improvement over Somalia, since the separate U.S. and international forces are at least not operating in the same physical territory, but it represents a clear regression from what was achieved in Haiti; Bosnia; or, in particular, Kosovo. By the same token, the overall results achieved to date in Afghanistan are better than those in Somalia, not yet better than those in Haiti, and not as good as those in Bosnia or Kosovo. However, the operation in Afghanistan is a good deal less expensive.

Duration

Another aspect in which these seven cases differ is in duration. Some began with clear departure deadlines that were adhered to, such as Haiti. Some began with very short time lines but saw those amended, such as Germany, Japan, Somalia, and Bosnia. And some began without any expectation of an early exit, such as Kosovo and Afghanistan. The record suggests that, while staying long does not guarantee success, leaving early ensures failure. To date, no effort at enforced democratization has taken hold in less than five years.

And if democratization takes hold, does that provide the ultimate exit strategy? As these case studies suggest, not necessarily. U.S. forces have left clear failures behind, such as Somalia and Haiti, but remain present in every successful or still-pending case: Germany, Japan, Bosnia, Kosovo, and Afghanistan. These five interventions were motivated by regional or global geopolitical concerns. Democratization alone did not fully address such concerns. Germany and Japan were disarmed and consequently required U.S. help in providing for their external security long after they became reliable democracies, fully capable of looking after their own internal affairs. Bosnia, Kosovo, and Afghanistan may also require assistance with their external security long after internal peace has been established.

Whether this help will take the form of an external troop presence, an external security guarantee, or external leadership in forging new regional security arrangements remains to be seen. But some security relationship is likely to continue long after the democratic transformation is completed. Indeed, if Germany and Japan are any guide, the more thorough the democratic transformation the more deeply forged the residual links may be. The record suggests that nation-building creates ties of affection and dependency that persist for a substantial amount of time.

Conclusions

With these considerations in mind, we draw a number of general conclusions, in addition to the numerous case-specific lessons contained in the chapters:

- Many factors influence the ease or difficulty of nation-building: prior democratic experience, level of economic development, and national homogeneity. However, among the controllable factors, the most important determinant seems to be the level of effort—measured in time, manpower, and money.

- Multilateral nation-building is more complex and time consuming than undertaking unilateral efforts but is also considerably less expensive for participants.

- Multilateral nation-building can produce more thoroughgoing transformations and greater regional reconciliation than can unilateral efforts.

- Unity of command and broad participation are compatible if the major participants share a common vision and can shape international institutions accordingly.

- There appears to be an inverse correlation between the size of the stabilization force and the level of risk. The higher the proportion of stabilizing troops, the lower the number of casualties suffered and inflicted. Indeed, most adequately manned post-conflict operations suffered no casualties whatsoever.

- Neighboring states can exert significant influence. It is nearly impossible to put together a fragmented nation if its neighbors try to tear it apart. Every effort should be made to secure their support.

- Accountability for past injustices can be a powerful component of democratization. It can also be among the most difficult and controversial aspects of any nation-building endeavor and should, therefore, be attempted only if there is a deep, long-term commitment to the overall operation.

- There is no quick route to nation-building. Five years seems to be the minimum required to enforce an enduring transition to democracy.

APPLYING THESE LESSONS TO IRAQ

After reviewing these experiences and seeking to draw the most-important lessons, we conclude by suggesting how these best practices might be applied to future operations and, in particular, to Iraq. Although the military phase of the war against Iraq went very well, and the regime collapsed much faster than many expected, the United States has been left with an unenviable task in seeking to build a democratic, economically vibrant Iraqi state. The British spent several decades forging an Iraqi state out of the remains of the Ottoman Empire, but neither they nor their Iraqi successors managed to forge a real Iraqi nation.

Nation-building in Iraq faces a number of challenges. Iraq has no tradition of pluralist democracy; politics has always been about authoritarian rule and the settlement of disputes by force. Although a sense of Iraqi national identity does exist, it does not override communal forms of identity along ethnic, geographic, tribal, or religious grounds. The majority of the population, the Kurds and Shia, have no real tradition of representation in national Iraqi politics but will now have to be brought into the polity. To make matters worse, organized crime and banditry are strongly rooted in Iraqi society. The past decade of sanctions and dictatorship have denuded Iraq of its once-strong middle class, which had a stake in the development of a civil society.

In addition to these particular Iraqi problems, the country faces the familiar challenges of a society emerging from a long period of totalitarian rule. The military, security services, and bureaucracy need to be radically reformed and purged. Justice needs to be achieved for victims of human rights abuses, and the economy has experienced two decades of turmoil. These challenges are significant. Because of the diplomatic circumstances of the conflict, the United States must also cope with unsympathetic neighbors—Iran, Syria, and Turkey—who have an interest in shaping Iraqi politics and perhaps destabilizing a smooth transition. At the international level, the prewar splits in the UN Security Council make it much harder for the United States to adopt the burden-sharing models adopted in Bosnia, Kosovo, or even Afghanistan. At the same time, the United States was unable to undertake many of the prewar preparations that would have eased postwar transition, such as coordinating humanitarian relief with the UN and nongovernmental organizations, organizing international civil police forces, and establishing an international political authority to rebut Arab suspicions of U.S. imperialism.

Nonetheless, Iraq does have some advantages for nation-builders. First, it has a nationwide civil administration, which is relatively efficient. This administration needs to be rebuilt but not to be reconstructed from scratch. Staffed mainly by Iraqis, it will reduce the need for direct international intervention and facilitate security and development across the country. Second, the civil administration and the extensive links with UN agencies mean that the humanitarian issues should be soluble. Third, Iraq's oil means that the country will not remain dependent on international aid in the medium term.

As it embarks on its most ambitious program of nation-building since 1945, the United States can learn important lessons from the case studies we have examined. It has staked its credibility on a successful outcome in Iraq. This will require an extensive commitment of financial, personnel, and diplomatic resources over a long period. The United States cannot afford to contemplate early exit strategies and cannot afford to leave the job half completed. The real question for the United States should not be how soon it can leave, but rather how fast and how much to share power with Iraqis and the international community while retaining enough power to oversee an enduring transition to democracy and stability.

PROGRESS TO DATE

In its early months, the U.S.-led stabilization and reconstruction of Iraq has not gone as smoothly as might have been expected, given the abundant, recent, and relevant U.S. experience highlighted in this study. This is, after all, the sixth major nation-building enterprise the United States has mounted in 12 years and the fifth such in a Muslim nation. In many of the previous cases, the United States and its allies have faced similar challenges immediately after an intervention. Somalia, Haiti, Kosovo, and Afghanistan also experienced the rapid and utter collapse of central state authority. In each of these instances, local police, courts, penal services, and militaries were destroyed, disrupted, disbanded, or discredited and were consequently unavailable to fill the postconflict security gap. In Somalia, Bosnia, Kosovo, and Afghanistan, extremist elements emerged to fill the resultant vacuum of power. In most cases, organized crime quickly became a major challenge to the occupying authority. In Bosnia and Kosovo, the external stabilization forces ultimately proved adequate to surmount these security challenges; in Somalia and Afghanistan, they did not or have not yet.

Over the past decade, the United States has made major investments in the combat efficiency of its forces. The return on investment has been evident in the dramatic improvement in warfighting demonstrated from Desert Storm to the Kosovo air campaign to Operation Iraqi Freedom. There has been no comparable increase in the capacity of U.S. armed forces or of U.S. civilian agencies to conduct postcombat stabilization and reconstruction operations. Throughout the 1990s, the management of each major mission showed some limited advance over its predecessor, but in the current decade, even this modestly improved learning curve has not been sustained. The Afghan mission can certainly be considered an improvement over Somalia but cannot yet be assessed as being more successful than Haiti. It is too early to evaluate the success of the postconflict mission in Iraq, but its first few months do not raise it above those in Bosnia and Kosovo at a similar stage.

Nation-building has been a controversial mission over the past decade, and the intensity of this debate has undoubtedly inhibited the investments that would be needed to do these tasks better. Institutional resistance in departments of State and Defense, neither of which regard nation-building among their core missions, has also been an obstacle. As a result, successive administrations have treated each new mission as if it were the first and, more importantly, as if it were the last.

This expectation is unlikely to be realized anytime soon. Since the end of the Cold War, the United States has become increasingly involved in nation-building operations. In the 1990s, the Clinton administration conducted a major nation-building intervention, on the average, every two years. The current administration, despite a strong disinclination to engage U.S. armed forces in such activities, has launched two major nation-building enterprises within 18 months. It now seems clear that nation-building is the inescapable responsibility of the world's only superpower. Once that recognition is more widely accepted, there is much the United States can do to better prepare itself to lead such missions.

ACKNOWLEDGMENTS

Numerous people made significant contributions throughout the course of this project. Carl Bildt encouraged and helped design the project from its outset. Outside RAND, Robert Perito helped deepen our understanding of civilian police operations with his comments and writings as well as providing excellent source suggestions. James Carafano provided valuable insights on the occupation of Germany. Edward Drea and James Knight helped us find data on troop strength and casualties in Japan. Derek Boothby and Scott Feil offered helpful comments. Various U.S. and coalition military officers, civilian officials, and representatives from international and nongovernmental organizations provided important insights during Jerry McGinn's fall 2002 trips to various military units and headquarters in Tampa, Florida; Fayetteville, North Carolina; Atlanta, Georgia; and Kabul, Afghanistan.

A number of RAND colleagues contributed timely and valuable assistance. Bruce Pirnie and Steven Simon provided timely and thoughtful reviews. William Rosenau, James Thomson, and James Quinlivan provided helpful ideas or research leads. Miriam Schafer did a superb job researching economic data and issues for all the cases. Carl Bildt and Frank Carlucci, both members of the RAND Board of Trustees, cochaired an international conference to review the study's findings and gave generously of their time. Steven Simon and Elizabeth Whitaker organized the conference, and the participants provided valuable insights and comments during the two-day discussion which were factored into the final version of the study. Colleen O'Conner drafted the bibliography and list of abbreviations and helped put together the final report. Kimberley Alldredge, Jennie

Breon, Karen Stewart, and Amy Pett all provided excellent administrative support.

ABBREVIATIONS

ACJ	Allied Council for Japan
ANA	Afghan National Army
BPAK	Banking and Payments Authority of Kosovo
CENTCOM	Central Command
CIVPOL	Civilian Police
CMOC	civil-military operations center
CPA	Coalition Provisional Authority
DOS	U.S. Department of State
EU	European Union
FBI	Federal Bureau of Investigation
FRG	Federal Republic of Germany
GARIOA	Government Aid and Relief in Occupied Areas
GDP	gross domestic product
HNP	Haitian National Police
ICG	International Crisis Group
ICTY	International Criminal Tribunal for the Former Yugoslavia
IDP	internally displaced person
IFOR	Implementation Force
IMF	International Monetary Fund
IPTF	UN International Police Task Force

ISAF	International Security Assistance Force
JCS	Joint Chiefs of Staff
KDP	Kurdish Democratic Party
KFOR	Kosovo Force
KLA	Kosovo Liberation Army
KM	*konvertibilnaja marka* (new currency of Bosnia-Herzegovina)
KPS	Kosovo Police Service
LDK	League for Democratic Kosovo
mbd	million barrels a day
MNF	Multinational Force
NATO	North Atlantic Treaty Organization
NGO	nongovernmental organization
OEF	Operation Enduring Freedom
OHR	Office of the High Representative
OMGUS	Office of the Military Government, United States
OSCE	Organization for Security and Co-operation in Europe
ORHA	U.S. Department of Defense Office of Reconstruction and Humanitarian Assistance
PIC	Peace Implementation Council
PRT	provincial reconstruction team
PUK	Patriotic Union of Kurdistan
QRF	quick reaction force
SACB	Somalia Aid Coordination Body
SCAP	Supreme Commander of the Allied Powers
SCIRI	Supreme Council for the Islamic Revolution in Iraq
SFOR	Stabilization Force
SPU	special police unit
SWNCC	State, War and Navy Coordinating Committee
TMK	Kosovo Protection Corps

UN	United Nations
UNAMA	UN Assistance Mission in Afghanistan
UNHCR	UN High Commissioner for Refugees
UNICEF	UN Children's Fund
UNITAF	Unified Task Force
UNJLC	UN Joint Logistics Center
UNMIH	UN Mission in Haiti
UNMIK	UN Interim Administration in Kosovo
UNOSOM	UN Operation in Somalia
UNSCR	UN Security Council Resolution
USAID	U.S. Agency for International Development
WMD	weapons of mass destruction

Chapter One

INTRODUCTION

Since the end of the Cold War, the United States has invested significant military, political, and economic resources into conducting operations in the aftermaths of conflicts or civil unrest. Numerous studies, articles, and reports have been published on various aspects of these operations, but most have focused exclusively on the post–Cold War period. This is the first effort of which we are aware to review the major U.S. experiences in nation-building exercises since 1945, compare and contrast the results of these operations, outline significant lessons and best practices, and then suggest how those lessons might be applied to the current challenges facing U.S. policymakers in Iraq.

Various terms have been used over the past 57 years to describe the activities we are seeking to analyze. The German and Japanese operations were referred to as *occupations*. The operations in Somalia, Haiti, and Bosnia were generally termed *peacekeeping* or *peace enforcement* missions. The current U.S. administration has preferred to use the terms *stabilization* and *reconstruction* to refer to its post-conflict operations in Afghanistan and in Iraq. In all these cases, the intent was to use military force to underpin a process of democratization. *Occupation, peacekeeping, peace enforcement, stabilization,* and *reconstruction* do not fully capture the scope of such operations. Neither does the term *nation-building*, but we believe it comes closest to suggesting the full range of activities and objectives involved.

We chose seven historical cases for this study: Germany, Japan, Somalia, Haiti, Bosnia, Kosovo, and Afghanistan. These are the most important instances in the post–World War II period in which U.S. military power has been used to underpin democratization. Furthermore, they include substantial variation in both the success of nation-building and such critical inputs as resources, manpower, and money. *Success* is defined as the ability to promote an enduring transfer of democratic institutions. We did not include the U.S. colonial experience in the Philippines because the societal transformation attempted there was intended to span several generations. We did not include the post–World War II occupation of Austria because we believed its lessons would largely parallel those of Germany and Japan. We did not include the Cold War interventions in Korea, Vietnam, the Dominican Republic, Lebanon, Grenada, and Panama because these were shorter lived and had more-limited political objectives.

The case studies themselves were designed to draw out "best practice" policies for democratizing states. To achieve this goal, we adopted a common approach for each case study. In each instance, we first described the nature of the settlement that ended the conflict. Second, we describe the scope of the problem. To develop a set of best practices, we needed to be able to compare the magnitude of the challenges facing the United States across the case studies. To do so, we outlined the security, humanitarian, administrative, political, and economic challenges that the United States faced at the end of the conflict. Third, we described the institutional arrangements and policies adopted during the operations. In particular, we described the roles the United States, other countries, and international organizations assumed during reconstruction. Fourth, we examined how each operation developed over time, how the security environment stabilized or grew more fragile, how the humanitarian situation evolved, how a civil administration was constructed, how the process of democratization developed, and how economic reconstruction progressed. Finally, we evaluated each operation. Then, using our evaluations of the various operations, we compiled the most important cross-cutting nation-building lessons.

In the final chapter, we applied these lessons learned to the case of Iraq. We first examined the challenges that the United States faces in assisting the reconstruction of Iraq. Then, based on best practices from the case-study operations, we provided recommendations concerning policies likely to be most effective for creating an economically healthy and democratic Iraq.

Chapter Two

GERMANY

World War II was the bloodiest conflict in European history. Millions of soldiers and civilians were killed in battle or in Nazi Germany's concentration camps. In May 1945, Germany surrendered unconditionally to the United States, the Soviet Union, and the United Kingdom. The Allies had already decided to occupy Germany militarily. The United States, the United Kingdom, and France occupied zones in the west, while the Soviets occupied the east. The capital of Berlin was also partitioned among the four occupying powers. Common Allied policy was developed in a series of summit meetings, most notably at Casablanca in January 1943, at Yalta in February 1945, and at Potsdam in August 1945. At Casablanca, British Prime Minister Winston Churchill and U.S. President Franklin Roosevelt had decided to accept only unconditional surrender from Germany. This decision was reiterated in subsequent meetings that included Soviet leader Josef Stalin. The Yalta Conference called for unconditional surrender, the destruction of Nazism, the disarmament of Germany, the speedy punishment of war criminals, reparations, and an economy able to sustain the German people but not capable of waging war. The Potsdam Conference elaborated on these political and economic principles and included agreements about occupation areas, the disposition of eastern German borders, population transfers, and the treatment of war criminals.[1]

---

[1]U.S. Department of State [DOS], *Occupation of Germany: Policy and Progress 1945–46*, Washington, D.C.: U.S. Government Printing Office, Pub. 2783, 1947, p. 3.

CHALLENGES

Germany was utterly defeated by the end of the war. The last years of conflict severely damaged the state's physical infrastructure, although later analysis suggests that the damage was not as extensive as first thought.[2] The more immediate problem was the collapse of the economy in 1945 as the German government was replaced by the occupying powers and as central fiscal and monetary management was in abeyance. In addition to the economic problems, Germany was awash in refugees; the Germans were a defeated people. This situation created tremendous challenges for the United States and its allies as the victors began to think about how they should act in the war's aftermath.

Security

As U.S. and other allied forces occupied Germany in the immediate aftermath of the May unconditional surrender, there was a great deal of concern about preventing a security vacuum in the country. The German military was defeated, but it needed to be disarmed and demobilized promptly and efficiently. As part of that process, Nazi war criminals needed to be identified and brought to trial. In addition, the Allies feared that renegade guerrilla groups of German military forces would re-form into small units and launch attacks against Allied forces. Consequently, the first order of business for the occupation was to have the occupying forces establish security for the military governments. This required, at least initially, a robust presence throughout the country. At the same time, however, there were tremendous external pressures on the United States and the other Allies to withdraw their forces as quickly as possible. The need to shift forces to Asia to finish the war against Japan and, especially, the domestic cry to "bring the boys home" created tremendous pressure on U.S. forces to withdraw as soon as the fighting stopped.

---

[2]John Killick, *The United States and European Reconstruction: 1945–1960*, Edinburgh, UK: Keele University Press, 1997, pp. 61, 88.

Humanitarian

The scope of the refugee crisis in central Europe at the end of the war is hard to overstate. The Inter-Allied Committee reported in mid-1941 that there were 21 million displaced persons in Europe. Millions of non-Germans, for example, had been brought to Germany as forced laborers. This situation worsened during the last years of the war as millions more people fled in the face of German scorched-earth withdrawals or in fear of Soviet military retribution. Moreover, the Soviets and other states were eager to expel ethnic Germans from their countries. Many of these refugees and displaced persons had no homes to which to return and no means of support. Native Germans, meanwhile, were facing massive food shortages and deprivations as economic activity ground to a halt after Allied forces invaded Germany proper. It was truly a humanitarian and refugee crisis of unprecedented magnitude.[3]

Civil Administration

During 1944 and 1945, debates raged both within the U.S. government and among the Allies about the shape of a postwar German government and a postwar Germany. The Soviets and, to a lesser extent, France advocated that Germany never again be given full sovereignty because of the potential danger it presented to Europe. There was considerable sympathy within the U.S. government for this view. Secretary of Treasury Henry J. Morgenthau advocated the deindustrialization of Germany; other U.S. government officials argued for the establishment of Germany along modern democratic and capitalist lines.[4] Managing these internal U.S. dynamics and trying to forge a consensus among the Allies were daunting challenges. In Germany, meanwhile, the Allies were determined to dis-

---

[3]Michael R. Marrus, *The Unwanted: European Refugees in the Twentieth Century*, New York: Oxford University Press, 1985, pp. 296–299.

[4]For detailed treatments of internal U.S. deliberations about occupation policy before the end of the war, see Edward N. Peterson, *The American Occupation of Germany: Retreat to Victory*, Detroit: Wayne State University Press, 1977, pp. 37–44; Earl F. Ziemke, *The U.S. Army in the Occupation of Germany 1944–1946*: Army Historical Series, Washington, D.C.: Center of Military History, 1975, pp. 98–108; and Thomas Alan Schwartz, *America's Germany: John J. McCloy and the Federal Republic of Germany*, Cambridge, Mass.: Harvard University Press, 1991, pp. 19–24.

mantle the Nazi state apparatus, prosecute war criminals, and rebuild the German state with people untainted by the Nazi regime. This would be a massive undertaking, and it was unclear what type of reception Allied efforts along these lines would receive.

Democratization

Germany had some experience with democracy in the years prior to World War II. The post-Versailles Weimar Republic had a parliamentary government with active political parties. It was a volatile form of government, however, because there were a number of radical splinter parties on the political right and left, and significant elements of German society did not fully embrace the Enlightenment traditions of personal liberty and self-government. Instead, Germans focused on the inner development of the individual and the unique cultural expression of the German nation.[5] Furthermore, the economic crisis during the interwar years, which was marked by high unemployment and rampant inflation, strengthened the extremist parties and wiped out a large portion of the German middle class. The assassinations of Matthias Erzberger in 1921 and Walter Rathenau in 1922 were symptomatic of the terrorist tactics that extreme nationalist groups adopted, many of whose members later joined the National Socialist party of Adolf Hitler. The failure of German society to fully embrace Enlightenment concepts and the economic crisis allowed antidemocratic forces in German society to wreck the Weimar Republic and facilitate the rise of Hitler. It was unclear whether the German people would accept Western democratic principles more readily after 1945.

Reconstruction

The Allied commands in Germany faced the problems of restarting the German economy after its collapse in early 1945, repairing war damage, and providing housing and employment opportunities for the influx of German refugees from the east. They also had to deal with demands from their own governments and other countries for reparations from Germany for the damage the war had caused.

---

[5]Gordon A. Craig, *The Germans,* New York: Meridan, 1982, pp. 32–34.

THE U.S. AND INTERNATIONAL ROLES

As described above, the United States and the other allied powers discussed and planned the shape of post-Hitler Germany extensively in 1944 and 1945. Unlike after World War I, the victorious powers, at least those in the West, were determined to play an active role in transforming the German state into a peaceful democratic state that would never again threaten Europe with military force. Indeed, a significant impetus for the reconstruction of western Germany was the increasing power struggle between the United States and the Soviet Union over the future of Europe—and particularly the future of Germany.[6]

Military

Each of the Allies established military governments in its respective sector. The U.S. sector was organized under the command of the Office of the Military Government, United States (OMGUS). After much internal discussion, the U.S. military Joint Chiefs of Staff (JCS) promulgated JCS directive 1067 in April 1945. Its stated objective was to establish a

> stern, all-powerful military administration of a conquered country, based on its unconditional surrender, impressing the Germans with their military defeat and the futility of any further aggression.[7]

In substance, JCS 1067 directed dissolution of the Nazi party; demilitarization; controls over communications, press, propaganda, and education; reparations for countries desiring them; and decentralization of the German government. On the matter of humanitarian assistance, the directive discouraged, but did not prohibit, the importation of relief supplies.[8]

---

[6]Marc Trachtenberg, *A Constructed Peace: The Making of the European Settlement, 1945–1963*, Princeton, N.J.: Princeton University Press, 1999, and Melvyn P. Leffler, *A Preponderance of Power: National Security, the Truman Administration, and the Cold War*, Stanford, Calif.: Stanford University Press, 1992.

[7]As quoted in Ziemke (1975), p. 104.

[8]Ziemke (1975).

Civil and Economic

After Germany's unconditional surrender on May 7–8, 1945, the victorious Allies—initially the United States, the United Kingdom, and the Soviet Union—assumed supreme authority over Germany on June 5. (France would become one of the occupation powers in the months following Potsdam.) Acting by the authority of their respective governments and "in the interest of the United Nations [UN]," the United States and the other two allies declared their primacy over the conquered nation, "including all the powers possessed by the German Government, the High Command and any state, municipal, or local government or authority."[9] This gave the Allies authority to occupy and completely control German political, economic, and cultural life until they decided when or if Germany would regain national sovereignty. Germany was divided into four zones, which the four powers administered separately. Berlin was to be occupied jointly, with each power administering a sector of the city, and was to be governed by an inter-Allied authority.

The chief agency for coordinating Allied policy toward Germany during the war had been the European Advisory Commission, created in November 1943. It met in London and helped guide decisions about the determination of the zones of occupation and such issues as reparations policy. The Council of Foreign Ministers replaced the Commission in July 1945. To coordinate the occupation, the Allies established the Control Council. The purpose of the Control Council was to ensure "appropriate uniformity of action by the Commanders-in-Chief in their respective zones of occupation and [to] reach agreed decisions on the chief questions affecting Germany as a whole."[10]

WHAT HAPPENED

In the immediate postwar period, the Western Allies pursued nation-building in Germany by demobilizing the German military, holding war crimes tribunals, helping construct democratic institutions, and providing substantial humanitarian and economic assistance. In

---

[9]DOS (1947), pp. 8, 79–80.

[10]DOS (1947), pp. 3–5, 81. See also Peterson (1977), pp. 36–37.

time, the Federal Republic of Germany (FRG)—consisting of the former U.S., British, and French zones—developed into a robust democratic state with a thriving economy. These achievements, however, took several years, and the early international efforts were not uniformly successful.

Security

The Soviet and Western troops that had defeated the German *Wehrmacht* remained in country and took up occupation duties. In the Western zones, U.S., British, and French forces established military governments in their respective sectors.[11] OMGUS oversaw the U.S. sector. On V-E day, General Dwight D. Eisenhower had 61 U.S. divisions (1,622,000 men) in Germany out of a total of 3,077,000 men in Europe. These soldiers became the occupation force for the U.S. sector. They manned border crossings, maintained checkpoints at road junctions, and conducted patrols throughout the sector. The occupation was comprehensive and demonstrated the scope of the German defeat.[12]

Rapid U.S. demobilization, particularly after the Japanese surrender in August, quickly reduced the levels of U.S. forces in Germany. U.S. planners developed an Occupational Troop Basis goal of 404,500, later reduced to 370,000, to be reached a year after surrender. This goal, however, was overtaken by events. The domestic pressures for bringing U.S. soldiers became acute in late 1945 and into 1946. The plan for a nine-division force in Germany was reduced quickly to a forecast of five divisions.

As a way to meet the U.S. sector requirements while still reducing the Occupational Troop Basis, U.S. military leaders began to consider adopting a constabulary or police-type occupation force in Germany in fall 1945. The purpose of the constabulary force was to fill the law-

---

[11]We concentrated on the Western occupation zones in this analysis because the data for these areas are more accurate and more readily available.

[12]The U.S. Army, at first reluctantly, began developing doctrine and training for potential military governments in the early 1940s. As the U.S. military pushed across North Africa and then Europe, the military found itself in control of all functions of government. (Ziemke, 1975, pp. 4, 320, and Robert B. Oakley, Michael J. Dziedzic, and Eliot M. Goldberg, eds., *Policing the New World Disorder: Peace Operations and Public Security*, Washington, D.C.: National Defense University Press, 1998, p. 27.)

and-order gap until a professional German police force could be trained. General George Marshall asked General Eisenhower to develop a plan for this possibility. Commanders in Germany objected to the concept as inefficient, uneconomical, and impractical, but personal intervention by Marshall and Eisenhower overcame these reservations. The constabulary was planned to be a mobile reserve force that could respond to incidents of civil unrest, conduct mounted and dismounted patrols, interdict smuggling operations, and assist in intelligence gathering.[13] The planned force of 38,000 was calculated on the basis of one constabulary soldier per 450 Germans.[14] This would be enough to ensure civil order in the U.S. sector. Three tactical divisions and headquarters elements would back up the constabulary force, but the Occupational Troop Basis would drop significantly, from 370,000 to under 290,000.

The U.S. Constabulary was established in January 1946, but initially comprised only the commanding major general and his staff. They established a school to train soldiers on constabulary duties. These troops received training on law enforcement and military government issues. The constabulary was organized into three brigades and was equipped along the lines of mechanized cavalry, possessing jeeps, armored cars, and some light tanks.[15] The force was formally established in July 1946, with just over 30,000 soldiers, and was deployed throughout the American sector. The constabulary peaked at 31,000 troops. It played an effective role in the U.S. sector despite significant personnel turnover resulting from rapid demobilization. Although the constabulary's troop strength remained constant, overall troop strength dropped to around 200,000 by the end of 1946.[16]

---

[13]James J. Carafano, *Waltzing into the Cold War: The Struggle for Occupied Austria*, College Station, Tex.: Texas A&M University Press, 2002, p. 75.

[14]Ziemke (1975), pp. 334–335, 339–341. There were approximately 16 million Germans in the American sector.

[15]Carafano (2002), p. 75.

[16]James M. Snyder, *The Establishment and Operations of the United States Constabulary, 3 October 1945–30 June 1947*, Historical subsection C-3, United States Constabulary, 1947. See also Oakley, Dziedzic, and Goldberg (1998), pp. 27–28, and Ziemke (1975), pp. 339–341, 421–424. For a first-hand account, see Ernest N. Harmon, *Combat Commander: Autobiography of a Soldier*, Englewood Cliffs, N.J.: Prentice-Hall, Inc., 1970, especially pp. 279–294.

Initially, the U.S. occupation forces focused on demobilization of the vast German army, denazification of German society, and the prevention of the reemergence of Nazi elements. The Western zones quickly demobilized the German military, with little resistance. The *Wehrmacht* and all other military and paramilitary organizations were dissolved, and the German General Staff was abolished. The Allied Control Council promulgated a series of laws that codified this disarmament and demilitarization of Germany.[17] The constabulary force, meanwhile, trained a new German police force that was soon able to conduct routine police duties. This allowed the constabulary to focus on border control and law enforcement among displaced persons and U.S. servicemen.[18]

Ironically, by 1949 the United States began to push for the rearmament of West Germany as the Cold War began to heat up. With the signing of the North Atlantic Treaty and the creation of the FRG in 1949, the United States saw West Germany as an additional bulwark against the perceived Soviet military threat to Central Europe. Initially, France and the United Kingdom were unreceptive to the idea of rearming Germany. Moreover, Germany did not yet have full sovereignty because U.S. and other Western occupation forces remained in country, although at reduced numbers.

The Korean War brought the issue of German rearmament to a head. The June 1950 invasion from North Korea shocked the United States and its European allies. It transformed the security of Western Europe into an imminent problem in the minds of government officials on both sides of the Atlantic. In the central region of Germany, the Western allies had only 11 divisions, and most of these forces were not combat ready. The British High Commissioner noted that the central region had "only 4 weak Anglo-American divisions and practically no air force stood between the Channel ports and the 22 Soviet divisions poised a few miles from our zonal boundary."[19] The consensus estimate of Soviet forces, meanwhile, was that Moscow had 2.5 million men (175 divisions) under arms. Although Soviet

---

[17]DOS (1947), pp. 13–16, 89–108.

[18]Harmon (1970), p. 289.

[19]Quoted in Robert McGeehan, *The German Rearmament Question: American Diplomacy and European Defense After World War II*, Urbana, Ill.: University of Illinois Press, 1971, pp. 6–7.

divisions were significantly smaller than Western divisions, the disparity in force levels was on the order of 10 to 1. In response, North Atlantic Treaty Organization (NATO) countries developed conventional and nuclear forces to face the perceived Soviet threat.[20] France and other Western allies eventually acceded to the rearmament of Germany under the condition that all German forces would be under the control of NATO.[21] The FRG and other NATO members positioned troops along the FRG's eastern border in defense against a possible Soviet-led invasion. These troops would stay there throughout the Cold War and remain there, in reduced numbers, today.

Humanitarian

Humanitarian assistance and aid to refugees in Germany were coordinated and financed through OMGUS. However, private relief organizations, such as the International Red Cross and religious organizations, were heavily involved in the actual provision of food, clothing, and health care and in assisting refugees and displaced people to find surviving family and friends. They also assisted people to emigrate or move to new locations.

The U.S. government provided financial support for these activities in the U.S. zone through the Government Aid and Relief in Occupied Areas (GARIOA) program and through grants of war surplus supplies. The British had their own program in their zone. Figures on gross flows to the U.S. zone under GARIOA and provision of surplus supplies ran to nearly $9 million in late 1946; Germany was allowed to purchase $875 million of military surplus for $184 million on credit.[22] However, on a net basis, the flows were smaller because Germany was supplying France and other European countries with coal and other supplies as part of reparations. When payments were made,

---

[20]For a thorough discussion of the development of Cold War NATO force posture, see John G. McGinn, *Balancing Defense and Détente in NATO: The Harmel Report and the 1968 Crisis in Czechoslovakia*, dissertation, Washington, D.C.: Georgetown University, 2002, and John S. Duffield, *Power Rules: The Evolution of NATO's Conventional Force Posture*, Stanford, Calif.: Stanford University Press, 1995.

[21]On the German rearmament question, see McGeehan (1971).

[22]Killick (1997), p. 76.

they came in the form of "credits" from the recipient countries. At the time, these were of dubious value.

The total number of German refugees was estimated at 15 million at the end of 1945. They consisted primarily of Germans who had been expelled or had fled from East Germany, German territories awarded to Poland and the Soviet Union, and traditional German areas throughout Central and Eastern Europe. By 1947, there were still 9 million refugees in Germany, although this number fell sharply over the course of the next few years.[23] The FRG continued to receive refugees throughout the post–World War II period.

Civil Administration

In addition to demobilization of the German military, initial Western policy focused on the denazification of German society. The basic principles of the denazification program were laid out in JCS 1067 and at the Potsdam Conference of August 1945. These principles focused on dismantling the political and legal structures that the Nazi Party had created in Germany, arresting and punishing Nazi leaders and supporters, and excluding active Nazis from public life. In August 1945, the Allied occupying powers met in London and signed an agreement creating the Nuremberg Tribunal, officially entitled the International Military Tribunal. The London Charter set the ground rules for the Tribunal. In early October 1945, the Allies issued an indictment against 24 men, charging them with the systematic murder of millions of people and with planning and carrying out the war in Europe. With two of the indicted dead or missing and one too frail to stand trail, 21 defendants were tried in Nuremberg beginning in November 1945. The tribunal concluded in October 1946. Ten Nazi leaders were sentenced to death by hanging, and all but three of the remaining received lengthy prison terms.

The United States and other occupying powers also envisioned denazification extending below the national Nazi leadership and therefore set up tribunals to punish offenders at various levels of society. Although denazification was one of the principal objectives of the early occupation period, the proposed scale of denazification

---

[23]DOS (1947), pp. 24–28.

quickly proved impractical. The occupying powers did not have the manpower or resources to accomplish such a thorough purging of German society, and U.S. forces found it impossible to administer the state without interacting with and utilizing competent bureaucrats and officials, at least some of whom were complicit in the Nazi regime.[24] Instead, German officials largely ran the sector-level tribunals, or *Spruchkammern*, with occupying power supervision. Of the 3,623,112 persons considered chargeable under the Law of Liberation from National Socialism and Militarism, the *Spruchkammern* tried 887,252.

All told, the *Spruchkammern* convicted 117,523 people as offenders of some degree during the two years of trials, although most were in the lower categories. These results have led some to question the thoroughness of denazification, but most analysts contend that scaling back U.S. and allied denazification efforts resulted from the recognition of what was attainable.[25] In the long run, this more-practical policy helped lead to a more-thorough repudiation of Nazi policies by the German populace and eliminated remaining support for the return of such an autocratic regime.

Until 1949, the military governments ran their respective sectors. Even after 1949, Germany was only gradually given its political sovereignty.[26] The Potsdam Conference called for the establishment of local self-government "on democratic principles and in particular through elective councils as rapidly as is consistent with military security and the purposes of military occupation," with later extensions of authority to regional and state administrations. The agreement stipulated that there would be central German administrative departments for finance, transportation, communications, trade, and industry but was silent on the future of a unified German state. Tensions among the four occupying powers, especially between the Soviet Union and the Western allies, precluded the establishment of any central German institutions, however.[27]

---

[24]Peterson (1977), Ch. 4, and DOS (1947), pp. 16–21.

[25]Ziemke (1975), pp. 445–446, and Peterson (1977), pp. 340–341.

[26]In fact, Germany did not receive complete sovereignty until the end of the Cold War and German reunification in 1989 and 1990, respectively.

[27]DOS (1947), pp. 43, 177–178.

In fact, cooperation between the Soviet Union and the other occupying powers broke down quickly in the years after the war. By 1947, the Control Council and the Council of Foreign Ministers had become hopelessly deadlocked and were only able to achieve consensus on a few issues. Reparations, the structure and timing of the creation of a German state, the length of military occupation, and other major issues became contentious among the Allies, especially between the Soviet Union and the Western allies. Coordination among the Western allies progressed slowly but steadily. The British and French initially resisted General Lucius D. Clay's entreaties to unify the Western zones. But the United States and the United Kingdom merged their occupation zones in January 1947, in part to coordinate a common economic policy across their respective zones and expand economic opportunities for German businesses in their areas.[28] The French relinquished some control over their zone with the creation of the FRG in May 1949.

Democratization

Central to the objectives of the United States and the other Western occupying powers was the transformation of German political life along democratic lines. The Potsdam Conference declared that "all democratic political parties with rights of assembly and of public discussion shall be allowed and encouraged throughout Germany." In its sector, U.S. policy focused on a "grass roots" approach, designed to build a German civil society from the bottom up. JCS 1067, for example, argued that one of the Allies' most important objectives should be "the preparation for an eventual reconstruction of German political life on a democratic basis."

This effort to inculcate and nurture democratic political structures was done in incremental steps. Political parties were initially limited to the county (*Kreis*) level but were later authorized at the state (*Land*) level. *Land* administrations were set up in fall 1945. The military government appointed *Länder* officials who were assigned full responsibility for internal affairs not concerned with security. OMGUS carefully scrutinized all aspects of the German administra-

---

[28]For the agreement codifying the economic merger of the American and British zones, see "Joint Statement by Secretary of State Byrnes and Foreign Secretary Bevin," in DOS (1947), pp. 169–174.

tion, and, over time, additional functions were transferred from OMGUS to the various *Länder* administrations. In November 1945, OMGUS set up a Council of Ministers–President (*Länderrat*) for the three states in the U.S. sector. At first advisory, the *Länderrat* had been assigned substantial executive functions by June 1946 and was the principal implementing agency for OMGUS.[29] In addition, elections for small communities of less than 20,000 people were scheduled in January 1946, with elections for larger communities held a few months later. The French and British took a slower approach to local elections in their zones, but active political life had resumed by late 1946.[30]

By 1947–1948, under military proconsul General Clay's leadership, the United States, and then the British and the French, continued to return more authority to the German people.[31] The military government attempted to strike a balance between the return of sovereignty with the need for denazification, but the former was in ascendance by 1948. Moreover, in the U.S. view, the increase in Soviet power in Eastern Europe necessitated the rapid reconstruction of Germany.

The Western allies permitted the first countrywide elections in the Western zones in 1949. These elections led to the creation of the FRG and the election of Konrad Adenauer as the first chancellor. Adenauer's government administered the new West German state at the national level, but ultimate sovereignty was vested in the Allied High Commission (i.e., the three Western occupying powers).[32] With the agreement of the Western powers, West Germany joined NATO and commenced rearmament in 1955.

Another part of the U.S. and international effort to promote democratic ideals and eliminate vestiges of the Nazi regime was to change the education system, encourage freedom of press, and foster free discussion of ideas. For example, textbooks that perpetuated Nazi ideas were removed, as were the majority of elementary- and secondary-level teachers. OMGUS strictly licensed and monitored newspapers and made special efforts to ensure that the press and

---

[29]DOS (1947), pp. 45–46, 181–186.

[30]DOS (1947), pp. 50–59, and Ziemke (1975), pp. 360–366.

[31]Peterson (1977), Ch. 5.

[32]McGeehan (1971), pp. 12–13.

radio were staffed with personnel with anti-Nazi backgrounds. These cultural efforts all worked to support allied goals of creating a peaceful and democratic German state.

Reconstruction

Disbanding the German government also meant disbanding German budgetary institutions. The occupying forces became responsible for economic and budgetary policies. On paper, the U.S. occupying force was only supposed to organize the economy to the extent needed to "meet the needs of the occupying forces and to ensure the production and maintenance of goods and service required to prevent disease and unrest."[33] However, General Clay, the military governor of the U.S. zone, ignored this directive, as did the U.S. military officers under his command who were in charge of various German municipalities. The U.S. military government directed its energies to reviving German output as quickly as possible to provide sustenance to the German population, including refugees. Financial pressures soon came into play as well, since both Britain and the United States wished to reduce the cost of feeding and clothing German populations in their zones.

The occupying powers continued to allow the German central bank to operate, but they, rather than the Germans, exercised control over it. As early as 1946, U.S. economists had plans for replacing the debased reichsmark with a new currency. The deutschmark was not introduced until 1948, in the context of the Ludwig Erhard's reforms, however, because the Allies and the Soviets had joint control over the currency until then. The Western powers were afraid that the Soviets would print large quantities of a new currency to purchase goods from the Western zones, negating the effects of a currency reform. Only in 1948 were currencies and central banking activities sharply divided between east and west.[34]

Because the national German government was, for all intents and purposes, dissolved, the military governors of the zones were not only responsible for civil and political affairs but also for the economic recovery of their sectors. In the U.S. sector, General Clay

---

[33]JCS Directive 1067, as quoted in Killick (1997), p. 60.

[34]Killick (1997), p. 117.

devoted substantial effort and resources to restarting German factories and mines. The same was true in the British sector. The French were more fearful and hence much less willing to see a resurgence of the German economy.

Despite initial discussions about prohibiting the reindustrialization of Germany, German economic output recovered rapidly in 1946 as plants and mines were reopened. By the fourth quarter of 1946, industrial output in the U.S. zone had risen to 2.4 times its fourth-quarter 1945 level, although it was still 45 percent of its 1937 level. In the more heavily industrialized British zone, output was up 50 percent. Nonetheless, the German gross domestic product (GDP) was only 40 percent of its 1944 level because of the disastrous economic situation in the first half of the year. British and U.S. economic policies quickly moved toward creating an economic environment favorable for business. U.S. policy, partially influenced by successful U.S. businessmen who were part of the Roosevelt and Truman administrations, was directed at creating a free-market economy in Germany. As part of this process, the German cartels were broken up. In addition, both zone commanders encouraged the development of trade.

Resources to support the German population were provided through GARIOA, surplus U.S. military supplies, U.S. and British military in-zone expenditures, and funds from the British budget. At the same time, the U.S. government recognized French and Russian claims for reparations. In particular, the U.S. government forced German mines to deliver coal to France and other nearby states for free. In return, the U.S. zonal authorities provided miners with food and wages. In addition, the Soviet Union dismantled German plants in both the British and U.S. zones and shipped the equipment back to the Soviet Union as part of reparations. Thus, some of what was given was taken away by other governments. The United States attempted to reduce the impact of these reparations payments by instituting a "first charge" principle. German export earnings were first used to pay for essential imports and only then for reparations.[35] The United States also provided very large loans to the United Kingdom in 1946, some of which helped defray its costs for running its zone.

---

[35]Killick (1997), p. 52.

Although annual economic statistics show double-digit growth in German GDP from 1947 to 1952, the statistics mask quarterly ups and downs. The winter of 1947 was very severe, and the following summer was very dry. A series of strikes and a slowdown in the rate of economic recovery in both Germany and Europe resulted in substantial concern about European recovery. This was enunciated in George Marshall's famous speech at Harvard University on June 5, 1947, calling for a massive commitment of funds from the United States to assist European reconstruction.

The Marshall Plan was finally passed on April 3, 1948. Because of concerns about control, the U.S. Congress did not want the UN Relief and Rehabilitation Administration to administer the funds. Consequently, the U.S. European Cooperation Administration administered the Marshall Plan, in conjunction with the Organization for European Economic Cooperation, which eventually became the Organization for Economic Cooperation and Development.

The Marshall Plan did contribute to rapid European (and German) economic growth and recovery between 1948 and 1951, when the program ended; however, in many ways, the period from 1946 to early 1948, before the official launch of the Marshall Plan, was more critical. During this period, the United States provided large loans and aid to a number of European countries, totaling $3.4 billion in 1946 and $4.7 billion in 1947. In addition, such international organizations as the International Monetary Fund (IMF), International Bank for Reconstruction and Development, and UN Relief and Rehabilitation Administration provided an additional $1.2 billion and $1.1 billion in 1946 and 1947, respectively. The United States also provided these funds and enabled Germany and the rest of Europe to pay for the large inflows of imports that were instrumental for the postwar recovery. As with other case studies in this report, external assistance was needed for a period when the economies were not yet able to generate sufficient export revenues to pay for the imports needed for recovery.

Some scholars have argued that German economic recovery was well under way by the time the Marshall Plan was passed. In addition, some consider the Erhard currency and fiscal reforms to have been more important for subsequent German economic growth than the Marshall Plan was, especially since Germany received less assistance than other countries on a per capita basis: $12 in 1948 compared with $45 in Holland.[36]

However, a more useful way to assess the U.S. role in German economic recovery is to assess the full panoply of assistance and policies. In fact, in policy discourse in the United States, the term *Marshall Plan* has become a shorthand term for U.S. economic policies in the aggregate, not just the specific 1948–1951 program. Under this definition, the "Marshall Plan" provided substantial resources directly or indirectly through loans and assistance to the United Kingdom to finance the imports needed to get the German economy on its feet. U.S. policies in its zone helped contribute to freer markets in Germany by breaking up major cartels and providing an environment in which private businesses could flourish. The U.S. insistence on trade liberalization and support for the creation of the European Payments Union in 1950 played important roles in European economic integration and the eventual European decision, in 1951, to create the European Coal and Steel Community and to sign the 1957 Treaty of Rome, which established the European Common Market. Trade liberalization, economic integration, and the creation of the European Union (EU) have been primary factors in post–World War II European and German economic growth.

LESSONS LEARNED

An examination of Allied reconstruction efforts in Germany highlights a number of important lessons regarding democratization, civil administration, security, and economics:

- Democracy can be transferred, and societies can, in some situations, be encouraged to change.

- Defeated populations can sometimes be more cooperative and malleable than anticipated.

- Enforced accountability for past injustices, through such forums as war crimes tribunals, can facilitate transformation.

- Dismembered and divided countries can be difficult to put back together.

---

[36]This section draws heavily on Killick (1997), pp. 114–117.

- Defeated countries often need sizable transfers to cover basic government expenditures and quickly provide humanitarian assistance after the conflict.

- Reparations immediately after the end of the conflict are counterproductive. The economy must grow before a country can compensate the victims of the conflict.

- Permitting more than one power to determine economic policy can significantly delay economic recovery.

The most important lesson from the U.S. occupation of Germany is that military force and political capital can, at least in some circumstances, be successfully employed to underpin democratic and societal transformation. Furthermore, such a transformation can be enduring. U.S., French, and British efforts to help build democratic institutions in Germany and to encourage the establishment of political parties were incremental and began in 1945. Over the next several years, these powers oversaw local and national elections; the establishment of a constitution and a bicameral parliament; and, in September 1949, the election of Konrad Adenauer as the first postwar chancellor of the newly formed West German state. While U.S. and allied efforts were important in ensuring this outcome, the West German population obviously played a critical role. Indeed, by the late 1940s, Western allies increasingly gave sovereignty of political institutions to the German people, who continued to deepen the democratization process.

U.S. officials anticipated and planned to deal with significant residual German resistance following the surrender of its armed forces. Yet no resistance of consequence emerged then or at any time thereafter, much as in Haiti during Operation Uphold Democracy (see Chapter Five). The large number of U.S. and allied military forces in West Germany and the establishment of a strong constabulary force preempted most resistance. Indeed, the constabulary force was specifically created to respond to incidents of civil unrest, conduct mounted and dismounted police patrols, interdict smuggling operations, and aid in intelligence gathering. This contrasts starkly with nation-building efforts in such countries as Bosnia, which were marred by organized crime and civil unrest.

The institution of war crimes tribunals and the thorough purging from public life of those associated with the Nazi regime was messy, controversial, and occasionally unfair. However, it consolidated the democratization process by removing a potential threat to a nascent democratic political system. Furthermore, denazification eliminated virtually all support for the return of the Nazi regime and caused a thorough repudiation of Nazi policies in Germany society. In short, justice and retribution in postwar Germany facilitated the population's reconciliation with its history and its neighbors.

The division of Germany into four occupation zones with independent political, economic, and military authority took 45 years to overcome. This was largely because the German question became tangled in the Cold War struggle between the United States and the Soviet Union. As historian John Lewis Gaddis notes:

> What each superpower most feared was that [Germany] might align itself with its Cold War adversary: if that were to happen, the resulting concentration of military, industrial, and economic power could be too great to overcome.[37]

Even reassembling the three Western zones took nearly half a decade, lengthening the occupation and slowing many reforms. Consequently, it is clear that divided countries can be very difficult to put back together—even among allies.

The economic policies General Clay and the U.S. Army personnel under his command pursued were key to the economic recovery of West Germany. In the U.S. zone, Clay and his subordinates rapidly and efficiently organized the provision of humanitarian assistance and restarted government services and economic activity. The U.S. Army's focus on "getting things moving" was key to minimizing humanitarian suffering and accelerating economic recovery in its zone in the immediate aftermath of World War II. Similar efforts in the British zone were also constructive. The American and British zones were large net recipients of assistance in the first few years after World War II. These inflows were needed to cover the cost of government services and to provide minimum levels of food and other goods. They played a crucial role in jump-starting economic activity in West Germany.

---

[37]Gaddis, John Lewis, *We Now Know: Rethinking Cold War History*, New York: Oxford University Press, 1997, p. 115.

Other zones did not fare as well because of reparations paid to the Soviet Union, France, and other states. Germany was compelled to export coal for free or on long-term credit to other European states. Soviet forces dismantled a number of assembly lines and shipped them back to the Soviet Union. These reparations slowed German economic recovery.

Each of the occupying powers set its own economic policies. The Soviet Union controlled presses that printed reichsmarks, the German currency, which it used to print money circulated throughout all four zones. Consequently, German inflation did not come under control until the introduction of the deutschmark in West Germany in 1948, thereby depriving the Soviets of their ability to print money. The introduction of the new currency and Erhard's conservative fiscal policies were crucial ingredients for the German boom of the 1950s and 1960s.

Chapter Three

JAPAN

The U.S. use of nuclear weapons on Hiroshima on August 6 and Nagasaki on August 9, 1945, led to the conclusion of the war in the Pacific, which for Japan had started in northern China in 1931. Between the dropping of the two atomic bombs, the Soviet Union entered the war and began moving into Manchuria. U.S. troops had captured Okinawa and were poised to invade the home islands. The specter of defeat led to a crisis within the Japanese government and a decision by the emperor to accept the Allied terms of surrender. Under the pressure of these events, the emperor broadcast a call to the Japanese people on August 15, 1945, to "endure the unendurable." With General Douglas MacArthur and Fleet Admiral Chester Nimitz in attendance, representatives of the emperor and the Japanese military signed the articles of surrender on September 2, 1945, aboard the battleship USS *Missouri* in Tokyo Bay.

The final terms of surrender were agreed upon at Potsdam on July 26, 1945: unconditional surrender; a purge of the leadership that had advocated global conquest; an Allied occupation until a new order was established and Japan's war-making power was destroyed; the disbandment of Japan's empire; military disarmament; prosecution of war criminals; establishment of freedom of speech, religion, thought, and respect for basic human rights; and reduction of economic capacity to prevent rearmament.[1] The United States, the United Kingdom, and China were party to these terms; the Soviet Union signed on after its declaration of war. The Potsdam Confer-

---

[1]DOS, *Occupation of Japan: Policy and Progress*, Far Eastern Series 17, Washington, D.C.: U.S. Government Printing Office, Pub. 267, 1946, pp. 53–55.

ence in effect presented an ultimatum that threatened "prompt and utter destruction" if Japan did not surrender. It represented the culmination of a series of Allied meetings beginning in 1943.

Preserving the emperor and the imperial institution were of utmost importance to the Japanese leadership. Their first offer of surrender, communicated through the Swiss, conditioned acceptance of the Potsdam terms on a guarantee of the emperor's safety. U.S. Secretary of State James F. Byrnes responded by noting that the surrender would be unconditional and that both the emperor and the Japanese government would be subject to the Supreme Commander of the Allied Powers (SCAP) upon surrender. The ultimate form of government and, by inference, the fate of the emperor would be left up to "the freely expressed will of the Japanese people."[2]

CHALLENGES

Security

At the time of its surrender, Japan had mobilized between 3.6 million and 4.3 million troops to defend against the Allied invasion of the Japanese home islands, and these troops were still armed. U.S. Army intelligence estimated that an additional 3.5 million troops were dispersed throughout Japan's former empire, including 1.6 million in China and Manchuria; 365,000 in Korea; and 525,000 scattered across isolated islands in the Pacific.[3] It was not clear whether all would comply with the emperor's command to surrender.

Humanitarian

The Allied bombings of Japanese cities left nearly 9 million people, 30 percent of the urban population, homeless. In Tokyo, 65 percent of the homes had been destroyed. The national food distribution system had totally collapsed, and many faced hunger and starvation. Nearly 3 million civilians were stranded overseas, with the largest

---

[2]DOS (1946), pp. 57–58.

[3]Douglas MacArthur, *Reports of General MacArthur: Japanese Operations in the Southwest Pacific Area*, Vol. II, Pt. II, Washington, D.C.: U.S. Government Printing Office, 1966b, pp. 752–753.

concentrations in Manchuria (998,815), Korea (712,583), China (428,518), Sakhalin (373,223), and Formosa (307,147).[4] Since Japan's navy and commercial shipping had largely been destroyed, few vessels were available to transport the civilians home. Approximately 123,510 children were orphaned or abandoned.[5] Equally abandoned were the other Asian residents of Japan, including 1.3 million Koreans, many of whom had been brought over as conscripts to work in coal mines and other industries. Some 30,000 Allied prisoners of war held in camps in Japan were in need of food, medical attention, and evacuation.

Civil Administration

Despite the economic and humanitarian crisis that resulted from the war, the emperor still enjoyed the support of the vast majority of Japanese. The bureaucracy, the Diet (Japan's parliament), and the cabinet were intact, functioning, and prepared to cooperate. The key issues for U.S. decisionmakers were how to make use of the Japanese government, how extensive an oversight function would be necessary, and how they would assign responsibility for the war. Because of the Japanese attack on Pearl Harbor and the perceived ferocity of the subsequent war in the Pacific, there was substantial anti-Japanese sentiment among the U.S. public, particularly toward the emperor. An opinion poll conducted in June 1945 indicated that 77 percent of Americans wanted the emperor to be severely punished.[6] The U.S. public was also weary of war and supported an early return of the troops. There appeared to be little desire for the high economic costs that an extended occupation would entail.

Democratization

In principle, Japan had a constitutional, but not a fully parliamentary, form of government in 1945. The Meiji Constitution, adopted in

---

[4]Douglas MacArthur, *Reports of General MacArthur: Japanese Operations in the Southwest Pacific Area*, Vol. I, Washington, D.C.: U.S. Government Printing Office, 1966a, p. 459.

[5]John W. Dower, *Embracing Defeat: Japan in the Wake of World War II*, New York: W. W. Norton & Company, 1999, p. 63.

[6]Michael Schaller, *The American Occupation of Japan*, New York: Oxford University Press, 1985, p. 3. See also Dower (1999), p. 299.

1890, vested sovereign power in the emperor but divided political power among a small set of competing elites. The political parties vied for power with the military, the bureaucracy, the leading industrialists (*zaibatsu*), and groups close to the emperor. Since 1925, all men over the age of 25 had been granted the right to vote, but their representatives in the Diet could easily be outmaneuvered because the majority party in the Diet did not automatically have the right to form a government; instead, the emperor appointed the prime minister. The military was not legally subordinate to civilian control, a structural flaw that the military exploited to the fullest. Political freedoms necessary to sustain a democracy, such as freedom of speech and assembly, to the extent they existed at all, were severely curtailed.

Reconstruction

At the end of World War II, the Japanese empire lay in ruins. Roughly 3 to 4 percent of the prewar population of 74 million had perished. One-quarter of the country's wealth was destroyed. The Japanese civilian economy was near collapse. With imports of essential commodities and raw materials completely cut off, food, fuel, clothing, housing, and nearly all the necessities of daily life were in extremely short supply. Deprived of their colonies, which had served as both a source of raw materials and markets for finished goods, Japan's economic future looked bleak. What remained of Japan's equipment and factories was earmarked for reparations. Actions taken by the Japanese leadership at the end of the war compounded these problems. Military stockpiles were hidden or looted, and the Finance Ministry and the Bank of Japan printed currency to pay off government obligations to workers, soldiers, and contractors, setting the stage for rampant inflation.[7]

THE U.S. AND INTERNATIONAL ROLES

Because of its predominant role in the final phases of the war against Japan, the United States decided to take the lead in the occupation. Unlike in Germany, there would be no zones and no division of

---

[7]Dower (1999), pp. 112–118, 531.

responsibility. The United States hoped to avoid the most trouble-some aspects of the German occupation, where policy formulation and implementation was slowed and sometimes blocked by the need to forge agreement among the four parties. The United States was, however, willing to accept some international participation. Agreement on the formation of two international bodies for oversight and consultation, the Far Eastern Commission and the Allied Council for Japan (ACJ), was finally reached in Moscow in December 1945. The Far Eastern Commission was established in Washington in February 1946. Composed of representatives of the 11 countries that had fought against Japan, its role was to formulate policies to enable Japan to fulfill its surrender terms and to review SCAP directives and actions.[8] It was given no authority over military operations or territorial questions.[9] Nominally designed as a supervisory body, its effectiveness was undermined by the fact it was not constituted until after much of the initial policy toward Japan had already been decided. A further hindrance to its effectiveness lay in the requirement that a majority of members, including China, the United States, the United Kingdom, and the Soviet Union, concur before a policy could be adopted. Without such agreement, SCAP interim directives were allowed to stand. Although constrained on most other issues, the Far Eastern Commission was given the power to override SCAP on the issue of constitutional revision and did have some influence on the content of the final document. Otherwise, MacArthur largely ignored or maneuvered around the commission.

The ACJ, composed of China, the Soviet Union, the United Kingdom, and the United States, was established in Tokyo in April 1946 to consult and advise SCAP. Like the Far Eastern Commission, the ACJ never became an effective instrument of policy because SCAP, whose representative served as the ACJ's chair, was not obligated to consult with it or accept its advice. Thus, the ACJ largely languished during the occupation.

---

[8]The initial members were the United States, the United Kingdom, the Soviet Union, China, France, the Netherlands, Canada, Australia, New Zealand, India, and the Philippines. Burma and Pakistan became members subsequently.

[9]For more details on the workings of the Far Eastern Commission and ACJ, see Jane M. Alden, "Occupation" in Hugh Borton, ed., *Japan*, Ithaca, N.Y.: Cornell University Press, 1950.

Military

General MacArthur and his staff acted under military orders laid out in the U.S. JCS directive 1380/15.[10] The decision to rule Japan through existing Japanese government machinery, taken on the eve of the occupation to conserve U.S. forces and resources, meant that there was no military government like those that had been set up in Germany. As SCAP, General MacArthur presided over both the military occupation and the administrative superstructure. The General Headquarters of the Far East Command was responsible for the military forces in Japan, Okinawa, and Korea.

In the initial phase of the occupation, some of the troops were organized into "military government" teams distributed across Japan's eight regions and 46 prefectures.[11] Each local team had functional sections dealing with such areas as government, economics, information and education, and public health that were parallel to the structure of the local government. Decisions were made in Tokyo and sent to governors and mayors for implementation. It was the job of the local military government teams to observe and report back to headquarters on how well their decrees were being implemented at the local level. These teams were later renamed Civil Affairs teams and were staffed with civilians.

Although this was nominally an Allied occupation, the United States exercised unilateral control from the beginning. Military operational issues were specifically exempted from the jurisdiction of the Far Eastern Commission, the international supervisory body attached to the occupation. The first U.S. plan for the occupation called for 600,000 troops and anticipated that this would include 315,000 American, 135,000 British Commonwealth, 60,000 Nationalist Chinese, and 175,000 Soviet troops, all under U.S. command.[12] These numbers were later revised, since neither the Soviets nor the Chinese ever contributed forces. In the end, only the countries of the British Commonwealth shared occupation responsibilities. These troops

---

[10]Theodore Cohen, *Remaking Japan: The American Occupation as New Deal*, New York: The Free Press, 1987, pp. 8–10.

[11]The nomenclature reflected earlier ideas about their probable function. The eight regions are Hokkaido, Kyushu, Shikoku, Tohoku, Kanto, Chubu, Chugoku, and Kinki. Okinawa, Japan's 47th prefecture, was administered separately (as discussed later).

[12]Cohen (1987), p. 60.

began arriving in February 1946; eventually, 45,000 British and Commonwealth troops were assigned duties in and around Hiroshima.

Civil and Economic

It was the view of the U.S. government that Japan surrendered unconditionally by accepting the terms laid out during the Potsdam Conference. Furthermore, while the Japanese government was bound by these terms, Potsdam did not limit the actions the United States could take in carrying out the occupation. The Americans did not recognize any legal constraint on the range and extent of their authority, with the exception of international law governing the proper treatment of civilians. In fact, a message sent from Washington to MacArthur with President Harry Truman's signature reiterated that the authority of both the emperor and the Japanese government was subordinate to him.[13] The message continued by noting the following:

> you will exercise your authority as you deem proper to carry out your mission .... Since your authority is supreme, you will not entertain any questions on the part of the Japanese as to its scope.

In addition to the Potsdam Conference agreement, MacArthur had two other documents to guide his work. One was the work of the State, War and Navy Coordinating Committee (SWNCC), entitled the "United States Initial Post-Surrender Policy Relating to Japan" (SWNCC 150/4), which outlined an ambitious program of political and economic democratization. The second, JCS 1380/15, remained secret during the early phase of the occupation. It elaborated on SWNCC 150/4 and served as the military directive that guided the occupation's reform program. MacArthur's receipt of this "unexpected and breathtakingly broad" program for democratization caused him to rethink the framework for SCAP's general headquarters. Instead of simply adding a civil affairs section to his general staff, he created a new headquarters, which would exist side by side with the Far East Command. SCAP headquarters was responsible for

---

[13]DOS (1946), pp. 88–89.

nonmilitary matters, the primary focus of the occupation. It had nine sections, roughly parallel in structure to the Japanese cabinet, and was staffed largely by U.S. civil servants and officers who converted to civilian status. At its peak in 1948, it employed about 3,500 people, although only about one-quarter of them were actively involved in administering the reform program.

In August 1945, MacArthur instructed the Japanese government to establish a liaison office to interact with SCAP headquarters. The Central Liaison Office was established in Tokyo and was staffed by the Foreign Ministry. Liaison offices were also set up in each prefecture to serve the local military government teams. The Central Liaison Office functioned as the primary channel for communication between the SCAP special staff sections and the Japanese government until the office was abolished in December 1947. Thereafter, the staff sections communicated directly with the ministries and agencies they oversaw.

WHAT HAPPENED

Nearly all parties involved have deemed the U.S. occupation of Japan a success, as do those who today enjoy the fruits of those efforts. However, the positive results were not evident overnight, and the immediate effects struck many as chaotic. The occupation, which was presided over by an autocratic U.S. general, arguably had more success at demilitarization and democratization than it did at fostering a truly open and vibrant economic system. Yet, it also turned a former enemy into a reliable ally.

Security

The speed of the Japanese surrender caught the Americans somewhat by surprise. Large numbers of troops were being prepared for the invasion of Japan but were not yet in place. General MacArthur, who had been appointed SCAP with full authority to accept the surrender and direct the occupation, was in the Philippines.

MacArthur initially estimated that he would need between 200,000 to 600,000 troops in the first six months of occupation to pacify and patrol Japan. He requested that the troops planned for the two-phased invasion of Japan be made available to him for occupation duties. This included the Sixth Army under the command of General Walter Krueger and the Eighth Army under General Robert Eichelberger. The Americans believed that most Japanese soldiers would obey the emperor's order to surrender and cooperate with the occupation authorities. Nonetheless, there was some concern that the occupation forces could meet intermittent and possibly even concerted resistance from dissident elements. MacArthur's initial plan entailed a phased landing of 22 Army divisions and two regimental combat teams plus air and naval units, which would be dispersed over 14 major areas in Japan in sufficient force to quell any attempt to disrupt the occupation.[14]

In the two weeks that elapsed between the Japanese acceptance of the surrender terms and the arrival of the occupying force, a newly constituted cabinet under Prime Minister Naruhiko Higashikuni, the emperor's uncle, began the process of demobilizing Japan's army and navy, as stipulated by the Potsdam Conference. Members of the royal family were dispatched to China and elsewhere to oversee the surrender of Japanese troops stationed abroad. The Japanese government also engaged in a public relations campaign to counter pervasive rumors that the U.S. occupying force would be brutal and violent to Japanese civilians. At the same time there were separate reports of Japanese authorities encouraging families to keep their women inside or send them to the countryside prior to the arrival of U.S. forces.

During the last days of August 1945, an advance party from the 11th Airborne Division landed at Atsugi Airport, near Yokohama, where they received a courteous reception from Japanese officials and specially selected troops. Two days later, General MacArthur arrived. On September 1, 1945, the main forces of the U.S. Eighth Army began coming ashore and rapidly took up positions in the northern half of the country, from Nagoya to Hokkaido. On September 4, the Sixth Army began to arrive at the naval port of Sasebo and assumed positions at former Japanese military bases in the southern half of the country. This division of responsibility lasted until January 1946,

---

[14]Howard B. Schonberger, *Aftermath of War*, Kent, Ohio: The Kent State University Press, 1989, p. 48.

when the Sixth Army was deactivated. Okinawa was left under the control of Army Service Command I. At the end of 1945, approximately 354,675 U.S. troops were stationed throughout Japan.[15]

Among the first tasks of the occupation were the demobilization and disarmament of the 7 million men in the Japanese armed forces and their successful reintegration into Japanese society. At the request of the Japanese, MacArthur agreed to allow the Army and Navy Ministries, renamed the First and Second Demobilization Ministries, to handle the deactivation of their own forces. In quick succession, the Imperial Headquarters was abolished, the Combined Fleet and the Navy General Headquarters were formally dissolved, and the general headquarters of the army and navy were closed. Demobilization of the Japanese military was completed on October 15, 1945, and the two service ministries were abolished on December 1. By the end of 1945, the Japanese armed forces had ceased to exist. Paramilitary and ultranationalist organizations were also disbanded. Subsequently, demilitarization was enshrined in the new Japanese constitution. Article 9, the so-called "no war" clauses, pledged that Japan renounced war and the threat or use of force as a means of settling international disputes and, therefore, would never authorize the maintenance of land, sea, and air forces or other war potential.

The role of U.S. forces in demobilization and disarmament was to provide oversight and surveillance. Foot and motor patrols conducted surveillance, while intelligence inspection teams searched for concealed arms and munitions. Inventory and disposition teams were established to evaluate; inventory; and, where appropriate, destroy captured weapons and equipment. The Japanese handled the disposal of weapons. Ammunition was dumped into the sea, and equipment and other war material were cut up into scrap under U.S. supervision and turned over to the Japanese government.

By 1947, U.S. policymakers were increasingly concerned about the Soviet Union and the spread of communism in Asia. They began to see Japan as a future ally rather than a former enemy, especially since communism was expanding into neighboring countries, such as China. Pressure began to build on Japan to consider some level of

---

[15]U.S. War Department, Office of the Adjutant General, Machine Records Branch, *Strength of the Army*, Washington, D.C., December 1, 1945.

rearmament. While the JCS did not support full-scale remilitariza-
tion, they did advocate increases in civilian and coastal "police"
forces to handle domestic security matters. Japanese resistance to
this pressure was swept away by the Korean War. In July 1950, the
Japanese reluctantly agreed to the U.S. request that they establish a
National Police Reserve of up to 75,000 men, which would function
as a paramilitary force to fill the vacuum left by the rapid movement
of all but one division of U.S. occupation forces to Korea. MacArthur,
a staunch proponent of Japan's demilitarization, now found himself
overseeing the creation of a small army.

The war in Korea also served to remove the JCS's objections to a
peace treaty and thus paved the way for the end of the occupation.
MacArthur pronounced the aims of the occupation complete in 1947
and began advocating a peace treaty before 1950. Neither his calls
nor those of DOS were a consequence of the war in Korea. MacArthur
and the DOS had been calling for a peace treaty since 1949 because
they believed that the continued presence of U.S. forces in Japanese
towns and cities served as an irritant rather than a force for stability.
However, the Pentagon and the JCS demanded that Japan accept
rearmament and U.S. bases indefinitely in exchange for a peace
treaty. In the end, Prime Minister Shigeru Yoshida acquiesced in
principle, although he resisted, on economic, political, and philo-
sophical grounds, U.S. demands to create a military force of 300,000
to 350,000 men. In September 1951, the peace treaty and a separate
security treaty were signed in San Francisco. In April 1952, Japan
regained its sovereignty. The security treaty ensured continued U.S.
access to bases in Japan in return for U.S. protection should Japan be
attacked.

The peace treaty did not include Japan's southernmost prefecture of
Okinawa, which had been administered separately from the mainland since April 1945. Given its increasingly strategic location, U.S.
military policymakers focused on turning the island chain into a
major base for the U.S. military in the Pacific. The JCS argued for
annexation, while the DOS advocated eventual return to Japan. In
1947, the UN Security Council approved a U.S. trusteeship for an
indefinite period that would last until March 15, 1972, when it was
returned to Japan.

Humanitarian

Although few U.S. policymakers favored highly vindictive policies toward the Japanese, they initially did not plan to devote much money or attention to alleviating the suffering that most believed Japan had brought upon itself. The first priority of the occupation troops was to aid Allied prisoners of war and foreign internees being held in Japan. On August 25, even before occupation troops came ashore, the U.S. military began dropping relief supplies of food, medicine, and clothing over the camps where the prisoners were being held. In addition, "mercy teams" were organized to accompany the Eighth Army headquarters. They were responsible for interacting with the International Red Cross and the Japanese Central Liaison Office to expedite the release of prisoners and internees and ensure their speedy evacuation. By the end of October 1945, 31,617 American prisoners of war had been freed.[16]

The next order of business was to deal with the nearly 7 million Japanese troops, officials, colonists, and merchants who were stranded overseas at war's end. This task was left largely up to the Japanese government, which was also responsible for funding it. Under U.S. naval supervision, the Japanese assembled nearly 400 ships, including 200 liberty ships and landing ship tanks borrowed from the U.S. military, to repatriate these displaced people.[17] The available vessels were small, and the repatriation centers in Japan had limited capacity to absorb returnees. As a consequence, repatriation took more than two years. Between October 1945 and December 1946, over 5.1 million Japanese returned to their homeland. Another 1 million returned in 1947. Of the over 1.3 million soldiers and civilians who surrendered to the Soviet Union in Manchuria and North Asia, 300,000 were never accounted for. Many returnees found their former homes destroyed and their families shattered. Life in the overcrowded repatriation centers was grim. There was little food and medical attention, but for some, there was no other choice.

Koreans, Chinese, and other foreign nationals living in Japan, many conscripted to man mines and other war industries, found themselves adrift. The Japanese government did not consider them citi-

---

[16]Dower (1999), p. 54.

[17]Schaller (1985), p. 27, and Dower (1999), pp. 54–58.

zens and thus had made no provision for their support. U.S. troops were called upon to oversee the repatriation centers and ensure that the Koreans, Chinese, and others were fed, controlled, and given medical attention as they awaited transport home. By the end of 1946, 930,000 Koreans had returned, and roughly 60,000 Chinese had returned either to mainland China or to Formosa (Taiwan).

The national food distribution system had totally collapsed, and many faced hunger and starvation. Furthermore, 1945 witnessed the most disastrous rice harvest since 1910, about 40 percent below the normal yield.[18] Although Japanese assertions that 10 million might perish without assistance proved exaggerated, the situation was quite dire.[19] Washington planners, who were aware of their duty to provide for the civilians within their areas of control, recognized that they would have to supply food to Japan for some period of time. But food supplies were severely limited worldwide in 1945, and feeding the Japanese, the former enemy, was a low priority. The military orders governing the U.S. occupation, JCS 1380/15, instructed SCAP to limit Japanese food relief to what was needed to prevent a level of disease and unrest that could endanger the occupying force and interfere with military operations. Imports of fuel and medicine would also be kept at subsistence levels.

MacArthur, worried that his democratization program would be undermined by hunger, lobbied for more substantial assistance, arguing that the United States would have to supply either more food or more forces. He was initially able to supplement the meager supplies with 800,000 tons of surplus military food resulting from the rapid drawdown in occupation forces. His 1946–1947 budget request included $250 million for food, fertilizer, petroleum products, and medicine, an amount exceeding the combined budgets of the U.S. Departments of Commerce, Justice, and Labor that year.[20] He got it.

This food aid saved Japan from acute malnutrition, if not starvation. For many Japanese, particularly young children whose school lunches consisted largely of donated food, this assistance symbolized

---

[18]Dower (1999), p. 93.

[19]Dower (1999), pp. 89–97.

[20]Cohen (1987), p. 144. The figure was $330 million in 1947–1948 and $497 million in 1948–1949.

U.S. generosity and wealth. In addition to food releases from military forces, the food aid came primarily from GARIOA and food gifts from Japanese residents in the United States that were sent through Licensed Agencies for Relief of Asia. Occupation authorities in Germany had declined some GARIOA food shipments, which some described as hardly better than cattle feed. Japan, however, was too hungry to do the same. Japanese officials who had considered the GARIOA food an outright gift were somewhat dismayed to receive a bill for $490 million.[21] This food aid, together with the chocolate and chewing gum that U.S. soldiers gave away free and the other goods for the troops that found their way onto the black market, imprinted an image of U.S. affluence on the Japanese psyche that they admired and to which they aspired.

The occupation forces were not directly involved in providing shelter for the homeless. In fact, the costs of constructing houses and facilities for the U.S. troops, which the Japanese government was obligated to cover, probably impeded similar construction for the local population.[22]

Civil Administration

At the start of the occupation, MacArthur and his SCAP staff faced three critical issues on dealing with the existing Japanese government: (1) how to make use of the existing political and bureaucratic apparatus; (2) how to handle the emperor; and, intertwined with these two issues, (3) how to hold individuals responsible for war crimes accountable. The decisions on these issues would establish the framework within which MacArthur and his staff would conduct their larger mission: demilitarization and democratization.

The postwar status of the emperor and the imperial institution were the focus of particularly intense debates within the U.S. government before Japan's surrender. U.S. experts on Japan argued that retaining the emperor, at least during the initial stages, would be a low-cost, low-risk method of governing. Following a meeting with the emperor on September 27, 1945, MacArthur was also persuaded that retaining

---

[21]*Asahi Shimbun* Staff, *The Pacific Rivals*, New York: Weatherhill, 1972, p. 124.

[22]Dower (1999), p. 115.

the emperor would facilitate a smooth and successful occupation. Sentiment in the United States, however, was heavily against Emperor Hirohito, since most held him responsible for the war. Many in Japan likewise assumed that he would, and should, be forced to abdicate. To counter such views, SCAP launched a concerted campaign to change the emperor's public image, painting him as a democrat and peacemaker who had been duped by the militarists into waging a war he had not desired.[23] In January 1946, the emperor issued a statement denying he had divine attributes. Subsequently he began touring the country in an orchestrated effort to boost morale and support the objectives of the occupation.

The lack of U.S. personnel with both language and technical capability led to the decision to retain the existing government and give the occupation authorities a supervisory role. MacArthur quickly assembled a staff for this purpose, recruited in part from the demobilizing military occupation.[24] By April 1946, SCAP employed 1,550 officers and civilians. In addition, it engaged hundreds of enlisted men, Japanese, and third-country nationals. As mentioned above, staff levels peaked at around 3,500 in 1948. Such a small staff for such a large and complicated nation meant that power and the area of responsibility for each staff member was vast. In the first months of the occupation, SCAP communicated with the Japanese government largely via written directives that laid out, in bold and broad strokes, the tasks they were to accomplish. The details were left up to the bureaucrats to devise and the Diet to debate. SCAP, of course, retained the right to intervene and to push legislation in the desired direction if necessary. The indirect nature of SCAP's exercise of authority masked its true power. In the early years, SCAP staff reviewed all Japanese proposals to ensure compliance with SCAP policy. This iterative decisionmaking process provided the Japanese with an avenue to influence the final outcomes and, as the occupation progressed, to obtain considerable and increasingly cordial access to various levels of SCAP. After the initial reforms were implemented in mid-1947, MacArthur encouraged the Japanese gov-

---

[23]Tetsuya Kataoka, *The Price of a Constitution: The Origin of Japan's Postwar Politics*, New York: Crane Russak, 1991, p. 26. Bonner E. Fellers, MacArthur's military secretary and chief of his psychological-warfare operations, was a key proponent of this view.

[24]For details on the staffing of SCAP, see Cohen (1987), pp. 103–107.

ernment and agencies to reassume the normal powers of government for all domestic affairs, with the exception of the economy. The Japanese bureaucracy emerged stronger than ever. It was the one group among the political elites whose power grew both through the war and the occupation.

These two decisions—to retain the emperor and to rely heavily on the existing bureaucracy—necessitated that both escape responsibility and punishment for their roles in the conduct of the war. These decisions would have profound implications for the type of democracy SCAP set about to instill.

Following the precedent established at Nuremberg to hold individual leaders responsible for war crimes, the occupation authorities rounded up the leading suspected war criminals throughout the fall of 1945 in preparation for the Tokyo War Crimes Trials.[25] Former Prime Minister Hideki Tojo and 24 other prominent Japanese men were designated Class A criminals and were accused of crimes against peace and humanity. Representatives of all 11 Allied powers who fought against Japan sat in judgment, but the single chief prosecutor, an American, created the impression that the United States was in control. The process and procedures of the Tokyo Trials were exactly the same as those at Nuremberg. The nature of the defendants and their crimes, however, differed to such an extent that one historian has termed the Tokyo Trials "a murky reflection of its German counterpart."[26] Japan had no counterpart to the Nazi party, the Gestapo, or the SS—the Nazi party units in charge of central security and mass extermination. Japan had not operated death camps, although its treatment of prisoners of war was notorious. Nonetheless, after trials lasting nearly three years (three times longer than Nuremberg), all were found guilty by majority verdict. Unlike at Nuremberg, there were no acquittals.[27] Seven were hanged, and the rest received long prison sentences.

But the fact that the emperor was never brought to trial undermined the credibility of the proceedings in the eyes of many observers,

---

[25]Formally known as the International Military Tribunal for the Far East.

[26]Dower (1999), p. 449.

[27]For more on comparisons between Tokyo and Nuremberg, see Dower (1996), Ch. 15.

especially since the war was waged in his name. In the end, none of those imprisoned served out their terms. Five died in prison, and the remainder were released. About 5,700 individuals were indicted for Class B and Class C crimes at trials convened by the British, U.S., and Philippine governments across Asia. The United States tried 46 soldiers, mostly for crimes against prisoners, 41 of whom were sentenced to death. By the time the trials were largely completed, in October 1949, a total of 4,200 Japanese had been convicted of war crimes.[28]

A related aspect of democratization was ridding Japan of those who had been important proponents of militarism and aggression. The first in a series of purge orders targeting politicians, bureaucrats, police, and military officers was issued by SCAP on January 4, 1946. To the dismay of the Japanese authorities who implemented it, the purge was categorical rather than personal—based on wartime position, not actions. It targeted those in designated organizations, including wartime cabinet ministers and other high public officials; the Special High Police; governors of occupied territories; members of the ultrarightist Military Virtue Society; and officials of the Imperial Rule Assistance Society, an umbrella organization created midway through the war to unite all political forces behind the emperor. All those in leadership positions within these groups were removed from their positions and barred from participating in public life. The purge eventually affected 210,000 Japanese (0.29 percent of the population). This was much lower than the purges in Germany, which affected 2.5 percent of the German population. Over 167,000 (80 percent) of those purged were officers in the military.[29] The next-largest category consisted of politicians, which included 34,892 people (16.5 percent of the total). Many well-known conservative politicians fell victim to the first purge, including Ichiro Hatayama, who was purged the day he was recommended as the next prime minister. Nonetheless, the purges did not seriously undermine the strength of conservative political forces that continued to control the

---

[28]Alden (1950), p. 310.
[29]Schonberger (1989), p. 61.

Diet and the cabinet throughout most of the occupation.[30] Bureaucrats, responsible for its implementation, largely escaped the purge.
The 1,809 bureaucrats who were eventually purged represented less
than 1 percent of the total.

In contrast, the trials in Germany focused more heavily on the civilian party officials and politicians than in Japan. Although allied
intentions to purge the bureaucracy were also trimmed in Germany,
the results went much deeper than in Japan. Moreover, beginning in
1949, MacArthur authorized the Japanese government to review the
purges of 1946 and 1947. By 1951, most of those who had been
purged had regained their political rights, though the majority did
not return to their former positions of influence. Finally, the purge
program was countermanded after the peace treaty was signed
between the United States and Japan. The Japanese government
immediately released those still in prison with time served.

One final area of civil administration was the thorough reorganiza-
tion of the police. The SCAP Civil Liberties directive of October 4,
1945, led to the dissolution of the Special Higher Police, which had
been responsible for enforcing restrictions on speech and thought.
Its members were rendered ineligible for other public office. The
Home Ministry and the national police were purged of militarists,
and, to allow the unfettered growth of unions, police were banned
from interfering in labor affairs. The Home Ministry, which had
directed an extensive network of repressive police forces, was abolished in 1947, and the police were reorganized as a decentralized
force. The Japanese government fought decentralization, arguing
that the national police force was the "only stabilizing influence
available to the Japanese government" and envisioning an increase
in police strength from 94,000 to 125,000.[31] But SCAP's Government
Section and military intelligence overruled them. Decentralization of
the police, while successful in many ways, left Japan without a
domestic force capable of responding to large-scale internal unrest

---

[30]Hans Baerwald, "The Purge of Japanese Leaders Under the Occupation," in Jon
Livingston, Felicia Oldfather, and Joe Moore, eds., *Postwar Japan: 1945 to the Present*,
New York: Pantheon Books, 1974, pp. 36–42.

[31]Kurt Steiner, "Occupation Reforms in Local Government," in Livingston, Oldfather,
and Moore (1974), p. 48.

until the formation of the National Police Reserve in 1950. The police were recentralized at the end of the occupation.

Democratization

Taking their direction from the Potsdam Conference agreement and other formal guidance documents, General MacArthur and his staff assumed the task of demilitarization and democratization with what is often described as messianic zeal. The key tasks in the political sphere were seen as (1) reform of the political system, beginning with the constitution, and (2) reform of the education system. The powerful SCAP Government Section, headed by Major General Courtney Whitney, directed these changes. MacArthur's personality loomed large over everything.

The Civil Liberties Directive of October 4, 1945, called for the release of political prisoners; the removal of limits on freedom of speech and assembly; and, as mentioned above, the abolishment of the Home Ministry. The Higashikuni cabinet resigned rather than implement the directive, which the members believed exceeded SCAP's authority. But the new cabinet quickly acquiesced. These freedoms set the stage for the revision of the Meiji Constitution of 1889. This task was initially left in the hands of the Japanese government, but SCAP found its proposed revisions unsatisfactory. On February 3, MacArthur directed the SCAP Government Section, under General Whitney, to draft a constitution to guide the Japanese cabinet in its efforts. He urged extreme haste and secrecy because he wanted to go public with a Japanese-endorsed draft before the newly established Far Eastern Commission, the international advisory board attached to the occupation, which had been given jurisdiction over constitutional issues, convened in late February. The Government Section completed the entire document in two weeks and presented a draft to the Japanese on February 19.

The SCAP draft reduced the emperor from a sovereign to a mere symbol of the Japanese state and placed the Diet, as representatives of the will of the people, at the center of national sovereignty. Equal rights were also granted to women with regard to property, marriage, inheritance, and other aspects of family life. The most innovative aspect of the constitution was Article 9, which required the full and complete disarmament of Japan and the renunciation of war. The

Japanese eventually accepted this hastily written and poorly trans-lated document, as did the Far Eastern Commission, after suggesting minor revisions. On March 6, 1946, General MacArthur announced that the emperor and the government of Japan were presenting a new constitution to the Japanese people. Its SCAP origins were delib-erately kept quiet, but the awkward phrasing of the document made the secret hard to keep. Constitutional revision became a topic of fierce debate almost immediately, but many embraced this constitu-tion despite its foreign origins, and, most remarkably, the document has never been amended.

In December 1945, the election law was revised to give women the right to vote, a move MacArthur viewed as a sure brake on the revival of militarism, and to lower the voting age from 25 to 20. The first elections were held on April 10, 1946, seven months after the begin-ning of the occupation; 363 "parties" participated, and 2,770 candi-dates vied for 466 seats in the House of Representatives. Of those elected, 377 were first-time members and 133 were representatives of minor parties or had run as independents. In addition, 39 female members were elected. The turnout rate was 78.52 percent for men and 66.97 percent for women.[32] Conservative parties retained their control and created a cabinet under Prime Minister Shigeru Yoshida. A second election for both the Lower and the newly reconstituted Upper House, as well for local assemblies and executives, was held a year later, in April 1947.

Another essential component of democratization and demilitariza-tion was educational reform. Early efforts focused on removal of all traces of emperor worship (State Shinto) and militarism from the classrooms and curriculum. Lacking funds and time to replace text-books, teachers and students were directed to rip out or line through offending language. Saluting the flag, singing the national anthem, and bowing to the emperor's portrait were prohibited. Local U.S. "military government" teams were dispatched to schools in their districts to ascertain that these SCAP directives were being carried out. Decentralization of education was viewed as essential to perma-nent removal of the ability of the government to indoctrinate Japanese students in the narrow form of Japanese nationalism that

---

[32] *Asahi Shimbun* Staff (1972), p. 126.

was believed to have sustained support for the war. The Board of Education Law, passed in July 1948, freed education from the direct control of the Ministry of Education and vested authority in the hands of local school boards. SCAP also reformed the elementary and secondary school system along U.S. lines and extended compulsory (and free) education from six to nine years.

The original planners had envisioned an occupation lasting about three years. By early March 1947, General MacArthur believed that the military objective to ensure that Japan would never again menace international security had been achieved and that a framework had been established for a new democratic system. He advocated that work begin on a peace treaty. However, the beginning of the Cold War and Soviet insistence on being given a say in the content of the peace treaty prevented further progress, and the U.S. occupation continued.

Reconstruction

Efforts to restructure the Japanese economy were perhaps the single most controversial issue of the occupation.[33] Debates over the proper course pitted planners in Washington—who wanted to democratize the economy by freeing labor unions, destroying the ability of Japan to produce weapons and war materials, and giving peasants title to their land—against conservatives who argued that Japanese capitalists ought to be allowed to participate in the economic recovery of their country. The political clout of these two opposing forces would shift over the course of the occupation. In the initial phase, MacArthur and his staff focused their efforts on the democratization of economic opportunity. The goal was to provide the 80 percent of the population that had previously lacked an economic stake in the nation a reason to support the democratic status quo. U.S. policy was hands-off with regard to economic reconstruction. Economic controls were to be left solely in the hands of the Japanese, and SCAP's role in economic stabilization was to direct the Japanese government to make "every feasible effort" to curb the rampant inflation that massive printing of money at war's end had caused.

---

[33]See Schaller (1985), pp. 30–41.

The SCAP Economic Scientific Section was entrusted with carrying out the economic elements of the occupation. Headed by General William F. Marquat for most of the occupation, the organization was responsible for a broad range of economic functions that had taken three offices to cover in Germany. The main tasks were dissolving the large business combines (*zaibatsu*) that dominated the economy, expanding workers' rights, and instituting a comprehensive land reform. Reparations and a purge of the economic decisionmakers who had been instrumental to the war effort were also mandated.

JCS Directive 1380/15 instructed SCAP to seek both economic disarmament and reparations, but the drive to extract reparations emanated from Washington. In April 1945, President Truman created a special reparations committee, headed by Edwin Pauley, to implement industrial reforms in Germany and Japan. Pauley's goal was to use reparations to rectify economic imbalances between Japan and its former colonies and to remedy past abuses.[34] He urged MacArthur to rapidly begin a program against the *zaibatsu* to seize their excess capacity, but MacArthur opposed any mandated program, and a deadlock ensued. In April 1947 SWNCC directed SCAP to distribute some 16,000 machine tools to Japan's Asian claimants. This was seen as a down payment on the final settlement, but in the end, it represented the entire reparations program.[35] Identifiable looted property was returned to the original owners. Capital equipment from designated government arsenals was divided and distributed among certain Allied powers, in line with the U.S. interim directive. Some small Japanese naval vessels were also transferred. Further reparations were halted in May 1949 because they would have interfered with Japanese economic recovery.[36]

Perhaps the most controversial aspect of the economic reform program was the economic purge. SWNCC 150/4 applied the purge to "active exponents of militant nationalism and aggression." Paragraphs 23 and 40 of JCS 1380/15 mandated a purge of those in "positions of important responsibility or influence in industry, com-

---

[34]Schaller (1985), p. 38.

[35]Schaller (1985), p. 38.

[36]Alden (1950), p. 310.

merce, and agriculture."[37] SCAP staff charged with designing and implementing the economic purge puzzled over how to apply these broad directives fairly and appropriately. Fear that applying the purge too rigorously would disrupt efforts to rebuild the economy also stymied the Economic Scientific Section's efforts. In the end, MacArthur shifted responsibility for the purge to the Government Section and withstood a concerted assault from U.S. businessmen and the U.S. press to see it through. The economic purge affected only 1,898 members of the business elite and had no discernible effect on industrial production.

The Initial Post-Surrender Policy for Japan announced that Washington favored "a program for the dissolution of the large industrial and banking combinations which have exercised control over a great part of Japan's trade and industry." JCS 1380/15 directed SCAP to work through the Japanese government to implement this. It was argued that the *zaibatsu* had suppressed domestic consumption with low wages, and in their search for cheap raw materials and foreign markets, had supported overseas aggression. The continued overconcentration of economic wealth and power in the hands of a few families was perceived to be antidemocratic and dangerous. For the first 18 months of the occupation, Washington regarded the breakup of the *zaibatsu* holding companies as critical to the reconstruction of Japan. The top four *zaibatsu* and the Japanese government worked out a deconcentration plan in October 1945 and presented it to MacArthur, who approved it.

The plan dissolved the *zaibatsu* holding companies but left the operating subsidiaries intact, along with their interlinking managements and financing. The SWNCC and others in Washington, unhappy with the limited nature of the proposal, lobbied for the formation of an expert mission to devise a more far-reaching plan. The mission, led by economist Corwin Edwards, toured Japan in early 1946. Its final report advocated the sale of any large-scale diverse enterprise to small- and medium-sized entrepreneurs, investors, consumer cooperatives, or trade unions to lay the groundwork for the development of a Japanese middle class and democratic capitalism. By the time the report wound its way through the Washington bureaucracy,

---

[37]For an in-depth discussion of the economic purge, see Cohen (1987), Ch. 9.

however, the political climate had changed. MacArthur supported efforts to break up the *zaibatsu*, but Washington was more concerned with countering communism and promoting economic recovery.

In the end, 83 *zaibatsu* were broken up into their component parts, and antimonopoly laws were passed to prevent their reestablishment. But their financial linkages were left intact, and action against 1,200 other companies was abandoned. The end result of this process was somewhat ambiguous. The breakup of the family-owned *zaibatsu* helped share the wealth and spur the creation of many new companies, which in turn created greater wealth and led to a more-competitive domestic economy. On the other hand, the process did not eliminate all anticompetitive practices. Private industries seeking to strengthen their positions organized into loose groups known as *keiretsu*, which were distinguished by ties to a lead bank and the cross-holding of each others' shares. In an effort to foster rapid industrial development, the Ministry of International Trade and Industry allowed, and in some instances encouraged, such anticompetitive practices as supplier discrimination, industry price-fixing, production limits, and export quotas.

Another major focus of economic democratization efforts was the enactment of laws that gave labor the right to organize, as well as other protections. The Civil Liberties directives of October 4, 1945, eliminated some of the greatest barriers to organizing unions in Japan. MacArthur subsequently ordered the Japanese government to draft legislation to protect the rights of Japanese wage earners, in line with a SWNCC directive. The resulting Trade Union Law of December 1945 had some serious limitations, but it guaranteed workers the right to organize, to bargain collectively, and to strike.[38] In less than a year, almost 13,000 enterprise unions with 3.8 million members had been organized. By March 1949, 7 million workers—over 50 percent of the labor force—belonged to unions.[39] Trade unions immediately used their new freedoms to organize and agitate for change through the political process. This invigorated Japanese democracy but did not contribute to political or economic stability. Left-wing political

---

[38]Schonberger (1989), p. 114.

[39]Schonberger (1989), p. 115.

parties embraced the labor unions, and some were infiltrated by communists.[40]

For instance, the Japanese Council of Industrial Unions (*Sanbetsu*), which was organized in April 1946 as a federation of 21 national industrial unions and claimed a membership of 1.5 million, was known to have ties to the Japan Communist Party. As policymakers in Washington became increasingly nervous about the spreading influence of communism, SCAP officials attempted to rein in the increasingly left-leaning and activist unions. When officials of the well-organized government workers union called for a general strike on February 1, 1947, MacArthur intervened and demanded they call it off. This action is widely regarded as the beginning of the "reverse course," in which economic stability took precedence over democratization and demilitarization.

One of the most dramatic and sweeping reforms of the economic democratization period was the land reform instituted in 1946–1947. It was designed to undermine the political and economic power of landlords, who were viewed as the bulwark of feudalism and militarism. Land reform, it was believed, could ease the economic consequences of immediate demobilization and reduce future agrarian unrest among poor tenant farmers and small landholders. It gave farmers a stake in the preservation of the emerging democratic status quo. Approximately 70 percent of Japan's farmers rented part of the land they cultivated, and about 50 percent rented more than half.[41] In light of this situation, land reform had previously been contemplated in Japan, and SCAP found willing allies within the Ministry of Agriculture and Forestry. Landlord influence in the Diet, however, had weakened the first Japanese attempt at reform in November 1945. When the bill finally passed, SCAP found it insufficient and set it aside. A reworked SCAP-sponsored bill, passed in October 1946, became the major land-reform legislation of the occupation. Absentee landlords were required to sell their land to the government. The land could be bought at a fixed price, with tenants

---

[40]For details on the emergence of labor as a political force in Japan, see Cohen (1987), Chs. 11, 14, and 15.

[41]Cohen (1987), p. 65.

allowed to pay in installments over 30 years at a low rate of interest.[42] In a program that SCAP carefully monitored, redistribution took place in 1947 and 1948 with little incident. The percentage of owner-operated land rose from 54 percent in 1947 to 90 percent in 1950. The share of farmers who owned their own land rose from 38 percent to 70 percent of the total during this period. Land reform was completed in 1950. Even today, land reform is seen as the single most important factor for quelling rural discontent and promoting political stability in the early postwar period.

By 1948, U.S. taxpayers were beginning to perceive the costs of continued occupation to be an unnecessary and unsustainable burden. Early in 1948, during the same period that the U.S. Congress was debating the Marshall Plan, the U.S. government decided that it would be more economical in the long run to encourage, and even fund, Japan's economic recovery.[43] But to obtain maximum benefit from the funds to be appropriated for recovery, Japan's economy would have to be "stabilized," and inflation would have to be tamed. On December 10, 1948, the U.S. government issued an interim directive to SCAP instructing MacArthur to direct the Japanese government to undertake an economic stabilization program designed by Detroit banker Joseph Dodge. Its principal component was to balance the consolidated budget, which had been in substantial deficit. This very tough program prohibited any expenditures for which there was no proof of sufficient revenue to cover the costs incurred. The Japanese government was prohibited from providing any new subsidies. The Dodge plan, launched in 1949, was followed by massive layoffs of government and industrial employees; increased taxes; wage freezes; higher prices for rice, transportation, and other government-subsidized goods and services; and reduced public services. The immediate effect was a wave of strikes, demonstrations, and sabotage.

This economic recovery program had made significant progress by the mid-1950s. But serious problems in the expansion of Japan's international trade and restriction of its external activities because of the absence of a peace treaty undermined efforts to achieve a self-

---

[42]Cohen (1987), p. 65.

[43]Alden (1950), p. 308.

supporting economy.[44] The lack of trade with China was particularly devastating. Ultimately, U.S. orders for military supplies to support the Korean War provided the Japanese economy with the boost in external demand needed to accelerate economic growth. During 1951 and 1952, U.S. military purchases of Japanese products amounted to nearly $800 million per year. By the end of 1954, these purchases totaled nearly $3 billion.[45] This military spending benefited nearly every sector of the economy, from vehicle manufacturing to textiles. Occupation-engineered economic reforms had created the necessary conditions for this stimulus to have its desired effect.

LESSONS LEARNED

The reconstruction efforts the United States undertook in Japan were remarkably successful. In comparison to the German case, Japan's transformation was quicker; smoother; and, in many ways, easier than Germany's, although in the end Japan was less integrated with its neighbors. The experience yielded a number of important lessons:

- Democracy can be transferred to non-Western societies.

- How responsibility for the war is assigned can affect internal political dynamics and external relations for years to come.

- Co-opting existing institutions can facilitate nation-building better than building new ones from scratch.

- Unilateral nation-building can be easier than multilateral efforts.

- Concentrating the power to make economic policy decisions in the hands of a single authority can facilitate economic recovery.

- Delegating implementation of economic policy decisions to local governing elites, with their own priorities, can significantly dilute the effectiveness of changes.

- Idealistic reforms designed for the long-term improvement of the recipient nation must sometimes give way to the immediate, global concerns of the occupying power.

---

[44]Alden (1950), p. 311.

[45]Schaller (1985), p. 288.

Germany's post–World War II democratization was facilitated by the fact that Germans already had significant experience with democracy, were surrounded on at least three sides by well-established democracies, and were soon integrated into a dense network of democratically based international institutions, such as NATO and the European Coal and Steel Community. These opportunities did not emerge for Japan. Despite the absence of a long democratic history and the existence of an authoritarian culture, nation-building in Japan was successful. The speed and relative ease of the Japanese transformation had two primary causes: the U.S. decision to co-opt Japanese institutions and the unilateral process of nation-building.

First, the U.S. occupation authorities retained and adapted existing Japanese institutions. The paucity of U.S. personnel with both language and technical capabilities led MacArthur and his SCAP staff to retain the existing Japanese government and give the occupation authorities a supervisory role. Indeed, U.S. authorities made use of the existing political and bureaucratic apparatus rather than rebuild Japanese institutions from scratch, although they did engineer the drafting of a new Japanese constitution, reorganize the police, and purge some in leadership and key administrative positions. The occupation was managed through a fully articulated Japanese government, ranging from the emperor to the prime minister, ministries, parliament, and courts. This starkly contrasted with Germany, where most such institutions were abolished and then rebuilt from scratch.

Second, occupation authority was centered in one nation and, indeed, one man: Douglas MacArthur. This made the reconstruction process less troublesome than in Germany, since neither MacArthur nor SCAP were obligated to consult with other countries. The two most important international bodies for oversight and consultation, the Far Eastern Commission and the ACJ, had little power. Unilateralism allowed U.S. authorities to spend more time and energy overseeing reconstruction and less effort forging a consensus among partners. At the same time, however, the failure to involve any of Japan's neighbors and former enemies in its transformation contributed to a lack of regional reconciliation. None of these nations was involved in the reconstruction process and none has yet been fully reconciled to the reemergence of a prosperous and powerful postwar Japan. Indeed, the Japanese were not forced to break with their recent past as thoroughly as were the Germans. In addition, the decision to absolve the emperor in whose name the war was fought of all responsibility leaves the Japanese today somewhat less reconciled with their history, less ready to admit their war guilt, and consequently less reconciled with their neighbors than are the Germans.

The concentration of power in a single authority, SCAP, permitted more-consistent and -dramatic economic policy changes than in Germany, where economic policymaking authority was divided across the four zones the occupying powers ruled. In Japan, SCAP pushed through a land reform that destroyed the power of the land-holding classes and made the peasantry property owners. SCAP also greatly expanded workers' rights and forced through the dissolution of the large business combines (*zaibatsu*) that had dominated the economy.

From the beginning, there was some tension between the U.S. policymakers who advocated the democratization of economic opportunity and those who favored working with existing economic elites to bring about a quick economic recovery. Many of the actions SCAP initially took—breaking up the large land holdings, granting workers more rights and powers, and dismantling the largest industrial conglomerates—seemed designed to impede rather than foster economic reconstruction. Eventually, U.S. global interests trumped the desires of SCAP reformers. The fall of the Chinese nationalists and the growing recognition that Japan could be a good ally in the fight against communism led to a shift in emphasis within the U.S. government toward policies that would promote Japanese economic self-sufficiency and contributed to the consolidation of political and economic power in Japan by the conservatives.

Chapter Four

SOMALIA

The overthrow of the regime of Major General Muhammad Siad Barre in 1991 led to a bitter struggle among competing clans for the reins of power. Somalia rapidly descended into chaos. In the absence of a national government, the country fragmented into factions headed by various warlords, two of which, General Mohamed Farah Aideed and Ali Mahdi Mohamed, competed for control of Mogadishu. The combination of a drought and fighting among the many warlords created a massive humanitarian disaster. Widespread suffering from famine and civil war led to humanitarian intervention in April 1992 under UN leadership.[1] The UN Operation in Somalia (UNOSOM I) was created to monitor the cease-fire in Mogadishu, provide protection and security for UN personnel and equipment, and escort deliveries of humanitarian supplies.

The operation consisted of 50 unarmed military observers and 500 lightly armed infantry tasked with monitoring the cease-fire between Aideed and Mohamed. In August 1992, UNOSOM I's mandate was enlarged to include protecting humanitarian convoys and distribution centers throughout Somalia.[2] However, the situation in Mogadishu continued to deteriorate. General Aideed mounted opposition to this intervention, most notably when he attacked Pakistani peacekeepers at the airport in November and warned that

---

[1]The UN Security Council adopted Resolution (UNSCR) 751 on April 24, 1992.

[2]For a detailed treatment of UNOSOM I's experience, see United Nations Department of Public Information, *The Blue Helmets: A Review of United Nations Peace-Keeping Forces*, 3rd ed., New York, 1996, pp. 291–294.

any forcible UNOSOM I deployment would be met by violence.[3] It became clear that UNOSOM I could not provide adequate security for humanitarian activities.[4]

In response to the difficulties faced by UNOSOM I, the Security Council authorized the deployment of the U.S.-led Unified Task Force (UNITAF) on December 3, 1992 (UNSCR 794, 1992). The mission was to safeguard the relief effort and lasted until May 1993. UNITAF entered Somalia with the understanding that its responsibilities would quickly be turned back over to the UN. U.S. Special Envoy Robert Oakley negotiated with Somali clan leaders in Ethiopia in early January 1993 and achieved a general agreement on comprehensive disarmament, which included placing heavy weapons under international supervision. As UNITAF deployed to Somalia, however, it was not clear how or whether the general agreement would be implemented.

CHALLENGES

The primary challenge the U.S.-led UNITAF mission faced in Somalia was to reassert order in what had become a chaotic and violent society. For UNITAF, it was critical to establish a secure environment for relief supplies. Doing so involved securing the airfield and seaport in Mogadishu, then expanding the operation to secure cities and relief centers, such as Baidoa, Oddur, and Kismayo, throughout the country.

Security

As UNITAF began its mission, a number of tribes and factions were involved in the fighting. Both civilians and militias in Somalia were heavily armed, creating barriers to effective policing. The population was not required to disarm; there was no national government; and the foundations for transition to a reconstruction phase were never

---

[3]Walter Clarke, "Failed Visions and Uncertain Mandates," in Walter Clarke and Jeffrey Herbst, eds., *Learning from Somalia,* Boulder, Colo.: Westview Press, 1997, pp. 3–19.

[4]Unlike the other cases studied here, no settlement to the conflict was reached in Somalia. U.S. and international intervention occurred in the midst of the conflict in Somalia. This case will focus exclusively on the period of explicit or implicit U.S. leadership of international operations and when U.S. troops were on the ground.

implemented. The unstable security environment created significant challenges for UNITAF in securing major airports, seaports, installations, and food distribution points, as well as in providing protection for convoys and relief organizations.

Humanitarian

The collapse of the government following the overthrow of Siad Barre led to a widespread humanitarian crisis in the country. The ensuing civil war created approximately 2 million refugees, including internally displaced persons (IDPs).[5] This situation was exacerbated by a drought in 1991. The combination of events created a widespread famine, with more than 1.5 million people at immediate risk of starvation. An estimated one-third of all Somali children below the age of five died from starvation and diseases related to malnutrition during the worst periods of the civil war.[6] Farms were also destroyed; livestock was slaughtered; food harvests were burned; and houses were razed. The continuing civil war and rampant lawlessness impeded the ability of relief organizations to distribute food and supplies. In some areas, it became virtually impossible to deliver humanitarian aid because combatants looted supplies for their own use.

Civil Administration

The departure of Siad Barre left Somalia with no government. No dominant party or figure was able to exert authority, even over the capital of Mogadishu. The rehabilitation of government institutions was a daunting task and not one that the international community planned to tackle during UNITAF.

Democratization

Building democracy was also not an important UNITAF objective. An informal preparatory meeting, attended by 14 Somali political

---

[5] Andrew S. Natsios, "Humanitarian Relief Intervention in Somalia," in Clarke and Herbst (1997), p. 94.

[6] UN Department of Public Information (1996), p. 287.

movements, was convened in January 1993 to prepare a framework for the formation of a Somali government. But it made little progress. There was no tradition of democracy in Somalia. The lack of an existing political order allowed authority to remain in the hands of warlords, who had gained control through coercion. With the advent of large amounts of humanitarian assistance, warlords were able to increase their power by controlling distribution systems and to increase their wealth by stealing supplies for resale.[7] It was unclear how the general agreement the clan leaders had negotiated would be implemented and how any political authority, much less a democratic one, would be established in Somalia.

Reconstruction

The crisis that commenced in 1991 shattered the existing economy as government services collapsed and businesses closed. Civil war affected every aspect of Somali society. It destroyed at least 60 percent of the country's basic infrastructure. Perhaps 80 percent of Somali households' income came from their animal herds. The civil war led to a sharp decrease in the price of animals, drove up cereal prices, and led to a dramatic increase in food insecurity.

THE U.S. AND INTERNATIONAL ROLES

The initial U.S. intervention in Somalia through UNITAF was narrowly focused on providing and securing humanitarian assistance. This mandate eventually broadened under UNOSOM II, which took over for UNITAF in May 1993, to include democratization and development even as the number and capacity of U.S. forces dropped precipitously.

Military

UNITAF's mission, as stated in UNSCR 794, was to establish a secure environment for humanitarian relief operations in Somalia. The UN Secretary General pressed for UNITAF to enforce the negotiated disarmament agreement, but at the U.S. government's insistence,

---

[7]Natsios (1997), p. 83.

UNITAF's mandate was limited to securing humanitarian assistance and explicitly did not include instructions to disarm warring factions and other armed groups. Although UNITAF forces conducted some disarmament, this objective was not a priority.[8] UNITAF was authorized under UN Chapter VII to use "all necessary means" to secure humanitarian assistance. However, the United States also emphasized from the outset that UNITAF was a temporary presence that must be succeeded by a UN-led peacekeeping force.

UNSCR 814 (1993) established UNOSOM II, the UN-led force that was to inherit the operation from UNITAF. UNOSOM II lasted from May 1993 until May 1995. It had an authorized strength of 28,000 but never numbered more than 16,000. UNOSOM II was a UN force under the authority of the Special Representative of the Secretary General, retired U.S. Admiral Jonathan Howe. A Turkish general, Lieutenant General Çevik Bir, commanded the UNOSOM II military contingent. His deputy was an American, Major General Thomas Montgomery, who also commanded a separate U.S. quick reaction force (QRF) that was not under UN command. The United States contributed approximately 3,000 logistics soldiers to UNOSOM II but kept its combat forces distinct. Washington later deployed U.S. Army Ranger and Delta Force units. These did not fall under the local U.S. command but were controlled directly from the United States.

Civil and Economic

UNITAF did not have a mandate to develop civil institutions or to conduct economic reconstruction in Somalia. Its role was narrowly restricted to providing security for the relief effort. UNOSOM II, however, had a much more expansive mandate:

- While UNITAF focused on the southern parts of Somalia, UNOSOM II covered the entire country.

- While UNITAF strictly limited its activities to securing humanitarian aid, UNOSOM II had the authority to seize heavy weapons of organized factions and small arms of all unauthorized armed elements.

---

[8]Bruce R. Pirnie, *Civilians and Soldiers: Achieving Better Coordination,* Santa Monica, Calif.: RAND, MR-1026-SRF, 1998, p. 60.

- While UNITAF did not have any role in nation-building, UNOSOM II was mandated to assist the people of Somalia in rehabilitating their political institutions, rebuilding their economy, and promoting national reconciliation and a political settlement.

WHAT HAPPENED

U.S. forces participated in both UNITAF and UNOSOM II. UNITAF accomplished its objectives of providing security for relief efforts. Famine was averted through the provision of food and supplies to millions of people. But UNITAF did not focus on reconciliation for the warring factions in Somalia.

In contrast, UNOSOM II had a broader mission but a weaker force. It included only 16,000 troops at its height, not counting the 1,200 troops in the U.S. QRF. UNOSOM II's objectives involved nation-building and included disarming the warring factions; securing ports and airports necessary for the delivery of humanitarian assistance; and building up new political and administrative structures at the local, regional, and national levels.

Neither UNITAF nor UNOSOM II was able to end hostilities between warring parties. Moreover, armed factions in Somalia violently contested the authority of UNOSOM II. This resistance, coupled with an unnecessarily complicated command and control arrangement, led to the armed confrontation in October 1993 that resulted in 18 American deaths. This incident, which has been memorialized in the book and film *Black Hawk Down*,[9] triggered the U.S. withdrawal from Somalia and the ultimate failure of the UNOSOM II mission.

Security

UNITAF's mission was to provide security for the relief effort. The initial arrival in December 1992 of U.S. troops as part of UNITAF led to a substantial diminution of conflict between warlords and a period of relative quiescence. UNITAF included 28,000 U.S. troops, who were authorized to use decisive force if necessary. It succeeded in

---

[9]Mark Bowden, *Black Hawk Down: A Story of Modern War*, New York: Atlantic Monthly Press, 1999.

establishing a secure environment for providing humanitarian relief. The presence of U.S. troops in significant strength buttressed the authority of the operation and convinced such warlords as Aideed and Mahdi that challenging the U.S.-led operation would lead to disastrous results for their forces. Consequently, the Mogadishu warlords allowed UNITAF to conduct its operations with relatively little harassment. UNITAF also maintained limited objectives, enforcing what were called the "four no's": no banditry, no roadblocks, no visible weapons, and no "technicals" (trucks mounted with heavy weapons).[10]

Coordination between the coalition members and the UNITAF commander was maintained through liaison officers and other means of communication. The U.S. commander retained authority over the entire operation. Somalia was divided into nine sectors, with responsibilities for each given to different partners in the coalition. Significant autonomy was given to each partner within its sector.[11] The command structure remained relatively straightforward, despite the fact that UNITAF incorporated troops from 20 countries. The smooth relations created among coalition partners added to the effectiveness of this segment of the effort.

UNITAF operated for a brief period from December 1992 until May 1993. One of the major innovations of the UNITAF deployment was the establishment of a civil-military operations center (CMOC). The CMOC provided liaison between the military and international and nongovernmental organizations (NGOs). This provided a meeting place for civilian agencies and military forces to exchange information and coordinate activities.[12] CMOCs and similar mechanisms would become central to civil-military cooperation in coming post-conflict operations.

The UN began the transition from UNITAF to UNOSOM II in March 1993, and authority was formally transferred on May 4. UNOSOM II held a much broader mandate than UNITAF and was authorized to

---

[10]Nora Bensahel, "Humanitarian Relief and Nation Building in Somalia," in Robert J. Art and Patrick M. Cronin, eds., *The United States and Coercive Diplomacy*, Washington, D.C.: United States Institute of Peace Press, 2003, pp. 20–56.

[11]Nora Bensahel, *The Coalition Paradox: The Politics of Military Cooperation*, dissertation, Stanford, Calif.: Stanford University, 1999, Ch. 4.

[12]Pirnie (1998), pp. 60–61.

use force against armed combatants beyond cases of self-defense. Despite this expanded mandate, the authorized strength of UNOSOM II was 28,000, significantly smaller than that of UNITAF. At the time of transfer of authority from UNITAF to UNOSOM II, only 12,000 troops were present for the new operation, not including the 1,300-man U.S. QRF. At its height, UNOSOM II and the U.S. QRF totaled 17,500 troops, short of UNOSOM II's authorized strength and even shorter of its effective combat power.[13]

The transfer of responsibility to UNISOM II was psychologically devastating for the remaining forces. The replacement of well-equipped U.S. troops with a smaller number of poorly equipped Pakistanis led to a drastic decrease in patrolling.[14] The reduced troop presence translated into increased risk for the remaining U.S. and UN forces and into decreased effectiveness in disarming the heavily armed Somalis in Mogadishu. The preplanned exit of UNITAF in May 1993 led to a weak start for UNOSOM II, as other countries failed to rally around an operation lacking a strong U.S. core.

The transition from UNITAF to UNOSOM II was also accompanied by increasing difficulties resulting from complex command arrangements. The political objectives for the mission came under dispute, with the UN arguing that disarmament must precede the UNOSOM II takeover, and the United States arguing that this was not part of UNITAF's mandate. The command structure for UNOSOM II was also unwieldy and confusing. International troops were led by the Turkish UNOSOM II Commander (Bir), who had an American Deputy Commander (Montgomery). U.S. combat troops reported separately to Montgomery and were not under UN command.[15] The situation became even more muddled when Task Force Ranger later deployed to the country. Task Force Ranger was a special operations force that reported directly to U.S. Central Command (CENTCOM). Its mission was to capture Aideed because he had attacked Pakistani peacekeepers. Because this force did not report to Montgomery, distinct forces were now operating in Mogadishu with three distinct

---

[13]David Bentley and Robert Oakley, "Peace Operations: A Comparison of Somalia and Haiti," National Defense University, Institute for National Strategic Studies, *Strategic Forum*, No. 30, May 1995.

[14]Bentley and Oakley (1995).

[15]Bensahel (1999), p. 122.

chains of command. The highly problematic nature of this arrangement became clear shortly.[16]

The security situation grew increasingly unstable as Somali warlords became hostile to the UN troops. On June 5, 1993, Somali fighters, allegedly from Aideed's clan, killed 25 Pakistani peacekeepers. The UN Secretary General was outraged at these killings, which occurred when the soldiers were unloading food at a feeding station. The Security Council reacted by passing UNSCR 837 on June 6, which called for military action against Aideed's clan. UNOSOM II responded by launching a series of attacks, including the seizure of Radio Mogadishu and the destruction of seized militia weapons and equipment.[17]

In support of these UN actions, the United States deployed Task Force Ranger in late August 1993. U.S. forces conducted a series of raids in September but were never able to locate Aideed. On October 3, Task Force Ranger received intelligence about a meeting of senior officials from Aideed's clan. The United States launched an operation to seize these officials and possibly Aideed. During the operation, Somali militia shot down two Black Hawk helicopters, leading U.S. forces to delay their withdrawal as they worked to rescue the downed crew. The complicated U.S. and UN command structure created significant delays in coordinating the rescue effort. As a result, U.S. forces spent the night fighting off Somali militia before being extracted by UN peacekeepers the next morning. Eighteen U.S. soldiers were killed in the firefight, and one was captured alive.[18] This action caused the Clinton administration to set a deadline for the withdrawal of U.S. forces from Somalia by March 31, 1994.

Although UNOSOM II continued after the departure of U.S. forces, it downsized both its expectations and its force level. After subsequent unsuccessful attempts to negotiate an accommodation among the warring factions, the UN determined that sustaining an effective humanitarian operation was no longer possible with the resources at hand. In March 1995, the last UNOSOM II forces evacuated Somalia,

---

[16]For detailed discussions on mandates and command relationships, see Bensahel (1999), Ch. 4; Bentley and Oakley (1995); and Pirnie (1998), pp. 61–63.

[17]UN Department of Public Information (1996), pp. 299–300.

[18]For a gripping account of this episode, see Bowden (1999).

leaving a situation that soon reverted to the violence and chaos existing prior to U.S. and UN efforts.[19]

Humanitarian

Recommendations from the Office of Foreign Disaster Assistance, a part of the U.S. Agency for International Development (USAID), led to sharply increased amounts of food aid from the United States and NGOs from the summer of 1992 onward. The U.S. Operation Provide Relief from August 1992 to November 1992 provided military assistance and airlift for the emergency humanitarian effort, in conjunction with other aid agencies. The initial delivery of 88,000 metric tons of food by aid agencies was augmented by a new pledge for another 145,000 metric tons. Alongside free distribution of food to the most needy, limited monetization was also attempted through the sale of foods and through distribution in local markets. The monetization program was initiated to infuse money back into the local economy. Funds raised from the sale of food were to be used for mass employment programs, eventually integrating young men into the economy. Unfortunately, the result was continued looting of food supplies for hoarding and resale by warlords through their clan merchants.[20]

UNITAF secured deliveries of food and other humanitarian aid to hundreds of thousands of Somalis in rural and urban regions, continuing the cooperation with aid agencies. UNITAF troops built or repaired over 1,200 km of roads; built bridges; dug wells; and established schools, orphanages, and hospitals. UNOSOM II began humanitarian assistance in March 1993 through the Relief and Rehabilitation Programme, which focused on returning refugees and displaced persons, food security, health care, and potable water.

Civil Administration

UNITAF did not include a coordinated effort to help the people of Somalia reestablish national and regional civil institutions throughout the country. In contrast, UNOSOM II's mandate was "nation-

---

[19]For a detailed discussion of the UNOSOM II experience, see UN Department of Public Information (1996), pp. 296–318.

[20]Natsios (1997), p. 87.

building": a determined effort to build new Somali political and administrative structures at the local, regional, and national levels.[21] Unlike later efforts in the Balkans, no substantial international civil structure was created in Somalia during either UNITAF or UNOSOM II to oversee and coordinate U.S. and international efforts to rebuild civil authority.

Before UNITAF, the UN helped broker the January 1993 general agreement on disarmament, but little was done on the civilian side once UNITAF deployed in the country. During UNOSOM II, the Special Representative of the Secretary General periodically attempted to help the Somali factions achieve reconciliation and reestablish a national political authority. Plans for economic reconstruction and development also languished because of the lack of a critical mass of international civilian experts on the ground.[22]

UNOSOM II committed itself to work with all concerned agencies and organizations to strengthen coordination of all aspects of the UN efforts throughout Somalia, including humanitarian, political, and peacekeeping objectives. The Addis Ababa Declaration of December 1, 1993, established the Somalia Aid Coordination Body (SACB).[23] SACB's aim was to help donors develop a common approach for allocating the resources available for Somalia. The declaration envisaged the broad participation in SACB of donors, UN agencies, NGOs, and multilateral and regional institutions and organizations.[24] Neither SACB nor the UN was effective in this effort, however, because civil conflict continued throughout UNITAF and UNOSOM II. The absence of a functioning police force capable of maintaining security also contributed to a downward spiral into chaos.

One area in which the international community did make a somewhat more sustained effort was law enforcement. To address the lack of law and order in Somalia, the Mogadishu Police Committee was

---

[21]See Bentley and Oakley (1995).

[22]UN Department of Public Information (1996), pp. 298–311.

[23]The Addis Ababa Declaration of December 1, 1993, is the final document of the Fourth Coordination Meeting on Humanitarian Assistance for Somalia, organized by UNOSOM.

[24]UN General Assembly "Assistance for Humanitarian Relief and the Economic and Social Rehabilitation of Somalia," 50th Session, item 20(b) of the Provisional Agenda, A/50/447, September 19, 1995.

established to create a capital police force and to help build a judicial system. The reinvigorated police force in Mogadishu, comprising former officers from the Somalia National Police, numbered 3,000 by March 1993.[25] This police force, known as the Auxiliary Security Force, was hampered by low or nonexistent pay and the absence of a judicial system.

UNOSOM II's expanded mandate allowed institution-building and the establishment of police forces and civil authorities.[26] Beginning in 1993, salaries for the 3,000 police in Mogadishu and the additional 2,000 police stationed elsewhere in Somalia were allotted from UNOSOM II funds. UNOSOM II developed an ambitious plan to create a 10,000-member Somalia National Police Force, as well as necessary courts, prisons, and a Ministry of Justice.[27] Because of a lack of funding, these efforts were never implemented. By March 1995, the Somalia National Police consisted of 8,000 officers. When UNOSOM II withdrew in May 1995, efforts to create a national or Mogadishu police force or judicial system ended, and further initiatives were terminated because of the absence of financial and institutional support.

Democratization

Efforts toward political settlement of the situation in Somalia received sporadic attention during the UNITAF and UNOSOM II periods. Although no mechanism was established for implementation of the January 1993 general agreement on disarmament, the Conference on National Reconciliation in Somalia met on March 15, 1993, in Addis Ababa, Ethiopia. At the end of the conference, the leaders of all 15 Somali political movements reached an agreement that had four parts: security and disarmament, reconstruction and rehabilitation, restoration of property and settlement of disputes, and transitional mechanisms.[28] Furthermore, building democracy

---

[25]Martin R. Ganzglass, "The Restoration of the Somali Justice System," in Clarke and Herbst (1997), p. 24.

[26]Ganzglass (1997), p. 29.

[27]Robert M. Perito, *The American Experience with Police in Peace Operations*, Clementsport, Nova Scotia: The Canadian Peacekeeping Press, 2002a, p. 33.

[28]UN Department of Public Information (1996), p. 299.

was a stated objective for UNOSOM II, especially for the United States. This was reflected in UNSCR 814, which noted that it was important to set up "transitional government institutions and consensus on basic principles and steps leading to the establishment of representative democratic institutions."[29]

These efforts lapsed in implementation, in part because UNOSOM II devoted little time or effort to achieving societal change or a political settlement between fighting factions. As a result, preconditions for effective postconflict reconstruction were never met. The conflict endured throughout both UNITAF and UNOSOM II. UNITAF made some progress in tempering the chaotic situation to allow delivery of relief supplies. Indeed, its ability to decrease general crime, looting, and lawlessness was critical to build the semblance of a functioning society in Somalia.

In the delivery of humanitarian assistance, the warlords were generally the political arbiters for the population. When aid agencies dealt directly with such warlords as General Mohamed Aideed, clan loyalists and armed supporters were first in line for aid, leaving little for the remaining population. Thus, depending on the warlords to distribute humanitarian relief merely concentrated political and economic power in the hands of unscrupulous armed individuals. The warlords used the resulting economic leverage to expand their power base, recruit followers, and buy weaponry. In addition, sharp increases in the price of food resulting from the drought and the interruption of agriculture created incentives for the theft of food. Warring clans would steal food from aid stocks and, in conjunction with clan merchants, sell the supplies at inflated prices.[30]

In dealing with the warlords, the United States and the international community shifted their approach from co-option to confrontation over time. During UNOSOM I, they worked through the warlords and attempted to persuade them to ensure the safety and equitable distribution of food aid. This worked initially but became more problematic when tensions increased with Aideed's clan. By the time of UNOSOM II, the United States and the international community

---

[29]UNSCR 814 (1993).

[30]Natsios (1997), pp. 83–85.

were moving toward a more-confrontational approach, even as the number and capacity of U.S. forces were diminishing.

The political situation in Somalia did not improve over time. The March 1993 Addis Abba agreement was never implemented because of the increasing hostility and violence of General Aideed's clan toward the international presence. Moreover, the international community did not address the regional dimensions of the internal Somali struggle. A number of neighboring states maintained relationships with, and financially supported, various warlords. The United States and the other intervening powers did not invest the time and effort to understand these external connections and to exploit them to put pressure on the warlords to reach a settlement.

Reconstruction

Little progress was made on reconstruction during the three-year intervention in Somalia. Some international organizations and NGOs attempted small-scale reconstruction projects in targeted localities, but the immediate priority of the UN mission in Somalia was to provide security for humanitarian activities. In the absence of a central governing authority, the international community focused mainly on the implementation of community-based interventions aimed at rebuilding local infrastructures and increasing the self-reliance of the local population. For example, the UN Development Programme–funded Somalia Rural Rehabilitation Program established offices in numerous cities and had a positive impact on the daily lives of people through the rehabilitation of public buildings, schools, water supplies, and health centers.[31] The reconstruction effort ended, however, when the UN withdrew from Somalia in March 1995.

LESSONS LEARNED

U.S. and UN nation-building efforts in Somalia were not successful. There was no sustained effort to help Somalia reestablish national and regional institutions or civil administration, though the United States, UN, and other aid agencies did provide humanitarian assis-

---

[31]UN General Assembly (1995).

tance in such areas as Mogadishu. The lessons learned were predominantly negative:

- Nation-building objectives should be scaled to available forces, resources, and staying power.

- Military forces need to be complemented by civil capabilities for law enforcement, economic reconstruction, and political development.

- Unity of command can be as important in peace operations as in war.

- There can be no economic or political development without security.

Somalia was the first post–Cold War attempt by the United States to lead a multinational effort in nation-building. Military power alone proved insufficient; it needed to be complemented by adequate civil reconstruction efforts. U.S. forces were initially introduced with a purely humanitarian mission. That mission dramatically expanded following the introduction of UNOSOM II, just as the bulk of U.S. troops withdrew. U.S.-led forces were initially able to control feuding warlords and impose a modicum of security. However, there was no attempt during this period to build civil or political institutions.

No international police, judges, penal authorities, administrators, or technical experts were deployed to fill the governance gap or begin reconstruction. Unlike in Bosnia and Kosovo, no international structure was established during UNOSOM I, UNITAF, or UNOSOM II to oversee nation-building in Somalia. By the time even a few civil institutions were created, such as SACB, international military forces had been drastically reduced, the U.S. role had diminished, and the warring factions were no longer intimidated. Nation-building goals needed to be matched with adequate forces, funding, and time.

At both the political and military levels, the Somali operation represented, above all, an egregious failure in command. At the political level, U.S. policymakers believed the UN was in effective charge, while the UN looked to Washington for leadership. Neither U.S. nor UN officials had experience running an operation of this dimension. U.S. officials were in the midst of a presidential transition. U.S. forces conducting the hunt for Aideed were not under the control of the local American commander, and U.S. combat troops in Somalia were not under the control of the UN commander. Three separate international forces—two of them American—were operating from the same facilities on the same terrain in Mogadishu. Neither the UN nor the United States made arrangements to back up or rescue the operation on October 3, 1993. A relatively small military action and a limited operational setback became a strategic defeat for the Clinton administration. The result was a precipitous U.S. withdrawal, the eventual demise of the entire international effort, and greatly increased skepticism in the U.S. Congress and among the public about the engagement of U.S. military forces in nation-building activities.

Security also proved to be a basic prerequisite for economic growth. Development assistance is futile if businesses and households are constantly at the risk of seeing their goods appropriated by armed groups. In a lawless environment, neither production nor trade can proceed.

Chapter Five

HAITI

On December 16, 1990, Jean-Bertrand Aristide was elected president of Haiti in what was generally judged a free and fair election, receiving 67 percent of the vote. Nine months later, he was ousted by the Haitian military and forced to flee the country. Neither the United States nor any other government recognized the "de facto" military regime, led by General Raul Cedras, that had seized power. Over the following three years, the international community employed political pressure, economic sanctions, and eventually the threat of military force to secure President Aristide's restoration. On September 18, 1994, General Cedras signed an agreement in the face of an imminent U.S. invasion. The agreement, brokered by former U.S. President Jimmy Carter, allowed U.S. and other coalition troops to enter the country. On October 15, 1994, three weeks after the arrival of U.S. troops and three years after being ousted, President Aristide returned to power in Port-au-Prince.

CHALLENGES

Although the U.S. entry was peaceful and U.S. forces suffered and caused almost no casualties or physical damage, the three years of Cedras' rule and the ensuing international sanctions undermined Haiti's fragile economy and deepened tensions between its large, impoverished, mostly black majority and its small, wealthy, predominantly lighter-skinned social and economic elites.

Security

Haiti had no civilian police. Its army, which also functioned as a police force, was corrupt, abusive, and incompetent. The first tasks the U.S.-led coalition faced were to secure control over the country and to ensure the safe return and installation of President Aristide. The next was to maintain law and order without heavy reliance on the repressive Haitian security apparatus, whose abuses had been responsible for the intervention in the first place. The last was to reform old and create new civil institutions—police, courts, and penal authorities.

Humanitarian

Following the ouster of President Aristide, 68,500 Haitians fled their country in small boats between 1991 and 1994. Of this number, 20,000 put to sea during June and July 1994. Another 30,000 Haitians found refuge, sometimes under onerous circumstances, in the Dominican Republic; upward of 300,000 persons were internally displaced in Haiti. The "boat people" were primarily motivated by economic deprivation and a desire to enter the United States. The mounting level of repression under the Cedras regime also contributed to the exodus and made it difficult for the United States to continue its practice of dismissing all claims for asylum and forcibly returning intercepted "boat people." Consequently, U.S. authorities housed most of the Haitian asylum seekers at the U.S. naval base in Guantanamo Bay, Cuba. The continued exodus of refugees, the unwillingness of the U.S. authorities to either return them forcibly to Haiti or allow them to enter the United States, and the impossibility of accommodating greater numbers at the Guantanamo facilities were critical factors in motivating the U.S. intervention.

Civil Administration and Democratization

The Clinton administration argued that the purpose of its intervention was the restoration of democracy. This was something of an overstatement. President Aristide had been freely elected, but few other elements of a functioning democracy were available to be "restored." The Haitian parliament was corrupt and ineffective, the Haitian bureaucracy weak and incompetent, and the Haitian judiciary almost nonexistent. Among political parties, only Aristide's movement, Lavalas, had any grassroots constituency, and that was largely a product of his personal appeal. Finally, Aristide's record after his first eight months in office called into question his own stability, judgment, and democratic intentions.

Reconstruction

Two centuries of misgovernment had left Haiti's economy as weak as its polity. Three years of progressively draconian economic sanctions had driven out of the country the meager amount of foreign investment that had been attracted over the preceding two decades. Between 1991 and 1994, per capita GDP fell by over a quarter as manufacturing facilities shut their doors and tourism disappeared. Haiti began the 1990s as the most impoverished nation in the Western Hemisphere and one of the poorest in the world. By the time of U.S. intervention, its situation had deteriorated even further.

THE U.S. AND INTERNATIONAL ROLES

U.S. forces entered Haiti under the terms of a request from President Aristide, an agreement with the de facto Cedras government, and a UNSCR authorizing the use of "all means necessary" to restore the democratically elected government of Haiti. For six months, the U.S.-led coalition, the Multinational Force (MNF), provided security and supported the efforts of the Aristide government to reestablish itself. These responsibilities shifted on March 31, 1995, to a UN peacekeeping force, also led and largely manned by the United States.

During the summer of 1994, U.S. military planners began considering possible scenarios for a U.S.-led intervention in Haiti, even as U.S. soldiers were withdrawing from Somalia. Drawing on what they believed to be the lessons of the failed Somalia operation, U.S. defense planners were particularly anxious to avoid "mission creep," to establish an "exit strategy," and to set a fixed and early departure date. In an effort to relieve the military of some responsibilities and to ensure better support from civil agencies, military planners involved the departments of State and Justice in various aspects of the planning from an early date. This experience eventually prompted the development of more-formalized interagency procedures for planning and coordinating future such operations through-out the remainder of the Clinton administration.[1]

Military

On July 31, 1994, the UN Security Council authorized member states to use "all necessary means" to remove the Cedras government and restore the democratically elected Aristide government. At the same time, it authorized the subsequent establishment of a UN peace-keeping force intended to replace the initial forces once a secure environment had been established. The United States provided nearly all the initial MNF and the largest contingent of the follow-on force, which fell under the UN Mission in Haiti (UNMIH).

Civil and Economic

Both the U.S.-led MNF and UNMIH were responsible for establishing and maintaining a secure and stable environment in Haiti. UNMIH was also responsible for helping the Haitian authorities organize local and national elections. But UNMIH's responsibilities did not extend to economic reconstruction, which donor states supported, under the loose coordination of the World Bank.

WHAT HAPPENED

Operation Uphold Democracy achieved all its principal objectives on schedule. President Aristide was restored to power. The Haitian military was abolished, and a new civilian police force was created. Local and national elections were held. New mayors, members of parliament, a new prime minister, and a new president took office in accordance with the Haitian Constitution. With isolated exceptions, systematic violations of human rights ceased. U.S. and other international forces departed, however, before a competent Haitian administration could be created, self-sustaining democratic structures could be put in place, or meaningful economic reforms could be instituted.

---

[1] As discussed in the Kosovo case, these procedures would be codified in Presidential Decision Directive 56 in May 1997.

Security

Americans entered Haiti unopposed on September 19, 1994. A total of 28 nations and 23,000 troops participated in Operation Uphold Democracy and formed the MNF. Its initial task was to restore stability and ensure public safety in preparation for the return of President Aristide. To this end, units searched and seized weapon caches and conducted presence patrols. U.S. forces were committed to a two-year presence in Haiti. The U.S. military initially resisted conducting any law enforcement missions. As General John Shalikashvili, the Chairman of the JCS, stated:

> The task of keeping law and order in Haiti is the responsibility of the Haitian police force and the Haitian military. We are not in a business of doing day-to-day law and order.[2]

This position quickly became impractical.

Anticipated resistance to the U.S.-led intervention did not materialize. There were only a handful of violent incidents over the two-year U.S. presence. On September 24, 1994, only five days into the intervention, a patrol of U.S. Marines in the city of Cap Haitian fired on a group of Haitian soldiers who made threatening gestures, killing seven of them. Three months later, on December 26, a firefight broke out among elements of the Haitian Army in the vicinity of the presidential palace. The incident was sparked by tensions over pay and separation benefits, and U.S. troops and international police intervened to suppress the fighting. By the end of the day, three Haitians had been killed, seven had been wounded, and 83 had been taken prisoner; 500 weapons had been seized. A few weeks later a civilian trying to avoid inspection at a roadblock shot an American soldier to death.

Responsibility for security passed from the MNF to UNMIH on March 31, 1995. As noted earlier, the United States retained the military command and remained the largest contributor of forces to the operation. At its peak, in June 1995, UNMIH comprised 6,000 military

---

[2]As quoted in Pirnie (1998), p. 65.

personnel from 24 countries, 2,400 of whom were Americans.[3] Furthermore, some 820 police from 20 countries served as civilian international police monitors under the leadership of former New York City Police Department Commissioner Raymond Kelly, who reported to the military commander of the MNF. When authority passed from the MNF to UNMIH, the international police monitors gave way to a somewhat smaller number of UN Civilian Police (CIVPOL). In each phase, these international police were armed with both weapons and arrest authority, an innovation in international peacekeeping practice.

Recruiting international civilian police was time consuming and labor intensive. Few countries had entire units of police available for deployment abroad, and volunteers were often recruited individually. It was several weeks into the intervention before significant numbers of such police became available.

As noted earlier, the U.S. military intended to rely on existing Haitian Army units acting as police to maintain law and order until a sufficient number of international civilian police could be deployed. A few days into the intervention, these Haitian military units moved to break up a friendly crowd congregating to watch U.S. troops debarking on the Port-au-Prince waterfront. International camera crews filmed Haitian "police" savagely beating these individuals while U.S. soldiers, who had come to halt such abuses, stood passively by. In response to this incident, hundreds of additional U.S. Military Police were dispatched to Haiti to monitor; oversee; and, when necessary, substitute for Haitian security forces until enough international civilian police became available.

The United States also began to organize an Interim Haitian Police Force composed of superficially retrained Haitian military and lightly trained recruits drawn from among Haitian refugees held at Guantanamo Bay. Simultaneously, the United States selected and trained a new civilian police force, the Haitian National Police (HNP). HNP recruits were selected though a nationwide competition. They received 16 weeks of training by instructors from the U.S. Depart-

---

[3]For more information on UNMIH, see David Bentley, "Operation Uphold Democracy: Military Support for Democracy in Haiti," *Strategic Forum*, No. 78, June 1996. Also see the UNMIH Web site.

ment of Justice, the Royal Canadian Mounted Police, the French *Gendarmerie*, and other donor law enforcement agencies. The U.S. objective was to train and field 3,000 new police (a target subsequently raised to 5,000) by the time its troops were scheduled to depart after two years. When throughput at the new HNP Academy caused delays in the timetable, 2,000 recruits were transported to the U.S. Army's Fort Leonard Wood in Missouri, where they were put through a comparable 16-week course organized by the U.S. Department of Justice.

The task of creating a new civilian police force took on added urgency when, shortly after his return to Haiti, President Aristide decided to completely abolish rather than simply to reform the Haitian Army. As a result, the HNP was destined to become the only legal armed force in the country. Aristide's determination to disband the Haitian Army came in the immediate aftermath of the above-mentioned firefight among Haitian soldiers. This incident occurred within earshot of the presidential palace, providing the president an unsettling reminder of the coup d'état that had forced his departure three years earlier. Aristide's decision may also have been influenced by strong U.S. resistance, on human rights grounds, to the officers he wished to name as leaders of the reformed Haitian military.

Plans to build a new civilian police force were in place before the intervention was launched. The project was adequately funded, well staffed, and quickly launched. There was no comparable advanced planning or funding to reform the penal or judicial sectors. Belated and half-hearted efforts to do so produced indifferent results. Strengthened law enforcement efforts quickly produced more accused criminals than the prisons could hold or the courts could try. The HNP, whose recruits were selected, trained, and funded by the United States, became for a time the most honest and effective component of the Haitian bureaucracy, only to find itself slowly sucked back into the culture of corruption, incompetence, and politicization in which it was embedded.

Six months into the intervention, the bulk of U.S. troops departed and handed the MNF's responsibilities over to the smaller UNMIH force. This force, however, retained a core of U.S. troops and an American commander. A year-and-a-half later, the United States turned these responsibilities over to Canada, at which point all but a handful of U.S. military engineers and medics left the country. Both transitions went smoothly, although they greatly diminished Washington's capacity to oversee and ensure a lasting democratic transformation of Haitian society.

Humanitarian

The arrival of the MNF soon created conditions in which the United States was able to return the more than 16,000 asylum seekers held at Guantanamo Bay and other screening centers and to resume the direct and forcible repatriation of further Haitian migrants seeking entry into the United States. Over the succeeding weeks, the U.S. Coast Guard returned several hundred asylum seekers to Port-au-Prince each day, where they were provided transport, or the means to procure it, to their home towns and villages. Feeding and other humanitarian programs that had been in place during the "de facto" period continued.

Civil Administration and Democratization

The Clinton administration declared the goal of its intervention to be restoring democracy in Haiti. As a practical matter, this became defined as the return of President Aristide and then the renewal, through free elections, of all Haitian electoral offices: local, legislative, and executive.

Among Haitian politicians and parties, only Aristide and his Lavalas movement had any substantial national following. Parties other than Lavalas were numerous, small, poorly funded, and largely personal vehicles for their leaders. The United States brought in a number of NGOs, including its Republican and Democratic Party institutes, to help all the Haitian parties organize and mount the election campaigns of 1995 and 1996. Given Aristide's overwhelming popularity, however, Lavalas did not need or want such assistance. Opposition parties had little hope of prevailing electorally, with or without such outside advice and assistance.

Aristide's own tenure was a matter of debate. The Haitian Constitution precluded his succeeding himself at the end of his five-year term. Some of his supporters argued that the three years he spent in exile should not count in this calculation. However, the Clinton administration, international community, opposition parties, and key leaders within the Lavalas movement disagreed, insisting that Aristide step down in 1996. He eventually agreed to do so. Aristide subsequently broke with those in Lavalas and formed a new and even more personalized political movement.

Local and national elections were held in fall 1995, and another round of national elections took place in 1996. Despite UN oversight and U.S. assistance, the Haitian authorities responsible for organizing those ballots were incapable of doing so competently—or even of maintaining an appearance of impartiality. International observers found these elections technically flawed but basically fair. There is little doubt that the results generally reflected the intentions of the voters. Reactions in both Haiti and the United States tended to break down along party lines. In Haiti, opposition politicians who had not boycotted the process from the beginning contested the results. In the United States, the Clinton administration and its supporters in Congress defended the elections as an advance toward democracy, while the Republican opposition decried them as a failure and a fraud.

One complaint the Haitian opposition advanced was the fear of government-sanctioned intimidation. On March 28, 1995, six months after the arrival of U.S. troops, the Cedras regime's former spokesperson, Madam Mireille Durocher Bertin, was gunned down on a Port-au-Prince street in what appeared to be a professional assassination. Acting at the suggestion of the U.S. ambassador, President Aristide immediately requested Federal Bureau of Investigation (FBI) assistance in the investigation. He and his officials became progressively less cooperative, however, as the FBI began to delve into the possibility of complicity among elements of the Palace Guard. The United States did not develop sufficient evidence to bring charges, but U.S. officials did insist upon and secure the exclusion of suspected individuals from that force. Three years later, the assassination of two more opposition figures was more clearly traced to yet other individuals within the Palace Guard, at which point that entire force was purged and reorganized under close U.S. control.

With these notable exceptions, international observers believed that human rights were generally respected throughout Haiti in the years immediately following Aristide's return. Indeed, having only three politically connected killings over a three-year span was a significant advance over the de facto regime's average of three killings per day.[4] But the Clinton administration, which had so lavishly touted its "restoration" of Haitian democracy, could take little comfort in such comparisons. The Republican opposition, which had endured a decade of Democratic criticism during the Reagan and Bush administrations for allegedly having tolerated "death squads" in Central America, was not forbearing in tarring the Clinton's enterprise in Haiti with the same brush.

The Haiti intervention was controversial in the United States from the beginning. In this, it did not differ from many previous or subsequent such operations. Seldom, however, has the U.S. debate broken down so clearly along party lines. To build support for the intervention, the administration was compelled to oversimplify its rationale and exaggerate the scale of its early successes. The Republican opposition went to opposite extremes. Reasoned cross-party dialogue about how to deal with a desperately poor and miserably governed nation only a day's boat ride from U.S. shores became progressively more difficult. Partisan differences in Washington and Port-au-Prince tended to reinforce each other. Only seven weeks after the launch of the Haiti intervention, Republicans won control of the U.S. Congress. This change led to differences over the direction of U.S. policy toward Haiti between the Executive and Legislative branches, and funding for Haiti gradually diminished while legislative restrictions over its use increased.

Reconstruction

Following the entry of U.S. troops, Washington moved quickly to lift economic sanctions and mobilize a broad international assistance effort. The United States and other donors paid off Haitian arrears to the IMF and World Bank, thereby qualifying Haiti for further lending and allowing the World Bank to assume leadership of the international reconstruction process. The World Bank provided an Emergency Economic Recovery Credit of $40 million within a few months

---

[4]International observers estimated that 3,000 to 5,000 people died in politically related violence during the three years of de facto rule.

of President Aristide's restoration to power.[5] This credit was designed to provide balance-of-payments support to pay for priority imports. Aristide named a moderate probusiness figure, Smarck Michel, as his prime minister and appointed other qualified free-market reformers to key economic posts. The Haitian currency, the gourde, quickly stabilized. Subsequently, international financial institutions, such as the Inter-American Development Bank and the World Bank, provided larger-scale project financing.

The U.S. and international strategy for Haiti's economic revival centered on improving governance; targeting investments in infrastructure; and alleviating poverty, especially in rural areas where more than two-thirds of the population lived.[6] A key problem for donors and international financial institutions has been the ineffective operation of the Haitian government. The World Bank pressured the Haitian government to set up a special Emergency Implementation Unit to handle the disbursal of funds from the initial World Bank loan. Both European and North American donors decided to work more closely with NGOs, many of which had been active in Haiti for years, rather than government agencies. Channeling assistance through NGOs increased the accountability of donor funds and alleviated pressure (and funding) for reform of government operations.

A key objective of donor efforts was to privatize the public utilities, which had long been dreadfully mismanaged. The state also owned other enterprises, such as manufacturing plants, some of which were moribund. Encouraged by Prime Minister Michel and his government, privatization plans initially moved forward. However, they encountered growing resistance from entrenched interests, including "workers" in long-defunct national enterprises and ideologues within the Lavalas movement, with which Aristide eventually sided. Approximately 12 months after his appointment, Prime Minister Michel was forced to resign and the privatization effort was effec-

---

[5]World Bank, *Haiti-Emergency Economic Recovery Credit*, Washington, D.C., Report No. PIC1271, 1997.

[6]L. M. Garry Charlier, "Review of the Impact and Effectiveness of Donor-Financed Emergency Poverty Alleviation Projects in Haiti Related to Basic Infrastructure Rehabilitation and Employment Generation," in The International Bank for Reconstruction and Development, *Haiti: The Challenges of Poverty Reduction*, Vol. 2, 7242-HA, August 1998, pp. 141–148.

tively terminated after accomplishing nothing. This state of affairs has yet to change. In January 2003, the IMF still underscored the importance of privatizing state-owned enterprises to improve the environment for economic growth.[7]

One of the brighter spots in Haiti's economy in the 1970s and 1980s was the export sector. Foreign and domestic investors made modest investments in such light assembly industries as apparel and sporting goods, which were designed to take advantage of Haiti's low-cost labor force and proximity to the U.S. market. International sanctions drove nearly all this investment out of the country in the early 1990s. Much of it went to Central America. Postconflict foreign investment has been very limited, running $10 million a year or less, and a number of the manufacturers that left the country in the early 1990s have not returned.

Neither the Haitian government nor the donor community made serious efforts to attract foreign capital by investing in such necessary infrastructure as roads, ports, and airports or by making a concerted effort to improve the legal and business environments. In addition, any preferential access that Haiti had to U.S. markets in the 1980s had been extended to Central America by the mid-1990s, reducing incentives for foreign investors to consider Haiti as a location for operations.

U.S. assistance to Haiti was not generously funded, particularly compared with the reconstruction efforts in Bosnia and Kosovo. Per capita, Bosnia received five times more postconflict reconstruction assistance from the United States than did Haiti. Kosovo received ten times more U.S. aid. Once U.S. peacekeepers departed in 1996, U.S. aid to Haiti returned to preconflict levels. Indeed, U.S. assistance levels after 1996 were not notably higher than during the Cedras regime itself.

Neither was U.S. assistance to Haiti large as a proportion of total external aid to that country. Despite Haiti's geographic proximity to the United States, the exodus of refugees to the United States, and the existence of a large Haitian-American community that supported

---

[7]IMF,"IMF Concludes 2002 Article IV Consultation with Haiti," Washington D.C., Public Information Notice No. 03/23, March 3, 2003b, p. 4.

assistance, the U.S. proportion of total external assistance to Haiti in the mid-1990s was only 30 percent. This markedly contrasts with the European contribution to the Balkans, which lay on Europe's doorstep and to which Europe contributed 65 percent of total external assistance.

International transfers, which encompass private as well as public financial flows, were also substantially lower on both a proportional and absolute basis in Haiti than in Bosnia or Kosovo. Per capita transfers averaged $74 per annum between 1995, the first postconflict year, and 1998. In contrast, they averaged $265 in Bosnia and $317 in Kosovo. As a share of GDP, international transfers to Haiti were also smaller than transfers to Bosnia and Kosovo. Transfers to Haiti peaked at 23.7 percent of GDP in 1995 but fell to 13.7 percent by 1998, four years after the end of the conflict. In Bosnia, transfers as a share of GDP were still at least 20 percent in 2000 and 2001—more than 5 years after the end of the conflict. In Kosovo, they accounted for over 50 percent of GDP in 2000, the first postconflict year, and 44 percent in 2001.

While the Haitian government's resistance to privatization and other economic reforms contributed to U.S. and international reluctance to provide generous assistance, similar attitudes among the Bosnian authorities did not present a comparable obstacle to large-scale external aid. The simple fact is that an internally divided U.S. government assigned a lower priority to Haiti's democratic transformation than European—or even U.S.—governments did to Bosnia's and Kosovo's only a few years later.

LESSONS LEARNED

The Haiti operation began well, proceeded smoothly, and ended on schedule but left little residue in the way of transformation. While U.S.-led reconstruction efforts achieved some goals, such as restoring President Aristide to power, the mission was not very successful. U.S. and international forces departed before a competent administration could be created, self-sustaining democratic structures could be put in place, or lasting economic reforms could be instituted. As in Somalia, many of the important lessons from the U.S. experience in Haiti are negative:

- Short departure deadlines and exit strategies diminish prospects for enduring transformation.

- International police armed with weapons and the power to arrest can usefully supplement military peacekeepers.

- Broad justice-sector reform is necessary to bolster policing efforts.

- Where government is grossly ineffective, it needs to be reformed before reconstruction programs can be successful.

- Privatization can be a prerequisite for economic growth, especially where government officials use state-owned enterprises for their own private purposes.

Haiti was the fourth Caribbean intervention the United States had conducted since 1965 but the first for which it was able to secure a UN Security Council mandate. With that mandate came allied forces and large-scale financial burden-sharing. But in the wake of the failed Somalia operation, the U.S. military adopted an extremely narrow definition of its appropriate mission and a short timeline for accomplishing its objectives. U.S. military planners were anxious to avoid mission creep and therefore set a fixed and early departure date. The problem with this approach is that nation-building takes significant time, resources, and determination. Out of the seven cases examined in this report—Germany, Japan, Somalia, Haiti, Bosnia, Kosovo, and Afghanistan—no successful example took less than five years. Setting an early and abbreviated timetable in Haiti made it nearly impossible to build viable political and civil institutions.

Haiti was the first instance in which significant numbers of international police, armed with weapons and the power to arrest, were deployed in support of military peacekeepers. These police were able to supplement and reduce the burden on military forces. But reforming the police is not enough to create an atmosphere of security and protection of civil liberties. An effective justice system requires a functioning police force, as well as courts and prisons. If unreformed, any one of these elements can diminish the effects and even undo reforms in the other parts of the justice system. For example, improved law enforcement in Haiti created an untenable situation in which there were more accused criminals than the courts could try or the prisons could hold. Furthermore, in the absence of a competent judiciary that could bring accused criminals to trial and incarcerate lawbreakers, the HNP eventually reverted back to a culture of corruption and incompetence.

Under the aegis of the World Bank, foreign donors created a strategy for Haiti's economic revival centered on improving governance; targeted investments in infrastructure; and alleviating poverty, especially in rural areas. Because NGOs were more effective than the government in reaching the indigent—especially the rural poor—donors channeled funds through NGOs rather than through the government. However, widespread lawlessness, graft, and the inability of the government to provide basic legal and other government services forestalled economic recovery. Ultimately, the failure to make the Haitian government more effective also resulted in the failure of the reconstruction program.

In most instances, Haitian state-owned enterprises were either used to provide jobs for government supporters or as sources of cash for politicians. The Haitian government's continued resistance to privatizing these companies resulted in the diversion of resources to government supporters at the cost of maintenance and investment. Consequently, state-owned enterprises frequently failed to provide the goods and services, such as electric power and clean water, for which they were created. Had international donors successfully pressured the Haitian government to privatize these enterprises, economic growth would probably have been stronger and poverty less extreme.

Chapter Six

BOSNIA

With the end of the Cold War and the fall of communism, the internal contradictions and tensions of Yugoslavia became too much for a highly diverse, multiethnic state first created 70 years earlier from the remnants of the Ottoman and Austro-Hungarian empires. In the late 1980s, using highly explosive nationalism to fuel his rise, former communist apparatchik Slobodan Milosevic became prime minister of Serbia. In a speech given in 1989 on the 600th anniversary of the epic Battle of Kosovo, in which the Kingdom of Serbia lost its independence to the Turks, Milosevic exploited Serbian nationalism to push for the end to the special status Kosovo and Voidvodina had enjoyed within the Republic of Serbia. The speech also marked a pivotal turning point in internal Yugoslav relations, setting the country on a slow but unrelenting march toward dissolution. After a brief armed confrontation in 1991, Slovenia was the first Yugoslav republic to declare and achieve its independence. Croatia also declared independence from the Yugoslav federation, and this was followed by a vicious war during which Serbia seized important cities in eastern Croatia and sections of Croatia inhabited by ethnic Serbs, such as the Krajina. The fighting between ethnic Croats and Serbs was fierce and widespread and left substantial portions of the country in the hands of Serb militia forces until 1995. The struggle in Croatia, however, was merely a preview for the bloody fight that was to come in multiethnic Bosnia.

Following the lead of Slovenia and Croatia, Bosnia and Herzegovina held a successful referendum on independence in early 1992. Shortly thereafter, the European Community recognized Bosnia's independence, on April 6, 1992. The declaration of independence was immediately followed by civil war. The intermingling of ethnic groups in Bosnia led radical nationalist leaders to create a bloody new strategy called "ethnic cleansing."[1] By the winter of 1992, Serbs had seized almost 70 percent of Bosnia, "purifying" the land of Croats and Muslims as they went. The Bosniacs (Bosnian Muslims) and their sometimes-allies, the Bosnian Croats, held on to a large chunk of central Bosnia, the capital Sarajevo, and selected pockets of territory elsewhere. By 1994, over 200,000 soldiers and civilians were dead or missing and an estimated 2 million people were either refugees or displaced persons.[2] The stalemate was finally broken in summer 1995. After receiving significant Western training and equipment, the Croatian army drove Serbian forces out of the Croatian regions of Krajina and western Slavonia. Subsequently, a combined Bosniac-Croat offensive launched in August 1995 began to make significant advances in western and central Bosnia. In addition, NATO launched Operation Deliberate Force in response to an August attack by Serb forces on a crowded market square in Sarajevo and attacked Serb positions throughout the country using airpower. These Croatian-Bosniac advances, coupled with NATO air strikes, were followed shortly by the decision of the warring parties to go to Dayton, Ohio, for peace talks in November 1995.

The General Framework Agreement for Peace in Bosnia and Herzegovina, better known as the Dayton Accord, was initialed in Dayton on November 21, 1995, and signed three weeks later in Paris.[3] Dayton created two entities within the Bosnian state that were almost identical in size: the Bosniac-Croat federation, which controls 51 percent

---

[1]Muslims were the single largest ethnic group in Bosnia, but there were also significant numbers of Serbs and Croats. According to the 1991 Yugoslav census, Bosniacs constituted 43.7 percent of the republic's total population; Serbs, 31.4 percent; and Croats, 17.3 percent.

[2]Estimate of the UN Special Humanitarian Operation in the former Yugoslavia (Jolene Kay Jesse, "Humanitarian Relief in the Midst of Conflict: The UN High Commissioner for Refugees in the Former Yugoslavia," Washington, D.C.: Georgetown University, Pew Case Studies in International Affairs, No. 471, 1996, p. 1).

[3]The Dayton Accord is available through the Office of the High Representative (OHR): *The General Framework Agreement for Peace in Bosnia and Herzegovina*, December 14, 1995. For an insightful and highly readable account of the behind-the-scenes diplomacy that led to the accord, see Richard Holbrooke, *To End a War*, New York: Random House, 1998. For an excellent account of the same period from a European perspective, see Carl Bildt, "Holbrooke's History," *Survival*, Vol. 40, No. 3, Autumn 1998a, pp. 187–191.

of the country's territory, and the *Republika Srpska,* which controls 49 percent. The December 8–9, 1995, Peace Implementation Conference in London appointed a High Representative for the implementation of the framework agreement. NATO meanwhile established and deployed a 60,000-soldier Implementation Force (IFOR) to enforce the Dayton Accord's military articles.

CHALLENGES

Although the Dayton Accord formally ended the fighting in Bosnia, it did not satisfy everyone. Its articles and annexes were the subject of immediate and fierce debates among the former warring parties and among the countries and organizations implementing the agreement. Thus, the obstacles to the realization of the multiethnic goals of the Dayton Accord were significant and many. They included the separation and demobilization of warring ethnic militaries, the implementation of a complex and contested peace agreement, and the return of over 1 million refugees and IDPs. In addition, the civil war had destroyed substantial portions of Bosnia's infrastructure, and homes and apartments throughout the country were in ruins.

Security

When the civil war ended, the armies and militias that the three ethnic groups had created remained in place. Although Bosnian Serb forces had more heavy weapons and equipment at the beginning of the fighting, the Bosniac and Croat militaries had built up substantial forces by the war's end. These forces needed to be separated, demobilized, and reintegrated as a national military. More importantly, the paramilitary forces that had conducted most of the ethnic cleansing needed to be disbanded. Finally, the respective police forces had to be reorganized and retrained to ensure public safety for all Bosnian citizens.

On the surface, the security environment in Bosnia was fairly stable. The front lines had hardened after more than three years of war and ethnic cleansing. This allowed the respective ethnic groups to consolidate political power and, in turn, to establish the structures necessary to maintain law and order. Thus, there were established authorities within the two entities and within ethnic cantons with which military and civilian organizations could interact. The security situation was, however, very unstable just below the surface. Efforts to reconnect the separated communities, return refugees to their prewar homes, and reunite the country had the potential to make the security environment much more volatile.

Humanitarian

Ethnic cleansing had displaced almost one-half of Bosnia and Herzegovina's 4.4 million people.[4] About 600,000 were displaced within the country, and about 1,259,000 were refugees outside Bosnia.[5] At the time the Dayton Accord was signed, 80 percent of the population depended on international assistance for food.[6] Because of the 1990s conflict, 250,000 people—mainly men—had lost their lives and, consequently, the number of orphans and households headed by women had increased dramatically. Young people throughout Bosnia and Herzegovina lost years of schooling, and much of the population suffered physical disabilities and psychological trauma.[7] Land mines were another humanitarian issue because they affected all aspects of reconstruction, resettlement, and community development in postwar Bosnia. The Red Cross estimated that there were 750,000 land mines scattered throughout the country in 1997.[8]

Civil Administration

One of the fundamental problems of Dayton was that it did not settle the very issue that was the subject of the war: the identity of the Bosnian state.[9] Because the agreement created a very weak central government; highly autonomous entity-level governments; and, in

---

[4]UNHCR, *The State of the World's Refugees 2000: Fifty Years of Humanitarian Action*, New York: Oxford University Press, 2000, p. 219.

[5]Murat Praso, "Demographic Consequences of the 1992–95 War," *Bosnia Report*, No. 16, July–October 1996.

[6]World Bank and European Commission, *Bosnia and Herzegovina: 1996–1998 Lessons and Accomplishments*, Washington, D.C., 1999.

[7]World Bank and European Commission (1999).

[8]International Committee of the Red Cross, *The Silent Menace: Landmines in Bosnia and Herzegovina*, Geneva, 1997.

[9]Ivo H. Daalder, "Bosnia After SFOR: Options for Continued U.S. Engagement," *Survival*, Vol. 39, No. 4, Winter 1997–98, p. 6.

the federation (the half of Bosnia assigned to the Bosniacs and Croats), powerful cantons (regional political units), opposing groups could frequently opt to enforce certain provisions of the agreement while ignoring others.[10]

Reconciliation between the former warring parties was also a major challenge. Unlike the other former Yugoslav states, which all had a dominant ethnic group, Bosnia had a much more diverse ethnic mixture of Bosniacs, Serbs, and Croats. No single ethnic group accounted for a majority of the population, although, in most regions, one or the other of these groups formed a local majority. Before the civil war, the three groups had lived side by side in relative peace, and a third of all marriages in Bosnia were between individuals from differing ethnic groups. However, a great deal of Bosnian blood was spilled during the 20th century in the name of ethnic causes, especially during World War II.[11] Bosnia had never been an independent, sovereign state in the modern era. While the ethnic groups often coexisted peacefully under Turkish, Austrian, or communist rule, Bosnia was subject to external or strong internal authority under these governments. Although nationalist leaders distorted and exploited ethnic grudges before and during the recent conflict, these grudges did have a basis in history and, when paired with three years of bitter civil war, posed a significant challenge to prospects for reconciliation between the former warring parties.

Another obstacle to political reconciliation was the fact that Dayton was not negotiated directly by all the parties involved.[12] The Serbs and Croats argued that they did not sign the agreement, and the Bosniacs contended that they were coerced into it. Thus, each party was aggrieved even before the implementation process began.

---

[10]The Republika Srpska, the Serb half of the country, does not have cantons. The entity government fulfills the functions that the cantons fulfill in the federation.

[11]The bitter ethnic fighting in Yugoslavia during World War II led to the deaths of hundreds of thousands of soldiers and civilians, the majority of which occurred in and around Bosnia. See John R. Lampe, *Yugoslavia as History: Twice There Was a Country*, New York: Cambridge University Press, 1996, especially pp. 203–220.

[12]Serb President Slobodan Milosevic had the authority to negotiate for the Bosnian Serbs; Croatian President Franjo Tudjman was present to safeguard Bosnian Croat interests; and Bosnian President Alia Izetbegovic acted as the representative of the Croat-Bosniac federation. The United States helped to broker this federation, which Croat and Bosniac leaders signed in Washington in February 1994.

Democratization

Given the nature of the civil conflict, constructing a new multiethnic and democratic Bosnia from the ashes of three-and-a-half years of war was a daunting challenge. The Dayton Accord, for example, gave the Organization for Security and Co-operation in Europe (OSCE) important roles, such as preparing for elections, strengthening the legal system, and assisting in establishing firm democratic control over the armed forces. The long-term goal of the international community was to leave Bosnia and Herzegovina as a fully functioning and sustainable democracy that could integrate itself as a member of democratic Europe. This was not expected to be easy, however, because elections in the early 1990s had in part spawned the ultranationalist parties that started the civil war in the first place.

Reconstruction

As a result of the widespread destruction and dislocation between 1992 and 1995, Bosnia's economic recovery began from a very low level. Per capita GDP in 1995 was estimated at only $628 on a purchasing power parity exchange rate basis, one-third of prewar levels. Industrial production had been reduced to only a small fraction of its prewar level. Most major plants had closed or were operating at a small fraction of prewar capacity levels. The vast majority of the country's 1.3 million workers had lost their jobs; many had lost savings with the freezing of bank assets; and the houses of more than half had been damaged. The agricultural land was mined or left fallow for lack of supplies and equipment. Damage to such physical infrastructure as power plants, transmission lines, roads, railroads, and telecommunications systems was severe. Nearly two-thirds of the homes, one-half of the schools, and one-third of the hospitals were damaged or destroyed, along with power plants, water systems, agricultural land, and roads.[13]

---

[13]Priit J. Vesilind, "In Focus: Bosnia," *National Geographic*, Vol. 189, No. 6, June 1996, pp. 48–61.

THE U.S. AND INTERNATIONAL ROLES

The Dayton Accord consisted of a general agreement and 11 annexes dealing with the specifics of the implementation process. A number of international organizations, such as NATO, OHR, the OSCE, and the UN, played important roles in the operation.

Military

IFOR, an international force under the authority of NATO, was given responsibility for the military aspects of Dayton implementation. With the passage of Resolution 1031 on December 15, 1995, the UN Security Council authorized IFOR as a peace enforcement operation under Chapter VII of the UN Charter. In accordance with Dayton, IFOR's military mandate was relatively narrow. For instance, IFOR's primary tasks were to establish a durable cessation of hostilities, ensure force protection, and establish lasting security and arms control measures.[14] These tasks gave it responsibility for such activities as enforcing the zone of separation between the former warring parties and monitoring the withdrawal of heavy weapons into designated cantonment areas. IFOR was also assigned supporting tasks to be done "within the limits of its assigned principal tasks." These supporting tasks included: "to help create secure conditions for the conduct by others of other tasks," "to assist the UNHCR [United Nations High Commissioner for Refugees] and other international organizations in their humanitarian missions," and "to observe and prevent interference with the movement of civilian populations, refugees, and displaced persons."[15]

IFOR's mandate, however, did not specify law enforcement or police responsibilities. The UN International Police Task Force (IPTF) was responsible for law enforcement, and the UN Security Council authorized a 1,721-member CIVPOL operation in December 1995. As discussed below, the IPTF was mandated to monitor, advise, and train Bosnian police but had no executive authority to investigate, arrest, or perform other police functions.[16]

---

[14]Dayton Accord (1995), Annex IA.

[15]Dayton Accord (1995), Annex IA.

[16]Perito (2002a), pp. 50–51.

Civil and Economic

The overall approach to implementing civilian aspects of the Dayton Accord was highly fragmented. OHR was established to coordinate civilian implementation of the Dayton Accord. Former Swedish Prime Minister Carl Bildt was named the first High Representative.[17] His responsibilities were to "facilitate the Parties' own efforts" at reconstruction and reconciliation, not to rule Bosnia as a protectorate. His mandate was ambitious, but his real authority was initially limited.[18] His office and staff had to be created from scratch, and he had few resources with which to work. He reported to and derived his authority from the Peace Implementation Council (PIC), an ad hoc group of interested countries formed for the purpose and endorsed by the UN Security Council.

Another illustration of the fragmented nature of civil implementation was the number of different organizations that had responsibility for various aspects of the Dayton Accord. The OSCE was given responsibility for organizing and monitoring elections. It was also in charge of negotiating arms control agreements between the former warring parties. This was one of first major operations for the OSCE. The UNHCR, meanwhile, was designated as the lead agency for the explosive issue of refugee and IDP returns, as well as for providing humanitarian assistance. The World Bank and IMF assumed responsibility for most of the efforts to create effective economic and financial policy institutions and for economic reconstruction in Bosnia. These disparate organizations each had distinct agendas. OHR had limited authority to oversee and direct the overall effort.

The International Criminal Tribunal for the Former Yugoslavia (ICTY) would also play a major role in the effort to achieve justice and reconciliation in Bosnia. Acting in response to the serious violations of international humanitarian law committed during the breakup of Yugoslavia, the UN Security Council created the ICTY on May 25, 1993, when it adopted UNSCR 827. The objectives of the ICTY included

---

[17]For a comprehensive discussion of the problems he faced, see Carl Bildt, *Peace Journey, The Struggle for Peace in Bosnia*, London: Weidenfeld and Nicholson, 1998b.

[18]John G. McGinn, "After the Explosion: International Action in the Aftermath of Nationalist War," *National Security Studies Quarterly*, Vol. 4, No. 1, Winter 1998, p. 97.

- bringing to justice persons responsible for violations of international humanitarian law
- rendering justice to the victims
- deterring further crimes
- contributing to the restoration of peace by promoting reconciliation in the former Yugoslavia.

The tribunal has jurisdiction over crimes committed since 1991 throughout the former Yugoslavia.[19]

WHAT HAPPENED

Although Dayton has been widely criticized for not producing results more quickly, especially regarding the return of refugees and displaced people and the arrest of high-ranking individuals charged with war crimes, it has achieved a number of important successes. Dayton stopped the fighting and has helped maintain peace since 1995. It has helped ensure a united, multiethnic Bosnia. It authorized a robust international effort to assist in rebuilding Bosnian society. At the same time, however, significant contradictions in the agreement and obstruction by the former warring parties inhibited implementation of the Dayton Accord. These problems have continued since Dayton and have weakened the Bosnian government. Bosnia and Herzegovina continues to be held together by the presence of a steadily decreasing number of U.S. and international troops and civilians.

Security

IFOR entered Bosnia in December 1995 and January 1996. NATO assembled 60,000 troops for IFOR and divided the country into three regional sectors, each with a lead nation. The United States commanded Multinational Division North; the United Kingdom controlled Multinational Division Southwest; and France directed Multinational Division Southeast. IFOR was created as a one-year mission, although it was widely recognized that an international military presence would be necessary for some time beyond that.

---

[19]Detailed information on the ICTY is available on its Web site.

Operation Joint Guardian was the first NATO ground operation conducted outside the alliance treaty area. In addition to NATO countries, Russia and several former Warsaw Pact countries contributed forces to IFOR. The first priority of IFOR was to separate the former warring military forces and establish a durable cessation of hostilities. A major part of this process was the demarcation and monitoring of the zone of separation established in Dayton. With the active cooperation of the former warring militaries, this withdrawal of forces from the front lines went very smoothly.

At first, IFOR did not involve itself in nonmilitary missions. Various NATO countries, not least the United States, had been concerned that IFOR would find itself gradually assuming responsibilities for civilian tasks, thus clouding its mission, confusing lines of authority, and possibly creating a "dependency culture" among the other international organizations and NGOs. These concerns about "mission creep" subsided somewhat once IFOR was established and had accomplished its initial military tasks.[20]

Nonetheless, the sharp civil-military distinctions in Dayton had several negative consequences. First, some important issues did not come under civilian or military responsibility and consequently fell through the cracks. This initially included responsibility for apprehending persons the ICTY had indicted. OHR did not have the capability to seize alleged war criminals, and IFOR was initially unwilling to involve itself in matters it considered to be law enforcement. As a result, virtually no individuals were arrested for possible war crimes during the first two years of reconstruction. Dayton left international oversight of policing entirely to the UN's IPTF, but the IPTF had little authority and took months to get in place. As a result, law and order were largely left to the suspect ethnic police forces.

When IFOR's mandate expired in December 1996, NATO did not withdraw from Bosnia. Although most of the formal military tasks were complete, the security situation in Bosnia was clearly not self-sustaining. A departure of NATO troops would almost certainly have led to a resumption of conflict between the former warring parties. As a result, IFOR was succeeded by another NATO-led force, the

---

[20]Gregory L. Schulte, "Former Yugoslavia and the New NATO," *Survival*, Vol. 39, No. 1, Spring 1997, p. 26.

Stabilization Force (SFOR), which was given an 18-month mission.[21] When SFOR was extended in June 1998, no end date was specified, and SFOR remains in Bosnia today.

SFOR assistance in the implementation of the civil annexes to Dayton increased significantly after 1996. NATO troops, for example, seized their first indicted war criminals in July 1997. Expanded SFOR activities included increased civil-military cooperation to restore essential public services and economic reconstruction and the use of military force to enforce aspects of the Dayton Accord (e.g., seizing extreme nationalist radio stations to dampen interethnic vitriol).[22] SFOR became more involved in civil affairs largely because its primary military tasks had been accomplished and policymakers perceived a need for more muscle to accomplish other tasks stipulated in the Dayton Accord.

At the outset, the police situation in Bosnia was not conducive to reintegrating the country. There were three ethnically based police forces that were not interested in protecting minorities or encouraging refugee returns.[23] IPTF had little precedence or experience on which to draw in confronting this situation. The UN operation in Haiti had involved the first large-scale use of international police and had demonstrated such inherent difficulties as lack of standard procedures and language differences.[24] Moreover, to emphasize their roles as advisers and facilitators rather than as actual law enforcement officials, IPTF monitors were unarmed.[25] It took eight months

---

[21]Some argue that exit strategies, such as the original one-year timeline for IFOR, are "misguided in theory and unhelpful in practice. Instead of obsessing about the exit, planners should concentrate on the strategy." (Gideon Rose, "The Exit Strategy Delusion," *Foreign Affairs*, Vol. 77, No. 1, January/February 1998, p. 56.)

[22]For a detailed discussion of the civil-military cooperation elements' contribution, see William R. Phillips, "Civil-Military Cooperation: Vital to Peace Implementation in Bosnia," *NATO Review*, Vol. 46, No. 1, Spring 1998, p. 22.

[23]Bosnia had almost 45,000 local police at the end of the war, three times the number before the war (Perito, 2002a, p. 54).

[24]Remarks of Ambassador James Dobbins, "Haiti: A Case Study on Post–Cold War Peacekeeping," remarks at the ISD Conference of Diplomacy and the Use of Force, Georgetown University, Washington, D.C., September 21, 1995.

[25]The task force does not have any executive authority and is not intended to establish conditions of law and order by itself but to assist local law enforcement agencies to

to get the IPTF to full strength. Once the monitors were in place, the IPTF continued to have difficulties with the local language and with the quality of some of their recruits.[26] The IPTF was still struggling to influence the local police forces in 1999, four years into the operation.[27] Eventually, however, the situation did improve. The IPTF had some success in transforming the Bosnian police, training 16,000 police officers to operate in accordance with internationally recognized standards of human rights and fundamental freedoms.[28] Additionally, once more-moderate political forces came into power, entity and cantonal governments began to pressure the new police forces to enforce the law on a more-equitable basis, and, consequently, problems related to interethnic differences in law enforcement declined.

As the security situation has stabilized over the past several years, the number of SFOR soldiers has dropped substantially. By 1998, SFOR had 32,000 troops, roughly half of IFOR's original strength. These levels have continued to drop, and approximately 18,000 troops remain in Bosnia as part of SFOR. These withdrawals have not adversely affected the security situation in Bosnia, but the continued presence of SFOR does clearly exert an important stabilizing influence in the country.

Humanitarian

The UNHCR has been the lead agency for most humanitarian issues in Bosnia since 1992. The return of refugees and IDPs, demining, and the resumption of basic needs (such as water, sanitation, school, medical supplies, and electricity) were the major humanitarian issues in the months after Dayton. The vast majority of initial returns were Serbs, Croats, and Bosniacs coming home to places where their ethnic group was in the majority. There were initially very few so-

---

achieve this. (Julie Kim, *Bosnia: Civil Implementation of the Peace Agreement*, Washington, D.C.: Congressional Research Service, 1996, p. 16.)

[26]On the challenges of getting the IPTF established and maintaining high-quality monitors, see especially, Perito (2002a), pp. 55–62.

[27]International Crisis Group (ICG), *Is Dayton Failing? Bosnia Four Years After the Peace Agreement*, Washington, D.C., October 28, 1999, pp. 58–67.

[28]Radio Free Europe/Radio Liberty, *RFE/RL Balkan Report*, Vol. 6, No. 47, December 20, 2002.

called minority returns—where people returned home to places where they were in the ethnic minority—during the first several years after Dayton. Despite strong international efforts to encourage minority returns, most people cited security concerns when they declined these offers. Persistent and often-violent attacks on those brave enough to risk returning kept these numbers extremely low.[29]

This situation has significantly improved since 2000, however. The Property Implementation Plan, which featured a more vigorous implementation of established property laws, greatly facilitated the return process between 2000 and 2002. The coordinated work of OHR, SFOR, the UN Mission in Bosnia and Herzegovina, the OSCE, and UNHCR has been the key element in creating an environment conducive to returns.[30] The UNHCR undertook various measures to support the return process, such as drawing up detailed return plans, addressing legal and procedural matters affecting returns, assisting the physical return of refugees and IDPs, and providing material assistance upon return. As a result, nearly 1 million people returned to their prewar municipalities as of February 2003, and have partially reversed the ethnic cleansing that occurred during the war.[31] For example, 2001 heralded a marked increase in the number of minority returns. UNHCR recorded a total of 92,061 minority returns, which represented an increase of 36.5 percent over the figures for 2000. This trend continued in 2002, when a record 100,000 refugees and displaced persons returned to their former homes, mostly in areas now controlled by an ethnic group other than their own.[32]

---

[29]ICG (1999), pp. 43–54.

[30]Moreover, the UNHCR has been working with several local government and non-governmental partners for assistance to returnees. These have included the Federation Ministry of Social Affairs; the Ministry for Refugees and Displaced Persons; the American Refugee Committee; the Hilfswerk Austria; the International Rescue Committee; Malteser Hilfstdienst; the Mercy Corps, Scotland; Swiss Humanitarian Aid; the European Committee on Training and Agriculture; Iustitia; Tango; Bosanski Humanitarni Logisticki; the Programme Implementation Unit; the Helsinki Committee on Human Rights; and the International Council of Voluntary Agencies.

[31]UNHCR, *Return Statistics*, Sarajevo, February 28, 2003b.

[32]About 39,000 Muslims went back to homes in the Republika Srpska, and a similar number of Serbs returned to places that are now part of the Croat and Muslim federation. Almost 11,000 Croats went home to areas in both parts of the country.

Demining has been a major emphasis of humanitarian activities in postwar Bosnia. Since 1996, 1,418 persons have been registered as mine victims, including 409 returnees and displaced persons, 34 percent of whom died of their injuries.[33] Although the process of mine clearance is very slow, significant progress has been made. In 1998, Slovenia established the International Trust Fund for Demining and Mine Victims Assistance with the aim of helping Bosnia and Herzegovina clear mines and provide assistance to mine victims. By September 2002, the trust fund had raised almost $100 million, cleared more than 29 million m² of land, and rehabilitated more than 600 mine victims. The United States has given significant humanitarian demining assistance to Bosnia and Herzegovina since early 1996.[34]

Civil Administration

At the international level, the London conference created the PIC to coordinate international efforts in Bosnia. It was envisioned that the PIC would meet periodically to make decisions about providing military, financial, or other assistance to the OHR or other international agencies operating in Bosnia.[35] A major weakness of the initial international effort was the fragmented nature of civilian implementation, poor coordination between the military and civilian elements, and disparity among the civilian elements themselves. The civilian implementation was problematic largely because of a U.S.-European split over the best approach to implementing the civilian annexes of the Dayton Accord. Most European countries were eager to give the EU responsibility for the entire civilian effort, but the United States did not want a European pillar competing with NATO for authority

---

[33]UN Office for the Coordination of Humanitarian Affairs, "Humanitarian Situation and Action 2003," December 31, 2002.

[34]As of April 18, 2000, the U.S. government had given over $40 million for humanitarian mine action support alone (DOS, "U.S. Humanitarian Demining Assistance to Bosnia-Herzegovina," media note, Office of the Spokesman, Washington, D.C., April 17, 2000). On March 22, 2002, the U.S. Congress again approved $14 million to continue support for demining efforts in the Balkans (DOS, International Information Programs, "U.S. Congress OKs Another $14 Million for Demining in Balkans," press release, March 22, 2002).

[35]Information about the history and composition of the PIC is available on the OHR Web site.

within the country. The result was a highly disjointed international effort from the outset. Initially, civil-military coordination was largely nonexistent. The military aspects of Dayton were under the control of NATO, while the civilian aspects were largely under OHR. There was little contact and no established coordination mechanism between the two organizations at the beginning of the operation. This created significant difficulties during the first year of the operation.

From the outset of the intervention, civilian implementation lagged behind the military effort. Apart from the difficulties in creating and staffing OHR, the complex and time-consuming nature of civilian implementation tasks contributed to the slow start, as did the poor civil-military coordination functions inherent in the Dayton framework. Following the language of Dayton, High Representative Bildt and his staff initially attempted to "facilitate the parties' own efforts" to reunite the country. Bildt's limited authority and the intransigence of many Bosnian leaders frustrated his efforts to get implementation of the civil annexes of Dayton on track. The result was continuing de facto military partition between the ethnic groups and little progress in reintegrating the country. The first national elections, held in September 1996, overwhelmingly returned wartime leaders to office.

The relationship between OHR and IFOR during the first postwar year was strained. OHR, for example, wanted IFOR troops to secure suspected mass gravesites and to conduct other operations in support of Dayton civilian implementation. IFOR, on the other hand, focused on completing the military tasks given to it in Dayton. In time, OHR and SFOR developed a closer working relationship, but it did not emerge during the difficult first year.

The intransigence of the former warring parties during the first two years after the peace settlement led OHR to take a more-intrusive role in Dayton implementation. The international community decided to adopt a condominium model. OHR was to oversee, rather than simply support, entity and cantonal governments. It would frequently make and enforce decisions, sometimes in direct opposition to the wishes of the ruling parties. Using authority that the PIC had delegated in December 1997, the second High Representative, Carlos Westendorp, began to make decisions that the former warring parties had been unable or unwilling to make. This more-robust power enabled Westendorp to impose binding decisions and dismiss public

officials.[36] Some of the High Representative's actions included decisions on a common Bosnian currency, a national flag, and national
license plates. These policy decisions facilitated greatly increased
integration between the entities. Common license plates encouraged
interentity travel (usually for commercial reasons), something that
had previously been difficult because cars marked by license plates
from a different entity were frequently vandalized, or their drivers
were harassed by police.

As the political situation stabilized, thuggish behavior was penalized,
the economy improved, and moderate political forces within Bosnia
began to gain strength. In the Republika Srpska and in Croat areas of
the federation, leaders began to take more-temperate policies toward
Dayton implementation. Nonetheless, centrifugal forces continued
to hamper the economic and political integration of Bosnia. Joint
institutions, such as a central bank and a common foreign policy,
remained feeble. Although railroads, highways, and bridges were
repaired, economic connections between the two entities and
between Bosniac- and Croat-dominated cantons remained tenuous
as relations between the ethnic groups continued to be strained.

Another element in the reconciliation process has been the tribunal
in The Hague. The ICTY publicly and later secretly indicted numerous officials who had allegedly committed atrocities during the
Bosnian war. Initially, few were arrested and brought to trial. Beginning in summer 1997, however, SFOR became more involved in
seizing indicted officials, and the number of prisoners at The Hague
increased. In addition, numerous indicted persons have turned
themselves in to the ICTY, most notably former Bosnian Serb President Biljana Plavsic. Former Serb President Milosevic was appre-
hended by Serbian national police in April 2001 and transferred to
the tribunal in June 2001, where he is currently on trial for war
crimes.[37] Although Milosevic was initially charged with war crimes
committed in Kosovo, he was subsequently indicted for incidents in
Bosnia as well. In total, 83 individuals have been tried or are awaiting

---

[36]ICG, *To Build a Peace: Recommendations for the Madrid Peace Implementation Council Meeting*, Washington, D.C., December 15, 1998, p. 2.

[37]For details on the ICTY process and proceedings, see its Web site.

trial in The Hague. Two principal indicted figures, Bosnian Serb leaders Radovan Karadzic and Ratko Mladic, still remain at large.

Democratization

Until 2001, the OSCE directly managed all election activities. The OSCE established various programs to promote the development of democratic political institutions at all levels of state government. These programs aimed at preparing, conducting, and supervising the country's postwar elections until an election law was adopted. The first few rounds of elections, however, largely resulted in returning to office the nationalist parties that helped spark the civil war. The situation improved in time as OHR and the OSCE removed candidates suspected of war crimes or believed to have "obstructed Dayton" from ballots and forced those in power with similar track records to withdraw from official positions. In October 1999, for example, the Provisional Election Commission refused to allow the Serb Radical Party to register for the April 2000 municipal elections on the grounds that its leaders were obstructing the Dayton peace process. With each subsequent election, the OSCE gave the national authorities greater control over the election process. Following the adoption of an election law in August 2001 and the appointment of the Election Commission in November 2001, the OSCE handed over the direct administration of the election process to national authorities.

Reconstruction

Because of the limited powers of the national government, the initial lack of authority on the part of OHR, and an international focus on providing humanitarian assistance and security, efforts to establish new economic policy institutions, a prerequisite for creating conditions for sustained growth, were slow to get off the ground. It was not until the end of October 1996, almost a year after the Dayton Accord was signed, that the three-member presidency of Bosnia and Herzegovina agreed to the appointment of an expatriate governor to the new Central Bank of Bosnia and Herzegovina.[38] However, the bank

---

[38]IMF, *Bosnia and Herzegovina: Selected Issues*, Washington, D.C., IMF Staff Country Report No. 98/69, August 1998, p. 8.

did not begin operations until August 11, 1997, almost a year later, at which time a currency board was introduced.

The currency board, mandated by the Dayton Accord, was to last for a minimum of six years. The stipulation that Bosnia adopt a currency board was taken to provide confidence in the new currency by anchoring it to the most widely used and trusted foreign currency, the deutschmark, and to remove the distractions and pressures involved in making decisions on monetary policy from the purview of the new Bosnian government. The currency board created a new currency, the *konvertibilnaja marka* (KM), which was pegged to the deutschmark at a rate of one to one; the currency now trades at a similarly fixed rate relative to the euro.[39] It took some time for the entities to adopt the new currency, however. New banknotes were introduced into the federation in June 1998. The Republika Srpska adopted the KM in 1999. The rapid depreciation of the Yugoslav dinar, which had been in widespread use in the Republika Srpska, led the government to ban the use of Yugoslav dinars in local payments and to adopt the KM.

During the years of the civil war, the Bosniac, Serb, and Croat authorities financed their operations by printing money. Not surprisingly, extraordinarily high rates of inflation ensued. All Bosnians preferred currencies other than the Bosnian dinar. Once the currency board was introduced and the KM was launched, however, the entity governments could no longer print money. Since no one was willing to lend to them, they were forced to exercise fiscal restraint, although both entity governments financed some expenditures by delaying payments and building up arrears. International financial institutions, working with OHR, provided the national, entity, and cantonal governments with considerable advice and help during this period. They helped set up a modern unified tax and customs administration, introduced simpler and more-transparent tax codes, and set up systems to audit and control government expenditures.

Although the new tax codes resulted in rapid increases in tax revenues in the federation, the increases came off a very low base. Con-

---

[39]IMF, *Bosnia and Herzegovina: First Review of the Stand-By Arrangement and Request for Waiver of Performance Criteria*, Washington D.C., IMF Country Report No. 03/04, January 2003a, p. 16.

sequently, the international community was an important source of budgetary finance in 1995 and into 1996. However, by 1997, foreign grants and concessional loans fell to just 3.6 percent of total expenditures, down from 7.1 percent in 1996 and a very large share of government expenditures in 1995. The substantial flows of economic assistance since 1995, still one-fifth of GDP in 2001, were quickly channeled into reconstruction and development programs that were handled through off-budget accounts. They were not used for direct support of ongoing government expenditures.

One of the failures of the new tax system was the incentives that it continued to provide for smuggling and excise tax evasion. Revenues from selling smuggled goods, contraband cigarettes, and other items were the primary means criminal gangs used to support their activities. The international financial institutions supported the use of customs tariffs to collect revenues for the Bosnian government. Customs revenues formed an appreciable share of total revenues—ranging as high as one-third in the Republika Srpska in 1996 but then declining to less than one-fourth. However, they remained small in absolute terms compared to overall levels of aid, which ranged from $125 million to $200 million annually. The additional cost to donors of making up revenues that were lost by eliminating customs tariffs probably would have been well worth it. Such measures would have deprived criminal gangs of their principal source of income, greatly hampering their ability to recruit and maintain the thugs they needed to wield their power.

In addition to creating a new central bank and revamping and improving fiscal operations, the Bosnian government has been revising its laws to make them more conducive to the operation of a market economy. In June 1997, the government passed a "quick start" package of key economic laws on the 1997 budget external debt, trade and customs policies, and on the central bank. However, many of these laws were not implemented until January 1998, more than two years after the Dayton Accord was signed.

Bosnian governments have continued to pass and modify laws to improve the operation of the economy and markets in Bosnia. A modern payment system has replaced the former regional payment bureaus. These semiautonomous units were frequently abused to make payments to favored institutions or individuals and to withhold payments from those less favored. More recently, tax rates have been unified, and tariffs have been reduced. Bosnia has signed a number of free-trade agreements with important regional trade partners, including Croatia, Serbia and Montenegro, and the EU and hopes to enter the World Trade Organization in 2004.

The Bosnian government has been slower to privatize state- or entity-owned businesses than to make other policy changes. Half of all tenders for privatization issued since 1999 were issued in 2002. Many state enterprises are not economically viable, but the government has been slow to restructure or close them. Control of entity-owned assets remains an important source of patronage and wealth for a number of Bosnian political parties and individuals. The December 1997 PIC decision to interpret the mandate of the High Representative to give him the authority to impose interim policy decisions, both in the political and economic spheres, was key to the passage and implementation of laws and policies in Bosnia conducive to economic growth. Without this authority, it would have been unlikely that the Bosnian governments (national, entity, and cantonal) would have agreed to the legal and other changes needed to make the Bosnian legal and regulatory systems conducive to the efficient operation of markets.

Despite the slow start in terms of legal and institutional changes, Bosnia's economic performance has been remarkable. By 1999, four years after the signing of the Dayton Accord, per capita GDP in Bosnia had reached $1,951 at purchasing power parity in 1995 prices, more than three times the 1995 figure. Although the rate of growth in GDP slowed sharply from 9.0 percent in 1999 to 4.5 and 2.3 percent in 2000 and 2001, respectively, it accelerated to 3.9 percent in 2002 and is projected to exceed 4 percent in 2003 and 2004. Inflation has plummeted from thousands of percent per year during the war to the low single digits or declines in the price level since.

The recovery was propelled by a $5.1 billion foreign-assistance package between 1996 and 1999. The slowdown in growth in 2000 and 2001 was in part due to reductions in economic assistance from abroad and in part due to base-year effects (as the economy grew, the same increment in output resulted in a smaller percentage increase). The resurgence in economic growth in 2002 and that projected for 2003 result from healthy growth in exports as manufacturing and agricultural output rise. The 2002 figures provided the first indications that Bosnia will be able to sustain solid economic growth even as external assistance declines.

LESSONS LEARNED

Nation-building efforts in Bosnia have had mixed success. NATO was well organized and effective, but adopted a limited view of its responsibilities. On the civil side, international responsibilities were more dispersed and slower to take hold. Bosnia has made political and economic progress but more than seven years after the Dayton Accord, it is not yet a self-sustaining political or economic entity. Important lessons include the following:

- Unity of command can be as important for the civil aspects of peace operations as for the military.

- Elections are an important benchmark in progress toward democracy. Held too early, they can strengthen rejectionist forces rather than promote further transformation.

- Organized crime can emerge as the greatest obstacle to trans-formation.

- It is difficult to put a nation back together if its neighbors are pulling it apart.

- Successful reconstruction in poor and divided countries requires substantial long-term commitment from donors.

- Foreign donors need to take an active role in economic policy in countries with stalemated or ineffective governments.

NATO was effective in ensuring broad participation, unity of command, and U.S. leadership on the military side of the Bosnia operation. On the civil side, however, the United States took the opposite approach. In a misguided effort, it sought to advance NATO authority at the expense of the EU, and U.S. influence at the expense of the Europeans. For example, there was no contact and little coordination between NATO and OHR at the beginning of the operation. The result has been endemic conflict among competing international agencies, indecisive leadership of the transformational effort, and unnecessary prolongation of the international military presence.

The Clinton administration originally set an arbitrary one-year deadline for the Bosnia mission. In an effort to meet that deadline, it pressed successfully for early and frequent elections at each level of governance. In most cases, the elections returned to office the nationalist parties that had helped spark the civil war and strengthened those resisting the creation of a democratic and multiethnic state. Holding elections before viable democratic political institutions were built created a number of problems that made democratization more—rather than less—difficult. Over time, however, OHR and the OSCE helped remove candidates suspected of war crimes and who attempted to obstruct implementation of the Dayton peace process.

As in other postcommunist societies, the emergence of organized crime accompanied Bosnia's transition to market economy. In the immediate aftermath of a conflict, governments have virtually no tax revenues because of the collapse in economic activity. However, foreign pressure to raise taxes to cover government expenditures can have unproductive side effects. In the case of Bosnia, the continued use of customs tariffs resulted in widespread smuggling, which provided the economic basis for the continued operation of criminal gangs and paramilitary groups. Bosnia now has free-trade agreements with all its major trading partners. The country would have been better off if it had immediately abolished tariffs and had donors temporarily funding the budgetary shortfall.

In the aftermath of the Dayton Accord, both the Serbian and Croatian governments continued to pursue their divisive and irredentist objectives in Bosnia through nonmilitary means. Only after replacement of the Milosevic and Tudjman regimes with democratic successors did Bosnia's neighbors begin to work with the rest of the international community to push it together rather than pull it apart.

The international community's long-term financial commitment has been crucial for economic growth in Bosnia. Economic growth was very rapid in the years immediately following the Dayton Accord, driven by the peace and by foreign assistance. In 2002, the Bosnian economy first showed signs that growth would be sustained as economic assistance is reduced. OHR and international financial institutions continue to play a key, positive role in economic policymaking in Bosnia.

Because of Bosnia's acrimonious interethnic politics and the weak constitutional authority of the national government, decisions to reform the economy were made very slowly, if at all. The logjam was broken only after the authority of OHR was significantly expanded. Key decisions on the national currency, taxation, budget, and privatization have only been made because of OHR. More than seven years after the Dayton Accord, OHR still plays a key role in economic policymaking in Bosnia. Moreover, like the Haitian government, Bosnia's governments have resisted privatization for political and personal reasons. Only with steady pressure from donors, international financial institutions, and OHR has privatization made progress in Bosnia. The process has still not been completed.

Chapter Seven

KOSOVO

Serbs and Albanians have wrestled for control over the territory of Kosovo for hundreds of years.[1] In 1989, then Serbian and subsequently Yugoslav President Slobodan Milosevic revoked Kosovo's autonomous status, disbanded its institutions of local government, imposed direct control from Belgrade, replaced Kosovar Albanians with Serbs in most official positions, and began to dispossess the Kosovar Albanians of their equity in most communally owned enterprises through a rigged process of "privatization." As Yugoslavia disintegrated in the 1990s, the majority Albanian Kosovar population's resistance to Serbian rule grew apace. Initially nonviolent, Albanian resistance began to take more-militant forms as the decade progressed, leading to the emergence of an armed insurgency, built around the Kosovo Liberation Army (KLA). Serbian efforts to extirpate insurgent activity produced significant civilian casualties and a mounting flow of refugees and displaced persons. By 1998, the international community felt compelled to intervene, initially through diplomatic means, then through economic sanctions, and finally with military force to stem the bloodshed. On March 24, 1998, NATO opened a bombing campaign over Kosovo and the rest of Yugoslavia. The bombing was triggered by Belgrade's rejection of an interim settlement for Kosovo that had been reached at an international conference in Rambouillet, France. NATO's objective was to force the removal of Serbian military and police forces and place Kosovo

---

[1]For a detailed treatment of Kosovo's turbulent history, see Noel Malcolm, *Kosovo: A Short History*, New York: HarperCollins, 1999.

under international protection until its final status could be determined.

On June 3, 1999, after 11 weeks of increasingly intense NATO bombing and facing the prospect of a Western military intervention on the ground as well, Yugoslav President Milosevic accepted NATO's conditions.[2] UNSCR 1244, passed on June 10, 1999, prescribed arrangements for Kosovo's postconflict governance, establishing a UN-led international administration, and authorized the deployment of a NATO-led military security force. Terms of this resolution postponed determination of the final status of Kosovo to the indefinite future. In the interim, the UN would gradually prepare the way for democratic, autonomous self-government, while NATO would provide external and, to the extent necessary, internal security.

CHALLENGES

A decade of Serbian repression, years of mounting civil conflict, and 11 weeks of NATO bombing had driven more than half of Kosovo's population from their homes and destroyed much of the infrastructure and housing stock. Ethnic tensions were white-hot, and the potential for retributive violence was very high. All elements of the Serbian administration were discredited, and most departed with Serbian forces, leaving Kosovo without the most basic structures of governance.

Security

Yugoslav military forces were required to withdraw immediately from Kosovo under the terms of the military technical agreement that Belgrade had signed with the NATO force commander.[3] There

---

[2]For analyses of the NATO air campaign, see Stephan T. Hosmer, *The Conflict over Kosovo: Why Milosevic Decided to Settle When He Did,* Santa Monica, Calif.: MR-1351-AF, RAND, 2001; Benjamin S. Lambeth, *NATO's Air War for Kosovo: A Strategic and Operational Assessment,* Santa Monica, Calif.: RAND, MR-1365-AF, 2001; and Ivo H. Daalder and Michael E. O'Hanlon, *Winning Ugly: NATO's War to Save Kosovo,* Washington D.C.: The Brookings Institution, 2001. For a first-hand account of the war, see Wesley K. Clark, *Waging Modern War: Bosnia, Kosovo, and the Future of Combat,* New York: PublicAffairs, 2002.

[3]International Security Force (KFOR) and the Governments of the Federal Republic of Yugoslavia and the Republic of Serbia, Military Technical Agreement, 2002.

was concern that Serbian forces would undertake punitive actions as they withdrew or that ethnic Albanian guerrillas would launch reprisal attacks against Serbian civilians once the Yugoslav forces left. The entire police force in Kosovo, being Serbian, was also required to leave the province. As Serbian forces moved out, KLA elements moved in, seeking to install themselves in positions of authority before the UN Interim Administration in Kosovo (UNMIK) was in a position to assume its new responsibilities fully.

Humanitarian

By war's end, close to 1 million Kosovar Albanians, about 45 percent of the prewar population, had fled or were expelled from their homes.[4] As Serbian forces withdrew, about half the Serbian population fled with them. These new refugees settled in Macedonia, Serbia, and Montenegro. Other Serbian residents fled their homes to congregate in Serbian enclaves elsewhere in Kosovo. All told, approximately 130,000 Serbs and 100,000 other minorities remained in the provinces.[5] The conflict also resulted in massive damage to the housing stock; two-thirds of all homes in Kosovo were damaged or destroyed.[6]

Civil Administration

Kosovo had no civil administration. Serbian administrators had fled and would, in any case, have been wholly unacceptable to the bulk of the population. Former Kosovar Albanian administrators had been out of office for a decade. KLA elements, few of which had any administrative or political experience, felt entitled to assume positions of responsibility and moved quickly to seize municipal and provincial facilities. The UN was assigned the responsibility of gov-

---

[4]Some 863,000 Kosovar Albanians fled Kosovo for Albania, Macedonia, or Bosnia and Herzegovina. Several hundred thousand more were internally displaced in Kosovo. (OSCE, *Kosovo/Kosova as Seen, as Told: The Human Rights Findings of the OSCE Kosovo Verification Mission*, Pts. I and II, Vienna: OSCE Secretariat, 1999, Ch. 14.)

[5]ICG, *Return to Uncertainty: Kosovo's Internally Displaced and the Return Process*, Washington, D.C., ICG Balkans Report No. 139, December 13, 2002c, p. 1.

[6]Dimitri G. Demekas, Johannes Herderschee, and Davina F. Jacobs, *Kosovo: Institutions and Policies for Reconstruction and Growth*, Washington, D.C.: International Monetary Fund, 2002, p. 2.

erning Kosovo only as the conflict ended and, consequently, had no opportunity to plan, organize, or recruit in advance.

Reconstruction

In the decade before the conflict, Yugoslavia's GDP decreased by one-half because of a combination of its involvement in wars in Croatia and Bosnia and its poor economic policies at home. Kosovo began and ended the decade as the poorest region in the former Yugoslavia. In addition to the general decline in the Yugoslav economy, discrimination against ethnic Albanians and an overall climate of unrest resulted in an exodus of people, especially the better educated. Investment during this period fell sharply. As a consequence, the stock of both human and physical capital had deteriorated substantially before the conflict, making postconflict recovery all that much more difficult.

THE U.S. AND INTERNATIONAL ROLES

NATO and the UN shared responsibility for Kosovo's postconflict security and governance: the former overseeing all military activities, the later all civil. UNSCR 1244 built in an intentional overlap between the two organizations' mandates for policing and internal security. The UN was to have primary responsibility for the police and law-and-order functions, but NATO was to fill gaps in the UN's capabilities as and when necessary. The intent was to avoid a situation that had so often occurred in Bosnia. Both the military and the civil authorities declined to perform important security-related tasks (for instance, riot control and combating organized crime): the military because it lacked the mandate and the civil because it lacked the capacity.

Military

UNSCR 1244 set forth detailed guidelines for what it termed an international security presence. Although the resolution itself did not so specify, it was understood that NATO would assume responsibility for fielding and controlling this presence. NATO's Kosovo Force (KFOR) was responsible under the terms of this resolution for

- deterring renewed hostilities, enforcing the cease-fire, ensuring the withdrawal, and preventing the return of Yugoslav military, police, and paramilitary forces
- demilitarizing the KLA and other armed Kosovo Albanian groups
- establishing a secure environment in which refugees and displaced persons could return home in safety, the international civil presence could operate, a transitional administration could be established, and humanitarian aid could be delivered
- ensuring public safety and order and supervising demining until the international civil presence could take over
- supporting the work of the international civil presence and coordinating closely with it
- conducting border monitoring duties
- protecting its own freedom of movement and that of the international civil presence and other international organizations.

KFOR entered Kosovo on June 12, 1999, numbered almost 45,000 troops by the end of that year, and organized itself into five multinational brigades, each led by a major NATO ally: the United States, the United Kingdom, France, Germany, or Italy.

Civil and Economic

UNSCR 1244 gave broad authority to what it termed the "international civil presence," which was to operate under UN leadership. While formally acknowledging continued Yugoslav sovereignty over Kosovo, the resolution assigned all sovereign functions to either NATO or the UN. UNMIK was thus charged with governing and with representing Kosovo internationally. All international organizations operating in Kosovo (other than NATO) were subordinated to UN authority, and the most important were assigned specific places within UNMIK's hierarchy. The result was a four-pillar arrangement in which UNHCR assumed responsibility under UN oversight for humanitarian issues; the OSCE for democratization, the press, and elections; and the EU for reconstruction and development. The UN, in addition to overseeing the activities of the other three pillars, assumed direct responsibility for the security pillar: the police, courts, and prisons.

The U.S. administration wished to maximize European responsibility for Kosovo's reconstruction and democratization. In contrast with Bosnia, therefore, where two and eventually three of the top four international positions were American, all the top spots were European in Kosovo, including both the NATO and UN commands and the leadership of all four UNMIK pillars. This allowed the United States to reduce the scale of its financial and military commitments to only 16 percent of the reconstruction funding and peacekeeping troops, while retaining adequate influence because of the U.S. positions in the NATO and UN hierarchies and its unparalleled prestige among the population of Kosovo.

U.S. planning for postconflict operation in Kosovo was conducted in accordance the Presidential Decision Directive 56, which had been issued following the Haiti intervention in an effort to capture the major lessons of that effort and to regularize preparations for similar operations in the future. Many of the lessons of that and previous such operations were applied. Interagency debates over respective roles and missions were, consequently, much muted.

WHAT HAPPENED

NATO began to prepare for its role in postconflict Kosovo several months in advance. Forces were accordingly positioned in neighboring Macedonia and thus were able to move on a few hours' notice to ensure Serbian withdrawals, demilitarize the KLA, and establish a somewhat secure, if still somewhat chaotic, environment. The UN, given only a few days notice regarding its own role, was much slower to deploy administrators and police. This left a large disparity, for the first several months, between the capacities of the international military and civil presences, creating a governance gap that both Albanian and Serbian extremists moved to fill. Nevertheless, the fact that NATO was assigned backup responsibility for internal security ensured that basic law-and-order functions were fulfilled and that extremist elements were held in check.

Over time, the hierarchical UN-led structure for civil governance began to function—and with greater authority and coherence than did previous efforts in Somalia, Haiti, and Bosnia. Kosovars were associated with this international regime, first by selection and then by election. Local and then general elections were held. Kosovo's comparative tranquillity contributed importantly to the peaceful diffusing of crises on its periphery, in Macedonia, Serbia, and Montenegro. Progress in the democratization, economic development, and eventual integration of the Balkan region as a whole reduced destabilizing pressures within Kosovo and increased the prospect that its final status would be resolved peacefully someday.

Security

The immediate task for KFOR was to ensure that Yugoslav forces complied with the phased-withdrawal timeline outlined in the military technical agreement. This required KFOR to deploy quickly into the province to prevent a security vacuum in contested areas. KFOR elements met with Yugoslav's military liaison teams in Pristina and elsewhere to ensure proper transfer of military authority in the region. Yugoslav forces completed their withdrawal with few difficulties by June 20, 1999, the deadline under the agreement.

Within KFOR, however, there was an immediate crisis. Russian troops moved from Bosnia into Kosovo unexpectedly and seized the Pristina airport. NATO Supreme Commander General Wesley Clark directed that the KFOR Commander, UK Lieutenant General Sir Michael Jackson, compel the Russians to withdraw from the airport. General Jackson responded that the confrontation should be resolved diplomatically, in which view London and eventually Washington concurred. The Russian and U.S. defense and foreign ministers met in Helsinki on June 18, 1999, and agreed on the terms for Russia's participation in KFOR. As in Bosnia, the Russians agreed that their forces would serve formally under U.S., but not NATO, command.[7]

Having entered Kosovo to protect the ethnic Albanian majority from Serbian oppression, KFOR and UNMIK soon found that their most difficult and demanding task was protecting the Serbian minority from its former victims. Roughly half the Serbian population (which may have numbered about 250,000 to 300,000) had left with the Ser-

---

[7]For a detailed account of the Pristina airfield incident, see Clark (2002), pp. 375–403. See also the Agreed Points on Russian Participation in KFOR (Helsinki Agreement), signed by the Secretary of Defense of the United States and the Minister of Defense of the Russian Federation at Helsinki, Finland, June 18, 1999.

bian forces. Those who stayed gathered in enclaves, mostly toward the northern border with Serbia. This embattled population found itself subjected to a progression of deadly terrorist-type attacks. In response, the remaining Serbs organized their own defenses, while spurning UNMIK efforts to secure control of their areas and promote ethnic reconciliation. The government in Belgrade (at least until Yugoslav President Milosevic's ouster in October 2000) encouraged this militant and rejectionist attitude on the part of the local Serbian population.

Although the robust size of KFOR eventually allowed it to create a generally secure environment, pockets of tension remained. The principal flash point was the town of Mitrovica, where Serbs and Albanians faced off against each other. When the KFOR commander attempted to move U.S. forces from the U.S. sector to reinforce Mitrovica during the February 2000 crisis there, the U.S. military authorities balked and required the troops to return to the U.S. sector.[8] This was inconsistent with the mechanism established in the NATO Operation Plan, which gave the KFOR Commander such authority, and made it more difficult for him to shift forces across command boundaries to meet future emergencies.

KFOR moved quickly to demilitarize the KLA. As Serbian forces began to withdraw, the KLA leadership, at strong U.S. urging (President Clinton personally called KLA "Prime Minister" Hachim Thachi to clinch the deal), signed the "Undertaking of Demilitarization and Transformation" on June 21, 1999. This agreement provided for a "cease-fire by the KLA, their disengagement from the zones of conflict, subsequent demilitarization and reintegration into civil society."[9] Disarmament proceeded slowly and was never total, but by September 20, the KFOR commander certified that the KLA had adequately completed the process of demilitarization.

Many demobilized KLA personnel found their way into the newly created Kosovo Protection Corps (TMK), which was established for that purpose. This organization was given the authority to provide

---

[8]See, for example, Richard Beeston, Michael Evans, and Ian Brodie, "Pentagon Refuses to Send Troops to Serb Area," *London Times*, February 29, 2000, p. 1, and Robert Burns, "US to Limit Kosovo Patrols," Associated Press, February 29, 2000.

[9]Hashim Thagi and KFOR Commander Lieutenant General Mike Jackson, "Undertaking of Demilitarisation and Transformation by the KLA," Kosovo, June 21, 1999.

disaster response, conduct search and rescue, provide humanitarian assistance, assist in demining, and contribute to rebuilding infrastructure and communities. The TMK was allowed no role in defense, law enforcement, riot control, internal security, or any other task involved in the maintenance of law and order. Nevertheless, its members and the bulk of the Kosovar population regard it as the precursor of an eventual Kosovar military force. The TMK's maximum authorized strength is 5,000 (3,000 active, 2,000 reserve). In principal, it requires representation from all ethnic groups, but Serbs have been most reluctant to serve in an organization led and largely manned by former KLA members.

The UN CIVPOL effort took many months to become fully established. Donor countries quickly volunteered significant numbers of police, but it took considerable time for these personnel to begin arriving in Kosovo. In the interim, in accordance with UNSCR 1244, KFOR assumed policing duties in Kosovo. UNMIK CIVPOL took over direct responsibility for law enforcement in a phased process beginning in Pristina on August 23, 1999, and extending to several other major towns by summer 2000.[10] The CIVPOL operation was initially intended to consist of 3,110 international police officers. The authorization was raised to over 4,700 in late 1999. Reaching these authorized numbers proved difficult, but 4,450 UNMIK international police were in country by December 2000. UNMIK also moved to create and begin training a new local police force, the Kosovo Police Service (KPS). By mid-July 2000, the KPS had 842 officers.[11]

The UNMIK international police effort eventually consisted of three components: the UN CIVPOL unit, the UN Border Police Unit, and the UN special police units (SPUs). The traditional CIVPOL were distributed among regional commands throughout the province, where they progressively assumed responsibility for law enforcement and maintenance of public security from KFOR. The Border Police Unit worked in conjunction with KFOR units on Kosovo's international frontiers. The SPUs were responsible for crowd control and other tasks requiring more heavily armed police. Unlike traditional

---

[10]See UNMIK, *UNMIK Police Annual Report 2000,* 2000a, pp. 10–12.

[11]ICG, *Kosovo Report Card,* No. 100, Pristina, Kosovo, and Brussels, Belgium, August 2000, pp. 42–46.

CIVPOL, who were individuals intermingled with police from other countries, SPUs were formed units from single countries, consisting of Italian Carabinieri, the French Gendarmerie, the Spanish Guardia Civil and other such quasi-military police establishments.

In Bosnia, these heavier police contingents, labeled military specialized units (MSUs), had operated exclusively under NATO command in Bosnia, but NATO commanders had generally resisted using them for law enforcement. In Kosovo, these assets were deployed in KFOR and UNMIK, giving both international entities some capacity for riot control and other high-end policing tasks. The first of UNMIK's SPUs arrived in April 2000; by early 2002, ten SPUs were stationed throughout the province.

By August 2001, KFOR's total presence in the province had dropped to 38,820.[12] U.S. and other KFOR militaries began doing more dismounted and small-unit patrolling, especially along the border between Kosovo and Macedonia, where guerrillas were smuggling weapons or agitating for uprising against the Skopje government.

The level of international military forces remained stable through 2002, although there have been discussions about significantly reducing—possibly halving—the size of KFOR.[13] Additionally, the force-protection posture of KFOR units has loosened substantially since 1999. U.S. commanders, long viewed as much more concerned about force protection than European militaries are, reduced travel restrictions for soldiers and began to allow visits and interaction with the local populace. The UNMIK CIVPOL contingent, meanwhile, remains significant. As of September 2002, 4,466 UNMIK police officers were in the province working alongside the 4,933 KPS officers who have been trained and deployed.[14] The crime rate, initially quite high, has been dropping as the UNMIK and KPS police efforts have matured.[15]

---

[12]International Institute for Strategic Studies, *The Military Balance 2000–2001*, Washington, D.C., 2001, p. 30.

[13]Reuters, "NATO Eyes More Troop Cuts in Balkans," January 15, 2003.

[14]UNMIK Police Web site, 2003.

[15]Michael Steiner, "Address to the [United Nations] Security Council," April 24, 2002.

Humanitarian

Upon entering Kosovo, KFOR provided humanitarian assistance. KFOR's role in humanitarian assistance was turned over to international organizations, such as UNHCR and various NGOs, as soon as these became operational in the province. Once established in Kosovo, UNHCR supervised the return of refugees and IDPs and an emergency shelter program. KFOR continued to play a role by protecting historic cultural sites and by escorting and safeguarding ethnic minorities in various parts of the province.

One of the major success stories of the initial deployment was humanitarian assistance. As mentioned above, most Kosovar Albanian refugees and IDPs promptly returned home, 500,000 in the first month after the end of the conflict alone. UNHCR provided shelter assistance to 700,000 people over the winter. Meanwhile, other relief agencies distributed food aid to 1.5 million people across the province.[16] Although numerous refugees and IDPs remained, they were receiving adequate assistance. As a result, the humanitarian assistance "pillar" was phased out of the UNMIK structure by July 2000.[17]

Civil Administration

Because the UN, unlike NATO, could not draw on standing units to supply the necessary manpower, it was slower in establishing a presence in Kosovo. Personnel to serve in UNMIK needed to be identified and hired one by one. It took many months to complete this process. By November 22, 1999, there were approximately 1,169 personnel from the UN and partner organizations in Kosovo.[18]

UNSCR 1244 assigned UNMIK chief responsibility for all legislative, executive, and judicial authority in Kosovo. Initially, UNMIK focused on assembling staff and equipment for this unprecedented mandate. By the end of 1999, UNMIK had established a series of interim administrative structures for governing the province. Many of these

---

[16]ICG (2000), pp. 41–42.

[17]UNMIK, Bringing Peace to Kosovo Status Report, October 19, 2000b.

[18]UNMIK (2000b).

structures included councils with Albanian and Serbian leaders, but initially none of the Kosovars had decisionmaking authority. UNMIK scheduled municipal elections for October 2000.[19]

Democratization

Kosovo's ethnic Albanian majority was divided between members and supporters of the KLA and those who preferred to look to the civilian nonviolent resistance movement organized around the League for Democratic Kosovo (LDK) for leadership once the war was over. KLA leaders, who had fought for Kosovo's liberation and had emerged as war heroes, expected to participate in, indeed to dominate, postconflict governance. They moved quickly to install their own chosen ministers, mayors, and other officials throughout Kosovo. UN-appointed successors displaced these individuals only gradually and with difficulty.

First public opinion polls, then local and eventually general elections indicated that, while the vast majority of Kosovar Albanian population respected and were very grateful to the KLA for its role in their liberation, most preferred to return to the more-mature and -moderate leadership of the LDK for their postconflict governance. The UN and NATO performed with considerable if not uniform success the difficult task of persuading the KLA leadership to pursue its aspirations for power through the open and democratic means of free elections, in which their prospects of prevailing were poor.

Kosovars elected a parliament in November 2001. The moderate LDK party won a strong plurality of the votes, but its subsequent difficulty in forming a governing coalition was a harbinger of the long political road ahead.[20] The political situation remains challenging. The provincial government is functioning, and many responsibilities have been turned over to elected Kosovars, but tensions between

---

[19]ICG (2000), pp. 22–33.

[20]Andrew Gray, "Moderate Party Wins Plurality in Kosovo," *Washington Post*, November 20, 2001, p. A16; Radio Free Europe/Radio Liberty, *RFE/RL Balkan Report*, Vol. 5, No. 76, November 16, 2001; Fredrik Dahl, "First Kosovo Assembly Session Marred by Walkout," Reuters, December 10, 2001; and Garentina Kraja, "Kosovo Fails to Elect President," Associated Press, January 10, 2002.

Albanians and Serbs remain high, as indeed do those among Albanian factions.[21]

Those who drafted UNSCR 1244 took the view that any attempt to determine Kosovo's final status would only destabilize the larger region, since the vast majority of the population would accept nothing but independence. Yet most neighboring countries, Albania accepted, strongly opposed such a development. By putting the issue of Kosovo's final status to one side, the international community has been able to promote a democratic transformation in Belgrade, work out an accommodation between Serbia and Montenegro, defuse a civil conflict in Macedonia, continue to build multiethnic institutions in Bosnia, and begin the integration of the region into both NATO and the EU.

Nevertheless, continued uncertainly over Kosovo's future status has only hardened its ethnic divisions and retarded its democratic development. At some point in the next few years, the international community will need to determine whether the region as a whole is stable enough to accommodate itself to a political future for Kosovo that is acceptable to its inhabitants, which almost certainly means independence or something very close to it.

Reconstruction

The EU, which had the lead responsibility for economic reconstruction, drew on the expertise of a number of donor countries and international financial institutions to manage the reconstruction and economic development effort. This effort involved a number of tasks, most of which were pursued simultaneously. On the institutional side, they included the creation of the Central Fiscal Authority, a nascent finance ministry; a new tax system and tax administration; and a new trade regime and customs department. As part of the new foreign trade regime, a flat 10 percent ad valorem tariff was imposed on all imports.[22] Because Kosovo technically remains part of

---

[21]For a summary of the current political situation and a proposed road map to a final settlement, see ICG, *A Kosovo Roadmap (I): Addressing Final Status*, Washington, D.C., ICG Balkans Report No. 124, March 1, 2002a.

[22]Dimitri G. Demekas, Johannes Herderschee, and Davina F. Jacobs, *Kosovo: Progress in Institution Building and Economic Policy Challenges*, Washington, D.C.: International Monetary Fund, December 6, 2001, p. 3.

Yugoslavia, imports from Yugoslavia (Serbia and Montenegro) have not been subject to this tariff.

The EU supervised the creation of the Banking and Payments Authority of Kosovo (BPAK) and the reform of the payment system. In addition to supervising all financial institutions in Kosovo, the BPAK operates 29 branches throughout the province. These branches, which were set up quickly, provide a substantial share of transaction services in the province.

A key element of the reconstruction of the financial sector was the decision made two months after the end of the conflict to legalize the use of all foreign currencies for domestic transactions. Because the deutschmark had been in wide use in Yugoslavia and Kosovo since the 1960s, it immediately became the de facto national currency. BPAK oversaw the cash conversion of deutschmarks for euros in early 2002, when the European Central Bank replaced national currencies with euro notes and coins. The EU also assisted in the reconstruction of housing and infrastructure. The bulk of economic assistance in 2001 and 2002 paid for materials, machinery, equipment, and construction services as part of this effort. To coordinate the tasks of reconstruction, a Department of Reconstruction was set up to coordinate donor assistance and prepare a public investment program.

In each of these institutions, well-qualified expatriate staff members were paired with Kosovars. After provincial elections were successfully completed in November 2001, the UNMIK began the process of transferring more authority to Kosovar government officials. However, a number of key decisions, including the overall budgetary framework, remain under the control of UNMIK.

The damage resulting from generations of communist mismanagement followed by a decade of Serbian looting proved difficult to repair. Facing disagreement within the international community on how to tackle these challenges, the UN administration delayed many of its decisions. By the end of 2000, Kosovo had a much-improved commercial code, the outcome of international development efforts. Nearly a year passed after the conflict before a criminal and civil code was put in place, and then it was the Yugoslav code dating from 1989, which had the virtue of being pre-Milosevic but the disadvantage of also being pre-postcommunist. A number of property disputes therefore remain unresolved even today.

Within two years of the end of the conflict, UNMIK had made substantial strides in creating a set of economic policy institutions in Kosovo. The institutional framework for fiscal policy had also been created, although the tax system was still under development. A value-added tax and taxes on personal income and on corporate profits had yet to be introduced. In 2000, tax revenues only covered half of recurrent government expenditures. Thus, the fiscal situation was unsustainable without continued foreign assistance. Moreover, Kosovo still lacked much in the way of a banking system at the time.

By January 2003, Kosovo had a budget and a functioning finance ministry, in the form of the Central Fiscal Authority. As of this writing, the tax system is being expanded to include personal and corporate income taxes.[23] Tax revenues were to cover over 90 percent of recurrent expenditures in 2002.[24] The financial system is solid, and the BPAK is considered very competent. Kosovars are taking increasing responsibility for economic policy decisions. As a consequence of these developments, Kosovo's economic institutions and policies have become completely independent from those of the Yugoslav government, a result that had not been officially envisioned at the time UNMIK was created.

International assistance for Kosovo's reconstruction proved more generous than for any earlier postconflict response or any since. The United States and international organizations spent $1.5 billion on financial assistance to Kosovo in 1999 and 2000, including funding for budgetary assistance, reconstruction and recovery, and peace implementation.[25] In addition to official assistance, Kosovars received an additional $350 million in financial assistance from expatriate family and friends. As a result, economic growth was very strong in both 2000 and 2001. Measures of aggregate output and consumption for Kosovo are fraught with great problems. Nevertheless,

---

[23]UNMIK, *The New Kosovo Government: 2002 Budget*, Pristina, Kosovo, 2002.

[24]Demekas, Herderschee, and Jacobs (2002).

[25]World Bank and European Commission, *Report on Progress Made in Committing, Contracting and Spending Donor Pledges to Kosovo*, Washington, D.C., May 2002, p. 1.

according to RAND estimates, per capita GDP may have been as much as three-quarters higher in 2000 than in the preconflict year of 1998. GDP rose by one-quarter in deutschmark terms in 2001 and in the neighborhood of 15 percent in real terms.[26] As a consequence, according to RAND estimates, per capita GDP had already exceeded 1990 levels by about 5 percent in 2001.

Substantial foreign assistance continued into 2001, still running 39 percent of estimated GDP. Expatriate Kosovars provided additional assistance, equal to about one-half that from official donors. On a per capita basis, assistance actually rose slightly compared to 1999 and 2000. However, assistance dropped in 2002 to about 25 percent of GDP and is projected to fall to 15 to 20 percent of GDP in 2004. As a consequence, rates of economic growth and increases in personal consumption have slowed.

Although the province now functions economically, it remains dependent on foreign assistance. Private economic activity, although expanding, has not yet reached the point of independently sustaining economic growth. A substantial share of consumption and investment continues to rely on official and private transfers of funds from abroad.

LESSONS LEARNED

Kosovo has been the best managed of the U.S. post–Cold War ventures in nation-building. U.S. and European forces demilitarized the KLA; local and national elections took place two years after the conflict ended; and economic growth has been strong.

Indeed, the experience yielded a number of important lessons regarding civil administration, democratization, and economic growth:

- Broad participation, extensive burden-sharing, unity of command, and effective U.S. leadership can be compatible.

- A slow mobilization of civil elements in peace operations can be costly.

---

[26]Demekas, Herderschee, and Jacobs (2002), p. 6.

- Uncertainty over final international status can hinder democratic transition.

- When countries lack effective governmental institutions, placing expatriate staff in positions of authority can facilitate economic policymaking and implementation.

- Large-scale assistance can rapidly restore economic growth in conjunction with effective economic institutions.

One of the most significant aspects of the reconstruction effort in Kosovo was the degree of collaboration and burden-sharing among participant countries and international organizations. Military unity of command was achieved through NATO, although U.S. troops represented only 16 percent of the force. While there were some disagreements among NATO countries over such issues as target sets and operational goals during the military campaign, postwar military cooperation was much smoother.[27] KFOR acted swiftly to demilitarize the KLA, some of whose members were integrated into the newly established TMK. Civil unity of command was established under UN auspices. Responsibility for economic reconstruction was assigned to the EU, acting under UN oversight. Again, U.S. economic assistance represented only 16 percent of the total. In sum, while Kosovo has been the best organized and best resourced of the post–Cold War operations, it has also been the one with the lowest U.S. contribution, in proportion to that of other participants.

Despite its comparative success, the Kosovo operation was plagued by slow start-ups in most aspects of civil implementation, such as CIVPOL. Italy, France, Spain, and other countries offered police contingents to perform such tasks as border patrol, law enforcement, and the general maintenance of public security. SPUs were established for more-difficult functions, such as crowd control, and included separate units from single countries, such as the Spanish Guardia Civil and the French Gendarmerie. It unnecessarily took several months for these units to become fully established. Fortunately, the international mandate contained in UNSCR 1244 explic-

---

[27]On alliance difficulties during the military operation in Kosovo, see Clark (2002); John E. Peters, Stuart Johnson, Nora Bensahel, Timothy Liston, and Traci Williams, *European Contributions to Operation Allied Force: Implications for Transatlantic Cooperation*, Santa Monica, Calif.: RAND, MR-1392-AF, 2001; and Lambeth (2001).

itly gave responsibility for the maintenance of law and order to KFOR, pending UNMIK's capacity to assume the responsibility. Yet, too much time was wasted for one of the operation's most important tasks.

Furthermore, Kosovo's final status was unresolved—and is still in limbo today. This postponement, essential for purposes of regional stability, has nevertheless retarded the process of ethnic reconciliation and democratic transformation in Kosovo. Bernard Kouchner, the UN administrator in Kosovo, has argued that, without greater clarity about Kosovo's status—including Belgrade's authority over the territory—it was difficult to administer the territory effectively.[28]

As a province of Serbia, Kosovo had no independent governmental budgetary or economic institutions. After the intervention, the international community helped Kosovo set up a central bank, treasury, and finance ministry within a few months. It also adopted a new currency for Kosovo, the euro. Reforming commercial law has proceeded more slowly. Competent expatriates initially staffed the new financial institutions. These individuals introduced systems and practices that have made the institutions function much more effectively than their counterparts in Haiti or even Bosnia. Early on, expatriate staff were paired with locals. This process enabled the expatriates to transfer their knowledge and management skills to nationals. It also enabled them to judge the competency of their eventual replacements and to recommend staffing changes, when appropriate.

With the exception of Germany, Kosovo enjoyed the most rapid economic recovery among the cases studied. Foreign assistance was also the highest as a share of GDP. The large per capita and absolute inflows of assistance to Kosovo, public and private, have been crucial to the rapid initial rates of recovery. The EU was largely responsible for economic reconstruction, and states and international organizations provided over $671 million during the last six months of 1999 and $704 million in 2000.

---

[28]Barbara Crossette, "UN Council Urged to Debate Political Future of Kosovo," *New York Times*, March 7, 2000, p. A6.

Chapter Eight

AFGHANISTAN

Whereas Yugoslavia was a strong state broken up by internal tensions, Afghanistan has been a weak state pulled apart by its neighbors. The 1979 Soviet invasion sparked a period of civil war and unrest that lasted over 20 years. After the Soviets withdrew, various factions occupied and then lost control of the capital, Kabul, until the rise of the Taliban in 1996. The Taliban gained control of the urban areas and most of the countryside and established an Islamic fundamentalist regime under Sharia law. Under this regime, women had no rights; there was no freedom of the press or religion; and the country was ruled by an autocracy. Afghanistan became a host for al Qaeda. Osama bin Laden and his terrorist network used their money and influence to support the Taliban regime; in return, they were permitted to train operatives and plan operations on Afghan soil.

Resistance to the Taliban rule came predominantly from the Northern Alliance, a coalition of Tajik, Uzbek, Hazara, and some Pashtun elements, supported by money, arms, and training from Iran, Russia, and India. By the latter half of 2001, the Northern Alliance controlled only a small area in the north and northeast of the country, which contained no major urban centers.

In response to the September 11, 2001, attacks on the World Trade Center and the Pentagon, the United States launched Operation Enduring Freedom (OEF), whose goal was to eliminate al Qaeda in Afghanistan. The operation began on October 7, 2001. With the assistance of U.S. money, airpower, and targeting from U.S. Special Operations Forces, the Northern Alliance was able to take Kabul in mid-November. The United States also instigated and supported smaller Pashtun risings in the south. Most Taliban resistance collapsed within a few weeks.

Expatriate and Northern Alliance Afghan leaders met in Bonn, Germany, in late November 2001 to establish an interim successor regime. On December 5, they signed the Bonn Agreement, which established a road map and timetable for achieving peace and security, reestablishing key institutions, and reconstructing the country. Hamid Karzai, a Pashtun leader then commanding the siege of Kandahar, was chosen as the chairman of an interim government. It was broadly based and generally representative, although Tajiks retained control of the three most important "power ministries": Defense, Interior, and Foreign Affairs.

On December 20, 2001, UNSCR 1386 created a framework for international assistance to postwar Afghanistan. The international community agreed to establish and construct a peacekeeping force, the International Security Assistance Force (ISAF), in the capital and to assist the interim Afghan government in its efforts to reestablish national structures and rebuild the economy.

CHALLENGES

Afghanistan was devastated after 23 years of conflict. The country had a long tradition of weak central government, tribalism, banditry, and ethnic tension. The triumph of the U.S.-assisted Northern Alliance had left the ethnic Pashtuns, the country's largest ethnic group and the principal base of support for the Taliban, feeling underrepresented in the successor regime.

Security

Security throughout Afghanistan was threatened from three sides: first, residual Taliban and al Qaeda elements; second, general banditry and lawlessness; and third, tensions among regional commanders operating, at least nominally, under the authority of the new interim government and fielding locally raised militias of 10,000 to 20,000 soldiers.

Humanitarian

The major humanitarian concerns as coalition forces entered Afghanistan in 2001 were the fate of refugees and IDPs, and the provision of food for the coming winter. Before the fall of the Taliban, millions of Afghans had fled to Pakistan and Iran. By late 2001, some 4.5 million Afghans lived as refugees in other countries. Most of these people went to Iran (2.4 million) or Pakistan (2.2 million), although some 30,000 were in other countries in the region, such as Tajikistan (16,000) and India (12,000). It was difficult to estimate with any accuracy the number of Afghans who were internally displaced, but the U.S. Committee for Refugees believed the figure to be about 1 million at the end of 2001.[1] There was serious concern about the food situation at the onset of winter. Many international assistance organizations believed that refugees returning home after years in Pakistan and elsewhere would be unable to find food or shelter.

Civil Administration

Few state institutions in Afghanistan were functioning at the end of 2002. Decades of civil war had decimated the civil service and government bureaucracy. The United States and the international community planned to support and buttress the new Afghan government, rather than rule the country as they had in Kosovo. This approach required significant resources to establish and strengthen a new Afghan government. In keeping with this focus, the international presence was small in Kabul and almost nonexistent elsewhere. Unfortunately, the international resources available to help build Afghan institutions for governance were also modest, at least compared to the amounts made available to Bosnia and Kosovo several years earlier.

Democratization

Although the Bonn Agreement had established democratization as a goal, the United States and the rest of the international community

---

[1]U.S. Committee for Refugees, *World Refugees Survey 2002*, Washington, D.C., 2002, p. 6. According to UNHCR, 52,927 Afghans filed asylum applications in Europe, North America, and Oceania during 2001.

focused on achieving a more-modest objective: the creation of a broadly based and representative regime whose base could be further broadened and whose legitimacy could be enhanced over time using traditional Afghan political processes, specifically the *loya jirga* (general assembly). The Bonn Agreement created a government that represented the various ethnic groups in Afghanistan and that was designed to help reduce intergroup tension. The Pashtuns were the largest ethnic group in the country, but many had supported the Taliban government and were therefore tainted in the eyes of others at Bonn. The Northern Alliance, on the other hand, was made up principally of ethnic Tajiks, Uzbeks, and Hazara. Northern Alliance forces arrived triumphantly in Kabul in late 2001. Relations between the various ethnic groups were expected to be delicate, and the continued viability and long-term prospects of the country depended in large measure on how these relationships were handled in the following months.

Reconstruction

Afghanistan's economy was ravaged by over 20 years of conflict. The country's infrastructure was crippled; roads were in severe disrepair; buildings had been destroyed or become run down through lack of maintenance; the availability of electricity and water was sporadic at best; and there were few employment opportunities for working-age individuals in the country. There was no stable national currency. Some of the regional commanders issued their own currencies. A multiyear drought, which began in 1999, resulted in widespread famine that had severely damaged Afghanistan's economy. The constant cycle of conflict over the past few decades had rendered the key economic institutions—a central bank, treasury, tax collection and customs, the statistical administration, the civil service, and the legal and judicial system—either weak or nonexistent.

THE U.S. AND INTERNATIONAL ROLES

From the outset, the United States and the international community attempted to keep a small international footprint in Afghanistan. Countries pledged significant financial assistance to Kabul at a Tokyo donor's conference in January 2002, but few donors had effective means in Kabul of delivering such assistance, and none, including the United States, had the capacity to deliver more than basic humanitarian aid to the larger country beyond the capital.

Military

A small international peacekeeping force of about 5,000 troops, initially under UK command, was established for the capital, Kabul. U.S. and coalition forces of about 8,000 troops continued to conduct counterterrorist operations against residual Taliban and al Qaeda elements throughout the country, mostly along the border with Pakistan. But they did not undertake any peacekeeping or stabilization responsibilities. The United States initially opposed establishing a countrywide international stabilization force for several reasons. There was some fear that Afghanistan's legendary xenophobia would manifest itself anew in resistance to any substantial foreign troop presence. The U.S. administration wanted to break with the pattern of ever-more-ambitious nation-building endeavors that its predecessor had set. Establishing even a modest countrywide peacekeeping presence would raise daunting logistical challenges. Because of the country's destroyed infrastructure, all troops, equipment, and sustaining supplies would initially have to be flown in. Few countries, other than the United States, had the airlift capacity to mount such an effort. Finally, the U.S. administration viewed Afghanistan as the opening campaign in a larger war against terrorism. U.S. policymakers did not want to tie down significant numbers of U.S. forces or logistical capabilities in Afghanistan.

Civil and Economic

On the civil side, as on the military, the United States and the international community decided to focus on building the capacity of the Afghan government and empowering it to expand control throughout the country. At Bonn, the Afghan parties had asked the UN to "monitor and assist in the implementation of all aspects" of the agreement.[2] To that end, UNSCR 1401, passed on March 28, 2002,

---

[2]UN, The Agreement on Provisional Arrangements in Afghanistan Pending the Re-Establishment of Permanent Government Institutions [the Bonn Agreement], December 2001, Annex II.

directed the UN Assistance Mission in Afghanistan (UNAMA) to integrate all UN activities in the country. UNAMA's limited mandate included promoting national reconciliation; fulfilling its responsibilities under the Bonn Agreement; and managing all UN humanitarian, relief, and reconstruction activities in Afghanistan in coordination with the interim authority. As part of the international effort, several countries volunteered to lead various aspects of the rebuilding of the Afghan government and infrastructure. Germany, for example, took responsibility for training the national police; Italy offered to assist with justice system reforms; and the United States volunteered to train a new national army and border force.

The Tokyo donor's conference on January 21–22, 2002, set the stage for the reconstruction effort. International representatives pledged more than $1.8 billion to rebuild Afghanistan in 2002 and a total of $4.5 billion over 5 years. Some donors made multiyear pledges, and a number of countries offered support in kind, without specifying a monetary value. A few specific pledges included:

- United States: $297 million in 2002

- Japan: $500 million over 30 months

- EU: $500 million in 2002

- Saudi Arabia: $220 million over three years

- World Bank: $500 million over 30 months.[3]

WHAT HAPPENED

With rare exceptions, U.S. and international military forces have been well received throughout the country. A national government has been established whose legitimacy, if not effective power, has been widely acknowledged throughout the country. A few battalions of the new Afghan National Army (ANA) have completed training. Reconstruction has begun, particularly in the capital. Despite these improvements, the situation in Afghanistan remains precarious. The

---

[3]Howard W. French, "A Nation Challenged: Donors," *New York Times*, January 22, 2002, p. A1; Ilene R. Prusher, "Rich Donors Try to Finesse Flow of $4.5 Billion into Afghanistan," *Christian Science Monitor*, January 23, 2002, p. 6.

national government controls only a small part of the country. Regional commanders and tribal chieftains retain authority throughout most areas outside Kabul and maintain militias that vastly outnumber the embryonic ANA. The lack of adequate security outside the capital has hindered the flow of international assistance and limited the resumption of normal economic activity.

Security

A number of armed forces operate within Afghanistan. To guarantee security within Kabul, a brigade of international peacekeeping forces, initially under British command, cooperates effectively with the Northern Alliance troops and police who took the city from the Taliban. Despite occasional incidents, including the murder of two cabinet ministers, the capital has generally been quiet, allowing the resumption of normal economic and political life. In other urban and rural areas, security, such as it is, is provided by militias and some few police under regional commanders, who for the most part pay nominal allegiance to the central government. Forces loyal to these commanders occasionally come into conflict with each other, although U.S. influence, exercised through its local military and civil representatives, has usually been sufficient to tamp down such outbreaks. Finally, the United States and its coalition allies have continued to operate, in cooperation with local forces, in actions centered around the border region with Pakistan, against residual Taliban and al Qaeda elements and, more recently, against extremist elements claiming allegiance to former mujahideen leader Gulbuddin Hekmatyar.

The International Security Force, numbering some 5,000 troops, has been well received by Afghans throughout the capital and has been highly effective at maintaining stability across the city. ISAF forces have conducted mounted and dismounted patrols, and their presence has had a significant psychological effect on the populace. As a result of these and other efforts, some Afghans trust ISAF more than their own police.[4] Approximately 8,000 U.S. and other coalition forces continue to conduct operations throughout the country. The

---

[4]Interviews with ISAF commander, deputy commander, and other staff officers, November 2002, Kabul, Afghanistan.

battles at Tora Bora in December 2001 and Operation Anaconda in March 2002, both of which occurred after the Taliban disintegrated, were major actions for OEF forces.

The principal way that U.S.-led coalition forces initially attempted to promote stability in the outlying regions of the country was through Special Forces and Civil Affairs teams stationed in major cities, such as Herat, Mazar-e Sharif, and Kandahar. The United States deployed these small elements (generally less than ten soldiers) to liaise with local leaders and gain influence through financial and humanitarian assistance. As discussed below, civil affairs units conducted small-scale reconstruction projects or other activities in these cities to build goodwill among the populace.

During spring 2002, the Afghan regime and various international groups pressed the United States and other governments to expand ISAF beyond Kabul. Critics argued that Afghanistan could not be reunified or rebuilt without the establishment of a secure environment throughout the country.[5] The ratio of peacekeeping forces to population in Afghanistan was significantly smaller than in any other operation examined in this study. While there were 18.6 peacekeepers per thousand people in Bosnia and 20 per thousand people in Kosovo, the 4,800 ISAF soldiers amount to 0.18 peacekeepers per thousand Afghanis—or one hundred times less. Even if OEF troops are counted in the total, the result is a troop-to-population density 50 times smaller. By spring 2002, the U.S. administration had moved away from its initial operation to any expansion of ISAF's area of responsibility, but it soon became clear that other nations were not ready to provide the necessary troops, particularly since the United States made clear that its forces were not going to participate in any peacekeeping or stabilization mission in Afghanistan.

As an alternative, the United States developed a concept for creating several 60- to 80-person provincial reconstruction teams (PRTs) in various regions of the country. These teams were to expand the "ISAF effect" to areas outside Kabul using U.S. and coalition military and

---

[5]For a good summary of the critique of the security situation in Afghanistan, see the Web site for the Future of Peace Operations Project at the Stimson Center. For a more recent critique, see CARE International in Afghanistan, "A New Year's Resolution to Keep: Secure a Lasting Peace in Afghanistan," policy brief, January 2003.

U.S. civilian officials. These PRTs contain a civil affairs section, a security section, and various USAID and DOS officials. They are intended to support the development of a more-secure environment in the provinces, facilitate cooperation between the Afghan interim authority, civilian organizations, and the military; and strengthen the Afghan government's influence through interaction with regional political, military, and community leaders. The first PRT deployed to southeastern Afghanistan in December 2002, a year after the fall of the Taliban and the installation of the Karzai regime. It is unclear, however, whether this strategy will be able to establish security throughout the country in the medium or long run.

The United States has also undertaken to lead the creation of a new ANA and to join with Germany in creating a national police force. Building the ANA has proved much more difficult than anticipated. The first several battalions that completed the 10-week instruction program, for example, graduated at half strength or less. There has been no sustained training program for the ANA battalions after graduation. This has resulted in further significant attrition in the first few battalions, as soldiers have drifted away from inactive garrison life. Although a sustainment program was eventually created, the goal of creating a 4,800-man "Kabul Corps" by the national elections scheduled for summer 2004 seems unrealistic. As of early 2003, roughly 1,500 minimally trained ANA soldiers were under arms.

The soldiers participating in training have generally been motivated and ethnically diverse. The officer corps, however, has largely comprised ethnic Tajiks from the northeastern Panjshir valley. Minister of Defense Fahim Khan, who also serves as the senior vice president of the Afghan government, has repeatedly pledged his commitment to the ANA. In practice, however, he has proved reluctant to divert money or equipment from the primarily Tajik forces who fought the Taliban under his command, currently garrisoned in Kabul and the surrounding region, and who remain loyal to him.

Within the U.S. government, the interagency process was not as detailed in its preparation for OEF as it was for prior operations in the Balkans and elsewhere. One reason for this lack of coordination was the short time between the attacks of September 11, 2001, and the start of OEF, on October 7, 2001. An additional factor was the fact that Presidential Decision Directive 56, the Clinton administration's planning document for complex contingency operations, had expired during the transition in administrations and was not renewed. The Bush administration eventually published a political-military plan, in March 2002, but this plan did not guide the planning or initial execution of postconflict activities in Afghanistan.

During the conflict, new coordination mechanisms were established between CENTCOM and coalition countries, as well as with domestic and international agencies. A "coalition village" of trailers was established in the CENTCOM headquarters parking lot in Tampa, Florida. While the focus of the coalition cell was on coordinating military support for OEF, the village also became a center for the coordination of humanitarian assistance. The UN and the U.S. NGO consortium, InterAction, for example, established a presence at CENTCOM and met regularly with CENTCOM and coalition staff. Although the UN and NGO presence ended at CENTCOM headquarters after the fall of the Taliban, the coalition village continued to play an important role in coordinating military and humanitarian activities in Afghanistan.

Such stability as Afghanistan has enjoyed over the past two years has derived significantly from a benign regional environment. In the aftermath of September 11, the United States persuaded Pakistan to abandon its support of the Taliban; provided decisive military might to the anti-Taliban coalition of the Northern Alliance, also supported by Iran, Russia, and India; and persuaded all of Afghanistan's neighbors to stop pulling it apart and support its consolidation under the Karzai regime.

Humanitarian

Nearly all the principal humanitarian assistance organizations were involved in Afghanistan before the global war on terrorism began. All the key UN agencies, including UNHCR, the UN Development Programme, and the Mine Action Service, had active programs in the country. Hundreds of NGOs were also present, some with sizable contingents. Afghanistan was the United States' top recipient of humanitarian aid even before September 11, receiving $174 million in fiscal year 2001.

As in Kosovo, the speed with which displaced Afghans and Afghan refugees returned home once the conflict ended took the international community by surprise. In addition to UNHCR, the International Office of Migration and the World Food Program played large roles in facilitating refugee and IDP returns. Almost 2 million Afghans returned during 2002, principally from Pakistan and Iran.[6] Financial aid, food, and other support needed to help the returnees fell short both in terms of requirements and international pledges, and the large influx exacerbated these shortfalls.[7]

Operationally, the UN faced a great challenge and had to prepare for massive shipments of humanitarian supplies to Afghanistan and the refugee areas on the border without knowing specific requirements, the security situation, or the status of infrastructure within Afghanistan. The UN Joint Logistics Center (UNJLC) was established to control the surge in activities required for large deliveries of food and other resources. The UNJLC included a large staff representing most UN agencies. It played an important coordinating role in the delivery of humanitarian aid to Afghanistan. By design, the UNJLC focused on logistical, not policy, issues. This limited the organization's broader influence. The creation of the UNJLC was the first full implementation of a concept that had been provisionally tested in Africa during the late 1990s outside that continent.[8]

Another area where states and international organizations played a critical role was in medical support. By summer 2002, a number of military resources that had been sent to the theater for military missions were also being used for humanitarian relief. Military doctors, for instance, were seeing more Afghan civilians for treatment than combatants of any type.[9] Some coalition members set up field hospitals to contribute to the humanitarian effort. At the one-year point in the conflict, for example, the Jordanian hospital in Mazar-e Sharif had treated over 105,900 civilians, the Spanish hospital in Bagram over 11,800, and the Korean hospital in Manes, Kyrgyzstan, over 2,000.[10]

---

[6]UNHCR, "Assisted Voluntary Repatriation Summary Report," January 31, 2003a.

[7]Carlotta Gall, "Food and Hope Are Scarce for Returning Afghans," *New York Times*, September 17, 2002.

[8]Interviews with UN and international officials, Kabul, Afghanistan, November 2002.

[9]Indira A. R. Lakshmanan, "Boredom Is Surgical Team's Ideal Battleground Scenario," *Boston Globe*, October 6, 2002, p. 16.

[10]Eric Schmitt, "In Afghanistan: What's Past and What's Still to Come," *New York Times*, October 13, 2002.

To coordinate military assistance to humanitarian activities in Afghanistan, the U.S. military established a civil-military operations task force.[11] This Kabul-based task force monitored four- to six-man coalition humanitarian liaison cells in key cities around Afghanistan. The cells were designed to provide immediate humanitarian assistance to the local populace and to provide a capability for ongoing coordination with international organizations and NGOs. These forces initially focused on reconstruction projects in Afghanistan. This was a departure from the traditional role of military civil affairs, which focuses on setting conditions for international organizations and NGOs to conduct humanitarian assistance. ISAF civil-military cooperation elements conducted similar activities to help build goodwill among the populace in Kabul. ISAF, unlike OEF forces, had a UN Security Council mandate for conducting peacekeeping and humanitarian activities, which facilitated its interaction with international and nongovernmental relief agencies.

The emphasis on such activities as rebuilding schools and digging wells led to a great deal of positive press for the U.S. military but also heightened the natural tensions between civilian organizations and the military.[12] Civil-military relations steadily improved from Somalia to Haiti and the Balkans, but operations in Afghanistan tended to renew old frictions.[13] Two aspects of this operation frustrated and sometimes alienated humanitarian organizations: the military focus on direct action, as opposed to facilitation, and the issue of military uniforms.

---

[11]U.S. Department of the Army, *Civil Affairs Operations*, Washington, D.C., Field Manual 41-10, January 11, 1993, and JCS, *Joint Doctrine for Civil-Military Operations*, Washington, D.C., Joint Publication 57, February 8, 2001. While Army and Joint doctrine has included the basic idea for some time, this was the first time such an organization was used in an actual operation. Initially, planners envisioned that the organization would be a wholesale clearinghouse for humanitarian shipments and would be based in Dushanbe, Tajikistan. This view was eventually discarded in favor of more direct facilitation and support of humanitarian activities.

[12]Susan Glasser, "Soldiers in Civilian Clothing," *Washington Post*, March 28, 2002.

[13]For excellent treatments of civil-military relations prior to Afghanistan, see Daniel Byman, Ian Lesser, Bruce Pirnie, Cheryl Benard, and Matthew Waxman, *Strengthening the Partnership: Improving Military Coordination with Relief Agencies and Allies in Humanitarian Operations*, Santa Monica, Calif.: RAND, MR-1185-AF, 2000; Pirnie (1998); and Chris Seiple, *The U.S. Military/NGO Relationship in Humanitarian Interventions*, Carlisle, Pa.: U.S. Army War College Peacekeeping Institute, 1996.

First, most of the civilian organizations preferred that the military concentrate on providing a secure environment and conducting such tasks as road and bridge repair, for which they had unique capabilities that the NGOs did not have. Many NGO officials understood the public relations need for the military to be seen rebuilding schools and other infrastructure. But these officials preferred that the military leave these tasks to the civilian organizations, which they believed were best suited for them.[14]

Second, civilian relief agencies vehemently objected to U.S. military personnel not wearing uniforms while conducting humanitarian tasks. During operations against the Taliban, some civil affairs teams wore civilian clothes because commanders were concerned that Taliban or al Qaeda forces would target uniformed teams that had little force protection. Civilian relief agency personnel in the field generally did not let this development affect their own activities. At higher levels, however, the uniform issue became a major sticking point for humanitarian organizations. They believed that such a posture set a precedent that threatened their impartiality and the security of their own representatives in the field.[15] The issue came to a head in April 2002, when the heads of 16 major U.S.-based relief groups wrote to U.S. National Security Advisor Condoleezza Rice to "express concern over U.S. military personnel conducting humanitarian activity wearing civilian clothes," arguing that it endangered aid workers.[16] On April 19, 2002, CENTCOM announced that it would modify the clothing prescribed for such personnel and would require uniforms.[17] This disagreement temporarily soured relations between the two groups, and although it has been resolved, the lingering effects remain unclear.

---

[14]Interviews in Washington, D.C.; Tampa, Florida; and Kabul, Afghanistan, September–November 2002.

[15]Interviews in Washington, D.C.; Tampa, Florida; and Kabul, Afghanistan, September–November 2002.

[16]InterAction, "Humanitarian Leaders Ask White House to Review Policy Allowing American Soldiers to Conduct Humanitarian Relief Programs in Civilian Clothes," news release, Washington, D.C., April 2, 2002.

[17]Peter Slevin, "U.S. Troops Working Relief to Modify Clothing," *Washington Post*, April 21, 2002.

Civil Administration

International coordination in Afghanistan was much more ad hoc and dependent on personal relationships. In Kabul, there was no overarching organization, such as Bosnia's OHR, or a robust and empowered UN presence, such as UNMIK in Kosovo. The U.S. embassy staff in Kabul was too small to accomplish its objectives. Constraints stemming from force protection concerns and the lack of space in the embassy compound further limited the embassy's ability to promote international coordination. Outside Kabul, cooperation hinged almost entirely on personal relationships. In some regions, international civilian relief organizations and military forces acted in close liaison with each other. In other regions, relations were tense, and there was little unity of effort.

As mentioned earlier, the international civilian presence in Afghanistan was deliberately modest. Individual states and international organizations launched initiatives, but there was no overarching framework for these efforts. UNAMA, for example, was initially small and had limited capacity. UNAMA has, however, grown in Kabul and elsewhere and has established pillars responsible for political affairs and relief, recovery, and reconstruction. The Secretary General's Special Representative, Lakdar Brahimi, has had advisers for human rights, gender, drugs, rule of law, police, and military and demobilization.[18] Still, UNAMA's role and authority in Afghanistan pale in comparison to those of UNMIK in Kosovo. The principal focus for the international civil effort during the first six months was organizing the *loya jirga*.

With the focus on building government capacity, individual states have volunteered to assist various Afghan authority institutions. Germany, for example, has taken responsibility for the training of the Afghan national police and has established an academy for retraining current police and training new recruits in accordance with international law-enforcement norms. Italy has begun to assist in the re-creation of the country's legal and justice system.[19] As part of its effort to assist the emerging ANA, the United States has begun devel-

---

[18]Information about UNAMA is available on its Web site.

[19]For a detailed discussion of Afghan judicial reform, see ICG, *Afghanistan: Judicial Reform and Transitional Justice*, January 28, 2003a.

oping a concept for the creation and training of an Afghan border security force. Although funding for this initiative has not yet materialized, the concept currently calls for establishing a 12,000-person force to guard Afghanistan's major border crossings.

Democratization

The Bonn Agreement established a framework for the political transition of Afghanistan. The agreement named an interim authority that would take office on December 22, 2001. This authority was to serve as the government until the convening of the emergency *loya jirga* six months thereafter. The *loya jirga* would

> decide on a Transitional Authority, including a broad-based transitional administration, to lead Afghanistan until such time as a fully representative government can be elected through free and fair elections.[20]

The *loya jirga* was set up to be both a process and an event. The process was designed to enable the broad and equitable participation of the Afghan people at every level of society through the convening of local and regional meetings during spring 2002 to choose representatives for the nationwide *loya jirga*. Over 1,500 participants were selected through such grassroots processes and participated in the *loya jirga* in June 2002.

Preparations for this *loya jirga* began as soon as the interim authority came into office. At the lowest local level, meetings of village elders decided on groups of electors. This was not a strictly democratic process but was broadly inclusive. The electors then met in late May and early June 2002 on a regional basis to choose district representatives for the *loya jirga*.[21] The emergency *loya jirga* convened in Kabul from June 10 to 16. A transitional administration was named, and Hamid Karzai was elected as its president. The disproportionate representation of former Northern Alliance leaders in the cabinet did abate somewhat, with the Tajiks retaining two of the "power ministries,"

---

[20]Bonn Agreement, paragraph I.4.

[21]For an in-depth discussion on the preparations for the *loya jirga*, see ICG, *The Loya Jirga: One Small Step Forward?* Washington, D.C., May 16, 2002b.

Defense and Foreign Affairs, but ceding Interior. Nevertheless, some Pashtun leaders remained skeptical about the central government and were reluctant to cooperate fully with Kabul.

An entire generation of civil servants was lost during the 1980s and 1990s and cannot be replaced quickly. It is also unclear how effectively the national government will be able to extend its authority to the regions over time. A constitutional *loya jirga* and national elections are tentatively planned for late 2003 and summer 2004, respectively. At this point it seems unlikely that either the security situation or the administrative capacity of the Afghan government will support a nationwide electoral process up to even minimal international standards.

Reconstruction

The rough estimate of Afghanistan's per capita GDP in 2002 was between U.S. $150 and $180, excluding illegal poppy cultivation and narcotics production. An estimated 60 to 80 percent of the population lives below the international poverty threshold of $1 a day. In 1996, Afghanistan ranked 169th out of 174 countries in the UN Human Development Index, and conditions deteriorated through 2001. The average life expectancy is a little above 40 years, and over 50 percent of children under the age of five are malnourished.[22] The country's infant mortality rate, life expectancy, and literacy rates are all among the lowest in the world.

The efforts at postconflict reconstruction have shown some signs of economic improvement. Inflation slowed markedly in the months after the intervention. According to the IMF, the Kabul consumer price index increased just 1 percent between March 22 and June 21, 2002. Indications of a recovery are strongest in certain sectors in Kabul, such as construction and services. The government's budgetary system is now being restored with assistance from the IMF and the U.S. Treasury, as part of efforts to establish the macroeconomic framework necessary for economic growth and to enable

---

[22]For details, see IMF, *Islamic State of Afghanistan: Report on Recent Economic Developments and Prospects, and the Role of the Fund in the Reconstruction Process,* Washington, D.C., Country Report No. 02/219, October 2002.

the country to receive and utilize foreign aid. On October 7, 2002, the Afghan government introduced a new currency, the afghani, a significant step toward facilitating and improving financial transactions. In addition, a basis for future economic growth is being created as schools are reopened. The numbers of students and teachers returning to school as a result of a donor-assisted back-to-school campaign have far exceeded expectations, with 3 million students enrolled and another 1.5 million looking for schooling opportunities.

Opium production and export have resumed in Afghanistan despite central government attempts to prohibit such activity. Drug smuggling is thus responsible, in some measure, for such economic growth as has occurred in a number of regions. In 2002, UK officials, backed by UK military units, implemented a program of enforced purchases and destruction of opium crops in certain high-production regions, with some limited success. The United States was unwilling to engage U.S. troops in similar efforts and has also been unwilling to allow newly trained ANA units to be used for counternarcotics missions. In 2003, the central government has chosen to rely on regional authorities to enforce an uncompensated crop destruction program. This is likely to have minimal effect in areas whose local commanders are complicit in drug operations or where Kabul's writ runs weakly.

U.S. military programs to reconstruct infrastructure in Afghanistan had received considerable coverage in the media by summer 2002.[23] U.S. Army civil-military operations of this type have principally concentrated on small-scale projects in areas the NGO community had difficulty accessing. "We go to many areas where the aid groups have never been," SGT Arthur C. Willis observed during a delivery of construction material to a remote village. What would have been an all-day drive from Kandahar took 50 minutes by Chinook helicopter. Willis added, "We get to go to places where they can't go, or won't go."[24] While such an approach can help avoid duplication of effort

[23]James Scott, "Rebuilding a Country, One Village at a Time," *Charleston* [S.C.] *Post and Courier*, July 14, 2002, p. 9.

[24]James Brooke, "U.S. Tasks In Afghan Desert: Hunt Taliban, Tote Plywood," *New York Times*, September 14, 2002, p. 1.

and mitigate civil-military competition over the delivery of assistance, helicopters can deliver only very limited aid, making aid that must be delivered this way largely symbolic.

Although there have been numerous achievements during the past year, aid for Afghan reconstruction has not been nearly as generous as for other recent operations. For example, per capita external assistance for the first two years of conflict was $1,390 in Bosnia and $814 in Kosovo but is only $52 in Afghanistan. Some countries and organizations are not even meeting the level of the pledges they made at the Tokyo donor's conference.[25]

LESSONS LEARNED

America's postconflict efforts have been effective in denying the use of Afghanistan as a launch pad for global terrorism at a relatively modest cost. But there has been little progress in the creation of democratic institutions, and the limited international military and economic assistance has not allowed the Afghan government to extend its authority throughout the country. It is too early to assess the results of postconflict operations in Afghanistan fully, but the following lessons suggest themselves:

- Low input of military and civilian resources yields low output in terms of security, democratic transformation, and economic development.

- The support of neighboring states can have an important influence on the consolidation of weak and divided states.

- In the absence of pervasive security, the prospects of widespread economic recovery or political development are very limited.

Some lessons from prior U.S.-led peace operations in the post–Cold War era have not been applied to Afghanistan. There is no unity of command on either the military or the civil side. U.S. assistance is focused heavily on a few high-visibility projects, such as the training of a new Afghan Army and the rebuilding of a road from Kabul to

---

[25]CARE International in Afghanistan, "Rebuilding Afghanistan: A Little Less Talk, a Lot More Action," policy brief, October 2002.

Kandahar. International peacekeepers have not been deployed beyond Kabul; international police have not been deployed at all; and the United States has declined to participate in such peacekeeping efforts as have taken place.

For a comparatively modest investment of troops and money, the United States succeeded in quickly installing a moderate and reasonably representative successor to the Taliban regime and in forestalling any resumption of large-scale civil conflict. This success has been greatly aided by the favorable regional environment that developed in the immediate aftermath of September 11, 2001. That November, the United States was able to add decisive weight to the military efforts of the Northern Alliance, which had hitherto relied on support from Iran, Russia, and India. At the same time, the United States was able to persuade the other principal regional protagonist, Pakistan, to remove its support from its Taliban clients. At the Bonn Conference, the positive actions of Iran, Russia, and India, along with the passive acquiescence of Pakistan, permitted the United States to broker a positive outcome. All these regional powers have since supported the Karzai regime and sought to dissuade regional leaders from overtly contesting his authority.

International assistance has spurred some growth, particularly in more-secure urban areas, such as Kabul. However, until entrepreneurs can travel freely and transport goods across the country without intimidation or theft, the economic growth of Kabul and other urban centers is unlikely to spread.

Government ministries have not been able to function effectively because of the lack of basic office equipment and funds to pay staff. To accelerate recovery, the government needs to be able to pay providers of government services, such as police, teachers, and medical personnel, regularly to ensure that the basic functions of government can proceed. Furthermore, Afghanistan's economy is already encountering barriers to growth because of the deficiencies of the country's infrastructure. The poor condition of all major highways greatly increases transportation costs. Most of the country is not linked to the electric power system. Where it exists, the system is in poor repair. Telecommunications is also rudimentary. Investment in these industries goes well beyond the current resources of the government or the domestic private sector. Unless donors step in, these deficiencies will quickly slow Afghanistan's economic recovery.

Chapter Nine

LESSONS LEARNED

This chapter compares the results of the operations in the seven cases—Germany, Japan, Somalia, Haiti, Bosnia, Kosovo, and Afghanistan—with the resources that the United States and the international community invested in them. We compare the cases in terms of five measures of inputs (military presence, police presence, total economic assistance, per capita economic assistance, and external assistance as a percentage of GDP) and four measures of outcomes (the numbers of postconflict combat deaths among U.S. forces, time until the first elections after the conflict, return of refugees and IDPs, and growth in per capita GDP). Because of the different sizes of the populations and economies of these countries, we have frequently used per capita, rather than aggregate figures. In many instances, we used time trends to help measure the speed at which and the extent to which nation-building efforts proceeded.

Most attempts to quantify inputs and outputs of complex processes suffer because available statistical measures are often poorly adapted to charting developments of consequence. This effort is no exception. The choice of metrics employed in this analysis was determined by the availability of data, as well as developments of interest.

MILITARY PRESENCE OVER TIME

Military force levels varied significantly across the cases. They ranged from 1.6 million U.S. forces in the European theater of operations at the end of World War II to the approximately 14,000 U.S. and international troops currently in Afghanistan. Gross numbers, however, are not always useful for making comparisons across the cases because the sizes and populations of the countries are so disparate. For purposes of comparison, we calculated the numbers of U.S. and, when the U.S. led a multilateral coalition, international soldiers per thousand inhabitants for each country. We used these numbers to compare force levels at specified times after the end of the conflict or after the U.S. operation began.

As Figures 9.1 and 9.2 illustrate, force levels varied widely across the seven operations. Large numbers of U.S. military forces were initially deployed to Germany, Bosnia, and Kosovo. Initial force levels in Japan, Somalia, Haiti, and Afghanistan were more modest—in some cases, much more so. In most cases, forces have stayed for very long periods. Forces were still in Bosnia five years after the conflict ended; U.S. forces remain in Germany and Japan today, more than 50 years after the end of World War II. In the cases of Haiti and Somalia, U.S. soldiers stayed for two years or less, and international forces left not long thereafter.

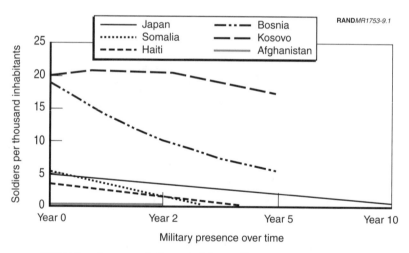

Figure 9.1—Military Presence over Time, Excluding Germany

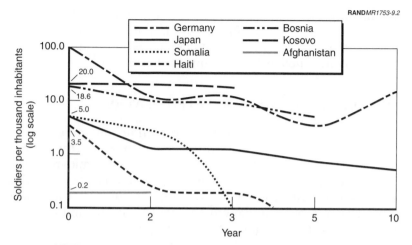

NOTE: In order to capture Germany in the same chart, we used a logarithmic scale because Germany started with a much higher troops-to-population ratio than all the other cases. The figures for Germany represent the level of U.S. troops at the end of the war as a proportion of the population in the U.S. sector.

Figure 9.2—Military Presence over Time, Including Germany

INTERNATIONAL POLICE PRESENCE OVER TIME

A more recent innovation has been dispatching U.S. and international police to supplement the efforts of military forces to provide security for local inhabitants. These initiatives have differed greatly in scope and scale. Some have principally consisted of training programs for local law enforcement officers; others have been major operations that have included deploying hundreds or thousands of armed international police to monitor, train, mentor, and even substitute for indigenous forces until the creation of a proficient domestic police force. Figure 9.3 shows numbers of foreign police per thousand inhabitants over time for the four cases that featured significant deployments of international police.

As Figure 9.3 demonstrates, it can take a year or more to build up and deploy a CIVPOL force once combat has ended. In Kosovo, for example, it took until the end of the second year of the operation to reach the target level for foreign police in the country. These delays can create a short-term vacuum of law and order and can increase the pressure on nation-building states to use their military forces, including military police, to maintain internal security.

POSTCONFLICT COMBAT-RELATED DEATHS

One of the most sensitive aspects of postconflict operations, especially after the 1993 U.S. retreat from Somalia, has been the issue of casualties. During the 1990s, the U.S. military, under guidance from its civilian leaders, placed tremendous emphasis on force protection to avoid U.S. casualties. As Figure 9.4 illustrates, casualty figures have not been high in postcombat environments. Somalia and Afghanistan top the chart with 43 and 30 deaths, respectively.

Afghanistan has the second-highest total for postconflict combat-related deaths, which reflects the nature of the operation. Although

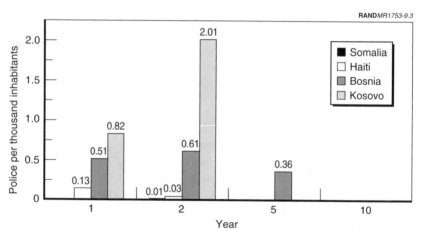

NOTE: Year 1 represents the end of the first year of military presence.

Figure 9.3—International Police Presence over Time

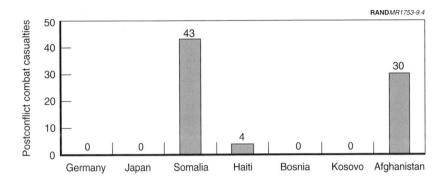

Figure 9.4—Total Postconflict Combat-Related Deaths

the fighting against the Taliban government ended in December 2001, combat operations against al Qaeda and Taliban remnants continue in what amounts to a low-level counterinsurgency campaign.

The highest levels of casualties have occurred in the operations with the lowest levels of U.S. troops, suggesting an inverse ratio between force levels and the level of risk. Germany, Japan, Bosnia, and Kosovo had no postconflict combat deaths. The postconflict occupations in Germany and Japan proved relatively risk-free because both Japan and Germany were thoroughly defeated and because their governments had agreed to unconditional surrender. The low numbers of combat deaths also show that postconflict nation-building, when undertaken with adequate numbers of troops, has triggered little violent resistance. Only when the number of stabilization troops has been low in comparison to the population have U.S. forces suffered or inflicted significant casualties.

TIMING OF ELECTIONS

Democratization is the core objective of nation-building operations. Central to this process has been the planning and conduct of democratic elections. The timing of these elections varied by case, as Figure 9.5 illustrates.

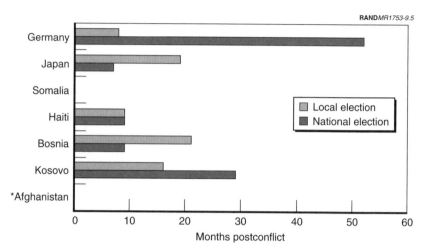

*In Afghanistan, the quasi-democratic *loya jirga* was held in June 2002, six months after the war. National elections are scheduled for June 2004, 30 months after the conflict.

Figure 9.5—Timing of Elections

In Somalia, the situation never stabilized long enough for elections to occur. In Germany and Kosovo, local elections preceded national polls by at least 18 months. National elections in Germany had to wait until a new country, the Federal Republic of Germany, was created from the Western occupation zones. As a consequence, national elections were not held until 52 months after the fall of Hitler, excluding the Soviet zone. In Japan, Haiti, and Bosnia, local elections were held at the same time or well after national elections.

The case studies suggest the desirability of holding local elections first. This provides an opportunity for new local leaders to emerge and gain experience and for political parties to build a support base. The extended preparatory periods in Kosovo and Germany appear to have facilitated the building of political parties and the establishment of other aspects of civil society, such as a free press. In contrast, the early national elections in Bosnia were probably counterproductive because they legitimated the nationalist governments responsible for the civil war in the first place. Early elections, driven by a desire to fulfill departure deadlines and exit strategies, can entrench spoilers and impede the process of democratization.

REFUGEES AND INTERNALLY DISPLACED PERSONS

All these conflicts caused citizens to flee, either abroad as refugees or to other areas of the country as IDPs. The number of refugees and IDPs a conflict generates is an important indicator of the degree of domestic instability. In almost all the cases, large numbers of people fled their homes. The exodus of people also had important political effects, especially if the destinations were countries that had the ability to intervene to reduce these flows. In Haiti, Bosnia, and Kosovo, refugee flows to the United States and EU, respectively, were a significant factor in the decisions to intervene to stop the fighting. The U.S. and European governments recognized that, until secure conditions were created in these areas, people would continue to flee, and refugees would not return.

Figure 9.6 shows the number of people who fled their homes during each conflict. For purposes of comparison, we calculated the number

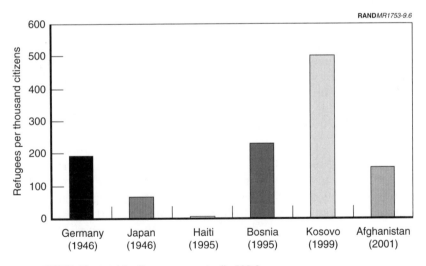

NOTE: The total for Kosovo was actually 500.9.

Figure 9.6—Refugees and Internally Displaced Persons

of refugees and IDPs per thousand population, rather than the total numbers of refugees and IDPs.

The wide range in the number of IDPs and refugees is noteworthy. Although Haiti had the smallest number of refugees per thousand inhabitants (1.9), the flow of refugees from Haiti seeking asylum in the United States was a major factor in the U.S. government's decision to intervene. At the other extreme, the Bosnian civil war led to the displacement of over a million people, 229 people per thousand, roughly one-quarter of the population. Similarly, millions of ethnic Germans fled their homes in regions outside Germany or that had been annexed from Germany at the end of World War II, creating an enormous problem of refugees in the immediate postwar years. Despite the number of refugees and IDPs in Germany following World War II, the most striking displacement occurred in Kosovo, where virtually half of the province's population fled their homes during spring 1999. By late May, 863,000 Albanian Kosovar had fled Kosovo and approximately another 250,000 were internally displaced.[1]

INITIAL EXTERNAL ASSISTANCE

In all the cases studied, substantial amounts of assistance in the form of grants of money, goods and services, or concessionaire loans were given to help revive the local economies. Assistance has been provided by private individuals, often emigrants from these countries, and from governments and international organizations, such as the IMF, UN, and EU. Figure 9.7 illustrates the total assistance in constant 2001 U.S. dollars provided to each of the countries in the two years immediately after the end of its conflict.

The amount of external aid varied widely between countries and postconflict situations. Germany, Japan, and Bosnia received the highest amounts of assistance in absolute terms during the first two postconflict years, at $11.6 billion, $4.1 billion, and $4.5 billion, respectively. In contrast, Haiti, Kosovo, and Afghanistan all received less than $2 billion.

---

[1]OSCE (1999).

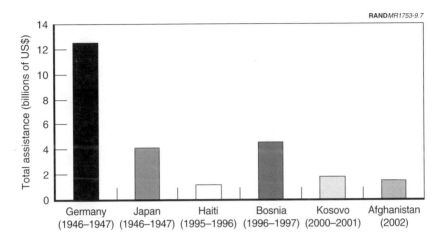

Figure 9.7—Total Assistance During First Two Postconflict Years

EXTERNAL PER CAPITA ASSISTANCE

Aggregate numbers are not always the most useful metric when comparing countries with very different populations. Consequently, Figure 9.8 provides data on assistance in constant 2001 dollars on a per capita basis.

On this basis, Germany, which was granted the most assistance in aggregate terms ($12 billion) after the first two years of conflict, does not rank as highly: Per capita assistance ran a little over $200. Kosovo, which ranked fourth in terms of total assistance, received over $800 per resident. Levels of per capita assistance have had some bearing on the speed of economic recovery. Kosovo, with the second-highest level of assistance on a per capita basis, enjoyed the fastest recovery in levels of per capita GDP following the conflict. In contrast, Haiti, which received much less per capita than Kosovo, has experienced little growth in per capita GDP since the end of the conflict.

EXTERNAL ASSISTANCE AS A PERCENTAGE OF GDP

Another useful measure is assistance as a percentage of GDP (Figure 9.9). Although the numbers vary, external assistance in relation to

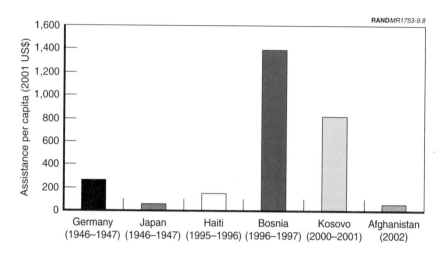

Figure 9.8—Per Capita Assistance in First Two Postconflict Years

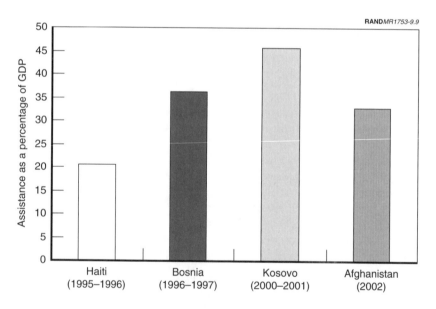

Figure 9.9—External Assistance as a Percentage of GDP

GDP has been substantial in many of the post–Cold War cases, running between 20 and 45 percent of the country's GDP in the first two years after the conflict. These levels of assistance were generally the outcome of donor conferences, during which international financial institutions presented assessments of need to potential donors. The levels illustrate both the depressed levels of economic activity after conflicts and the substantial sums that, according to experienced outside observers, could be profitably used to speed reconstruction and recovery.

CHANGES IN PER CAPITA GDP

One of the most important indicators of a country's economic revival after a conflict is the recovery of incomes as reflected in per capita GDP. Figure 9.10 tracks changes in per capita GDP in each country in the years following the conflict. The figure shows postconflict per capita GDP as a percentage of per capita GDP in the year immediately prior to the conflict.

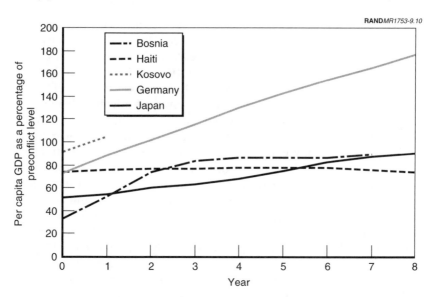

NOTE: Year 0 is the first year after the conflict.

Figure 9.10—Postconflict Per Capita GDP Growth

Although per capita GDP for all the countries increased during the immediate postconflict years, it did so to varying degrees. Haiti's per capita GDP recovered very slowly and then remained stable at about 75 percent of what it was prior to the conflict. On the other hand, Germany's per capita GDP jumped from 75 in 1946 to 175 in 1953. Although estimates of per capita GDP in the immediate aftermath of the conflict are prone to large margins of error, Bosnia appears to have experienced the sharpest drop in income over the course of the conflict. In 1995, per capita GDP was estimated at just one-third of preconflict levels. However, postconflict recovery was swift, primarily due to the large amounts of external assistance Bosnia received. By 2002, per capita GDP had reached close to 90 percent of prewar levels. In Japan, per capita GDP was half its 1939 level in 1945, but by 1952, incomes had risen to 80 percent of their levels in 1939. However, in contrast to Germany, Japan's initial economic recovery was slow.

CONDITIONS FOR SUCCESS

The German and Japanese occupations set standards for postconflict transformation that have not been equaled. One of the most important questions this study addressed is why these two operations succeeded so well, while those that have come after have fallen short to one degree or another. The easiest answer is that Germany and Japan were already highly developed and economically advanced societies. It is easier to reconstruct economies that have been modern than to foster rapid economic growth in economies that have never been developed. This may explain why it was easier to reconstruct the German and Japanese economies than it was to fundamentally reform the underdeveloped economies in the other five case studies. Note also that past difficulties fade with the passage of time. George Marshall was seriously concerned about the potential economic collapse of Germany in winter 1947, a concern that led to the passage of the Marshall Plan in 1948, three years after the end of the war. Japan had one of the slowest rates of recovery among the case studies. Per capita incomes in Bosnia have recovered much more rapidly; those in Kosovo exceeded preconflict levels within 24 months of the end of the conflict. In Japan, this did not happen until 1956, over a decade after the end of the war.

However, the successes of Germany and Japan are not primarily a matter of economics. Nation-building, as we have defined it, and, more importantly, as those responsible for the operations defined their objectives at the time, was not primarily about rebuilding a country's economy but about transforming its political institutions. The spread of democracy in Latin America, Asia, and parts of Africa suggests that this form of government is not unique to Western culture or of advanced industrial economies. Democracy can, indeed, take root when neither is present. No postconflict program of "reconstruction" could turn Somalia, Haiti, or Afghanistan into thriving centers of prosperity. But the failure of U.S.-led interventions to encourage democratic transitions in these countries has other than purely economic explanations.

Homogeneity is another possible variable to explain the differences in nation-building outcomes. Somalia, Haiti, and Afghanistan were divided ethnically, socioeconomically, or tribally in ways that Germany and Japan were not. But again, homogeneity is not a necessary condition. The kind of communal hatreds that mark Somalia, Haiti, and Afghanistan were even more marked in Bosnia and Kosovo, where, nevertheless, the process of democratization has made some progress. What distinguishes Germany, Japan, Bosnia, and Kosovo, on the one hand, from Somalia, Haiti, and Afghanistan, on the other, are not their levels of economic development, Western culture, or national homogeneity. Rather, what distinguishes these two groups is the levels of effort the international community has put into their democratic transformations. Successful nation-building, as this study illustrates, needs time and resources. The United States and its allies have put 25 times more money and 50 times more troops per capita into postconflict Kosovo than into postconflict Afghanistan. This higher level of input accounts, at least in part, for the higher level of output in terms of democratic institutions and economic growth.

Japan, one of the two undoubted successes, fully meets these criteria, at least in terms of the amount of time spent on its transformation. On the other hand, Japan received considerably less external economic assistance per capita than did Germany, Bosnia, or Kosovo. Indeed, it received less than Haiti and about the same as Afghanistan. Japan's postconflict economic growth rate was correspondingly low. U.S. spending on the Korean War, however, spurred

Japan's economic growth during the 1950s, which subsequently helped consolidate public support for the democratic reforms that had been instituted soon after the war. As with the German economic miracle of the 1950s, this experience suggests that rising economic prosperity is not so much a necessary precursor for political reform as a highly desirable follow-up and legitimizer.

The stabilization (or, as it was then termed, occupation) force in Japan was also smaller, in proportion to population, than those in Germany, Bosnia, or Kosovo, although it was larger than those in Haiti and Afghanistan. The willing collaboration of the existing power structures and the homogeneity of the population undoubtedly enhanced the ability to secure Japan with a comparatively small force. But the very scale of Japan's defeat was also important: years of total war had wrought devastation, including the firebombing of Japanese cities and, finally, two nuclear attacks. The result was a population tired of war and effectively beaten into submission. When conflicts have ended less conclusively and destructively (or not terminated at all)—as in Somalia; Afghanistan; and, most recently, Iraq—the postconflict security challenges have proven more difficult. It seems that the more swift and bloodless the military victory, the more difficult postconflict stabilization can be.

The pace of economic growth and political transformation in the German and Japanese cases suggests that the basics of democratization were put in place during a period of economic deprivation. The Marshall Plan did not begin until 1948, and per capita incomes in Japan did not exceed pre–World War II levels until after the economic boost from U.S. purchases of material for the Korean War. But in both cases, the basic political reforms were in place by 1947. Economic growth and the recovery in per capita incomes helped legitimize and consolidate democracy but were not necessary precursors.

Burden-Sharing Versus Unity of Command

When it was shouldering the burden of Japan's transformation and most of that for West Germany, the United States generated some 50 percent of the world's GDP. By the 1990s, when the number of nation-building cases increased, the United States accounted for about 22 percent of world GDP, although in absolute terms U.S. output was far higher than in the immediate post–World War II era. The decline in the U.S. share of global GDP and the concomitant rise in output and incomes elsewhere have made international burden-sharing both politically more important and more affordable for other countries.

Throughout the 1990s, the United States wrestled with the problem of how to achieve wider participation in its nation-building endeavors while also preserving adequate unity of command. In Somalia and Haiti, the United States experimented with sequential arrangements in which it organized, led, and largely manned and funded the initial phase of the operation but then quickly turned responsibility over to a more broadly representative UN force. These efforts were not successful, although Haiti was better organized than Somalia. In Bosnia, the United States succeeded in achieving unity of command and broad participation on the military side of the operation through NATO but made less progress toward that goal on the civil side.

In Kosovo, the United States achieved unity of command and broad participation on both the military and civil sides through NATO and the UN, respectively. While the military and civil aspects of that operation remained under different management, the United States ensured that the mandates and capabilities of the two entities—KFOR and UNMIK—would overlap and prevent a gap from opening between them.

None of these models was entirely satisfactory. Arrangements in Kosovo, however, seem to have provided the best amalgam of U.S. leadership, European participation, broad financial burden-sharing, and strong unity of command. Every international official in Kosovo works ultimately for one of two people, the NATO commander or the Special Representative of the Secretary General. Neither of these individuals is an American. But by virtue of its credibility in the region and its influence in NATO and the UN Security Council, the United States has been able to maintain a satisfactory leadership role while paying only 16 percent of the reconstruction costs and fielding only 16 percent of the peacekeeping troops.

The efficacy of the Kosovo and Bosnian models for managing a large-scale nation-building operation depends heavily on the ability of the United States and its principal allies to attain a common vision of nation-building objectives and to shape the response of the relevant institutions, such as NATO, the EU, and the UN, to those common objectives. When the principal participants in a nation-building exercise have a common vision, the Balkans models offer a viable amalgam of burden-sharing and unity of command.

More recently, in Afghanistan the United States opted for two separate military command structures and even greater variety on the civil side. An international force with no U.S. participation operates in Kabul, while a coalition and, mostly U.S., force operates everywhere else. The UN is responsible for promoting political transformation, while individual donors coordinate economic reconstruction—or, more often, fail to do so. This arrangement is a marginal improvement on Somalia, since the separate U.S. and international forces are at least not operating in the same physical space. But Afghanistan represents a clear regression from what was achieved in Haiti, Bosnia, and Kosovo. The overall Afghan nation-building operation is certainly more successful than that in Somalia, but not yet better than that in Haiti, and less advanced than the efforts in Bosnia or Kosovo at a similar stage. It is also considerably cheaper.

Duration

The seven cases also differed in duration. Haiti began with clear departure deadlines that were adhered to. Germany, Japan, Somalia, and Bosnia began with very short time lines but saw those amended. Kosovo and Afghanistan began without any expectation of an early exit. The record suggests that, while staying long does not guarantee success, leaving early ensures failure.

And if democratization takes hold, does that provide the ultimate exit strategy? Not necessarily. U.S. forces left clear failures behind in Somalia and Haiti, but remain present in every successful or still-pending case: Germany, Japan, Bosnia, Kosovo, and Afghanistan. These five interventions were motivated by regional or global geopolitical concerns. Democratization alone does not fully address such concerns. Germany and Japan were disarmed. They received American military support and financial assistance long after they became self-sufficient democracies because they were not capable of defending themselves unaided against the Soviet Union. This was because of their initially enforced and then voluntary disarmament, particularly their renunciation of nuclear weapons. Bosnia, Kosovo, and

Afghanistan may require assistance in maintaining their external security even after their internal peace is established. Whether this help will take the form of an external military presence, security guarantees, or leadership in forging new regional security arrangements remains to be seen. But international involvement in their external security is likely to continue long after the democratic transformation is completed.

Indeed, if Germany and Japan are any guide, the more thorough the democratic transformation the more deeply forged the residual links may be. The record suggests that building a nation creates ties of both affection and dependency that persist long after the end of the initial conflict.

Conclusions

With these considerations in mind, there are, in addition to the case-specific lessons noted at the end of each preceding chapter, some broader conclusions to bear in mind:

- Several factors influence the ease or difficulty of nation-building: prior democratic experience, level of economic development, and national homogeneity. However, among controllable factors, the most important determinant is the level of effort—measured in time, manpower, and money.

- Multilateral nation-building is more complex and time consuming than unilateral efforts but is also considerably less expensive for each participating country.

- Multilateral nation-building can produce more thoroughgoing transformations and greater regional reconciliation than can unilateral efforts.

- Unity of command and broad participation are compatible if the major participants share a common vision and can shape international institutions accordingly.

- There appears to be an inverse correlation between the size of the stabilization force and the level of risk. The higher the proportion of stabilizing troops, the lower the number of casualties suffered and inflicted. Indeed, most adequately manned post-conflict operations suffered no casualties.

- Neighboring states can exert significant influence. It is exceptionally difficult to put together a fragmented nation if its neighbors are trying to tear it apart. Every effort should be made to secure their support.

- Accountability for past injustices can be a powerful component of democratization. It can also be among the most difficult and controversial aspects of any nation-building endeavor and should, therefore, be attempted only if there is a deep and long-term commitment to the overall operation.

- There is no quick route to nation-building. Five years seems the minimum required to enforce an enduring transition to democracy.

Chapter Ten

IRAQ

In March 2003, a U.S.-led force invaded Iraq with the explicit aim of toppling the regime of Saddam Hussein. The rationale for the operation was that regime change provided the only sure means of disarming Iraq of its weapons of mass destruction (WMD). At the same time, the U.S. administration argued that the construction of a stable and democratic Iraq would promote reform and, hence, security in the wider Middle East. Having failed to secure support from the French, Chinese, and Russian governments, all veto-wielding members of the UN Security Council, for a second UNSCR explicitly authorizing the use of "all necessary means," the U.S. and British governments claimed authority for the operation under UNSCR 1441, the latest in a long line of resolutions calling for Iraqi disarmament.

A number of U.S. allies provided diplomatic support for the operation, notably the United Kingdom, Spain, Japan, and Australia. U.S. allies in the region, including Jordan and Saudi Arabia, expressed their behind-the-scenes support once they were convinced of the U.S. government's determination to "finish the job" but remained cautious in their public statements. Key U.S. allies, such as Turkey, France, and Germany, opposed the operation. After a long process of bargaining and internal political strife, Turkey eventually permitted U.S. overflights, as did France and Germany, and the resupply of U.S. ground forces in northern Iraq. But Turkey did not permit U.S. or British ground troops to use its territory to invade Iraq.

The deadlock at the UN and opposition from key allies reinforced the U.S. administration's desire to retain control of both military operations and postconflict planning. Therefore, even as combat ended, it was unclear to the international community whether the United

States saw a major role for the UN or for any but a limited number of U.S. allies in postwar reconstruction or political transformation.

As of this writing, the final shape of a postconflict settlement is still evolving. Nonetheless, the general outlines of the postwar situation are clear. U.S. forces are stationed in Iraq, undertaking both pacification and constabulary duties. Military assistance will be provided by an initially limited number of allies in a "coalition of the willing,"[1] operating under a U.S. military command. The Coalition Provisional Authority (CPA) has transitional responsibility for immediate reconstruction, reconstitution of the civil administration, and establishing an Iraqi transitional authority. The UN will have a role in advising on political transformation, but UN efforts will focus largely on providing humanitarian services and technical assistance through UN agencies.

CHALLENGES

Not since the occupation of Germany and Japan has the United States undertaken such an ambitious task: the military occupation of a sizable country and a stated commitment to wholesale political transformation. Bosnia and Kosovo are the most comparable in terms of ambition, but both are smaller entities and are in more-conducive strategic environments, and the interventions enjoyed more international support. As in Bosnia and Kosovo, there is no consensus on the nature of the Iraqi nation; Iraq has a deeply fractured polity, with entrenched sectarian and ethnic divides. Unlike the Balkans, Iraq is in an unstable and undemocratic region and is surrounded by neighbors who will be unsympathetic to democratization. Hence, Iraq combines many of the most troublesome features of the other cases analyzed in this report.

The challenges that the United States faces in Iraq can be grouped into those that are specific to Iraq, those that are common to societies emerging from totalitarian rule, and those that result from the postwar international environment.

---

[1]The United Kingdom and Poland have agreed to administer two of the zones into which the United States has divided Iraq for administrative purposes.

Some of Iraq's troubles mirror those in the Balkans, such as unresolved questions over national as opposed to communitarian identities. In Iraq's case, the political structures the British created after World War I did nothing to resolve these questions. Instead, Iraq was left with no tradition of pluralist democracy. Instead, politics have always been about authoritarian rule and the settlement of disputes by force. Although a sense of Iraqi national identity does exist, this does not override communal forms of identity along ethnic, geographic, tribal, or religious boundaries. The majority of the population, the Kurds and Shiites, have no real tradition of representation as communities in national Iraqi politics; they will now have to be brought into the polity. More generally, the vibrant Iraqi middle class that emerged in the middle of the 20th century and that provided the basis for a civil society has been hollowed out by over a decade of sanctions and two decades of turmoil under Saddam Hussein's dictatorship. In addition to these long-standing political problems, organized crime and banditry are now deeply rooted.

In addition to these particular Iraqi problems, the country faces the familiar challenges of a society emerging from a long period of totalitarian rule. The military, security services, and bureaucracy need to be radically reformed and purged. Justice needs to be achieved for victims of human rights abuses. The economy needs a major overhaul to make it competitive in global markets.

Any attempt to achieve transformation in Iraq would have had to face these challenges. Because of the diplomatic circumstances of the conflict, the United States has to cope with unsympathetic neighbors—Iran, Syria, and Turkey. All have an interest in shaping Iraqi politics and perhaps in destabilizing a smooth transition. The United States also needs to make sure that events in the wider region, such as in the Israeli-Palestinian conflict, do not undermine its credibility and position in Iraq. At the international level, the prewar splits in the UN Security Council make it much harder for the United States to adopt the burden-sharing models in Bosnia, Haiti, Kosovo, and Afghanistan. At the same time, the United States was unable to undertake prewar preparations that would have eased postwar transition, such as coordinating humanitarian relief with the UN and NGOs, organizing international civil police forces, and establishing an international political authority to rebut Arab suspicions of U.S. imperialism.

Nonetheless, Iraq does have some advantages for nation-builders. First, it has a nationwide civil administration that is relatively efficient. This administration needs to be rebuilt but not reconstructed from scratch. This administration, staffed mainly by Iraqis, will reduce the need for direct international intervention and will facilitate security and development across the country. Second, the civil administration and the extensive links with UN agencies mean that the humanitarian issues should be soluble. Third, Iraq's oil means that the country will not remain dependent on international aid in the medium term.

Meeting the Challenges

The postwar challenges—security, humanitarian assistance, creating a civil administration, political transition, and economic reform—can be considered in the short, medium, and long terms. In the short term, U.S. military preponderance is likely to ensure security from large-scale violence, but rapid action will be needed to reestablish law and order and to replace discredited Iraqi policing, internal security, and judicial structures. There will be a need to deal decisively with retributive violence and political power struggles that become violent. A functioning civil administration can rapidly be reconstituted based on the current administrative setup, once it is given an injection of external financial and technical aid. The United States, the UN, and NGOs will have to devote considerable effort to humanitarian assistance. Immediate economic efforts will focus on resuscitating the oil industry to generate export revenues.

In the medium term, all these issues, aside from the humanitarian one, become more challenging. Wide-scale conflict is unlikely if the United States manages to engineer a political agreement that meets the demands of the major armed groups in Iraq and forestalls overt Iranian or Turkish military intervention. However, there will be an ongoing struggle for influence within Iraq that will engage Iraq's neighbors, either overtly or covertly. Given the lack of experience in the country with resolving political differences peacefully and the proliferation of weapons and armed groups, it is likely that the protagonists in this struggle will use violence. Against this backdrop, it will be a priority to reform Iraq's police, military, and security services to allow U.S. and allied forces to stand back from constabulary and internal security duties.

Building a stable and lasting civil administration in the medium term will require a substantial overhaul of personnel systems, including purging senior Baathists and a careful integration of expatriate returnees. The long-term evolution of these administrative structures into real centers of power, free of the "shadow state," will be more difficult.[2] The United States will have to neutralize the informal networks of power that underlie and subvert the formal bureaucratic structures. Substantial reform of key sectors, such as education and health care, will also be vital.

Building the political superstructure will be a medium- to long-term challenge, since the development of the Iraqi nation has been stunted and since it is very difficult to foresee the nature of political dynamics in post-Saddam Iraq. A pluralist electoral process, perhaps starting from the bottom up, may be feasible, but there will be difficult balances to be struck between democratic legitimacy and accommodating current centers of power. It will be important to balance communitarian politics and identity with a commonly acknowledged national identity. Determining the polity's constitutional end-state will be vital but fraught with difficulties.

The Iraqi economy has potential for high economic growth, if its human capital can be harnessed, its oil sector modernized, and conditions created for sustained growth. This will require not only substantial investment but also deep structural reform of the legal and financial systems.

Security

Politics in Iraq have historically been bloody. One type of violence has been that between the regime and organized groups that resist authority. Another has been violence to effect regime change, with which Iraq has a long history. Iraq's coups and revolutions since the 1950s have been significantly bloodier than those of its Arab neighbors.[3]

---

[2]Charles Tripp, "After Saddam," *Survival*, Vol. 44, No. 4, Winter 2002–2003, pp. 23–37.

[3]As Charles Tripp has noted, "the use of violence in political life has ... been an important part of Iraqi history" (*A History of Iraq*, 2nd ed., Cambridge, UK: Cambridge University Press, 2001, p. 7).

Compared to other cases, such as Kosovo, Somalia, and Afghanistan, Iraq benefits from having a strong state capable of imposing order on society. Aside from the Kurdish autonomous zone, the central government controlled a nationwide internal security, policing, and judicial apparatus, backed up by strong military forces. In the medium term, there is no reason that this apparatus cannot be used to ensure a secure environment for the Iraqi populace and for the new regime. In the short term, however, the United States faces significant challenges in establishing a secure environment. These can be grouped into four categories: expressive violence, instrumental violence, force and regime protection, and law and disorder.

In dealing with these threats, the United States will have to take prompt action to restructure Iraq's military and security forces so that these can be deployed for national defense, internal security, and constabulary duties. However, removing senior Baathists and serious human rights violators from the officer corps of the Republican Guard and armed forces, security services, and police forces and demobilization of personnel will have to be systematic and politically sensitive.

Expressive Violence. The term "expressive violence" indicates that the perpetrators are unlikely to have realistic political objectives, and yet their violence goes beyond simple criminality. The United States is likely to face two types of expressive violence: regime holdouts and score-settling.

First are the regime holdouts. Despite the rapid and comprehensive military defeat of the regime's special military forces, there will be some capacity for regime loyalists to go underground and wage armed resistance against the occupation forces.[4] A long tradition of conspiratorial politics involving the military, widespread ownership of small arms, and a political-tribal culture of settling scores by violence means that episodic, guerrilla-style violence by those groups and individuals disenfranchised by the new status quo are likely. The regime's encouragement of suicide attacks in its dying days provided evidence of a planning for underground guerrilla-style operations.

---

[4]Perry Biddiscombe, *The Last Nazis*, Stroud, UK: Tempus Publishing, 2000

Second, score-settling is taking place and is likely to continue for some time. On previous occasions when the former regime lost control of the streets, such as during the 1991 *intifada* in the south or the Kurdish campaign in the north, large numbers of individuals associated with the regime or with the security forces were killed. Senior members of the Saddam regime are likely to be particularly in danger of retribution. Prominent families and tribes who have lost relatives will exact revenge on officials of the former regime and the *Ahl al-Thiqa* (people of trust), when they can be found.[5]

More generally, score-settling may involve two much broader groups. First, Iraqis are likely to take revenge on the legion of petty Baathist officials, secret policemen, and informers recruited by the security services throughout Iraqi society. The secret police informer network is reputed to have been as pervasive as the Ministerium für Staatssicherheit network in the former German Democratic Republic. Revenge killings began to take place soon after U.S. and British forces occupied the first towns. Second, many Iraqi citizens are likely to settle scores with the wider group of individuals who have benefited from the regime. For instance, the regime expelled thousands of Shiites to Iran in the early 1980s; their property and livelihoods were taken over by poor Iraqis, often of rural origin. In the north, the regime displaced thousands of Kurds in favor of Arab settlers. Kurdish property owners have already begun to reclaim their properties. If not properly regulated, such disputes are likely to turn violent.[6]

Instrumental Violence. It will not be surprising if organized substate groups or neighboring states actively promote their political, territorial, or strategic interests in part through violence. Such actors as the Turkish armed forces or, more likely in the face of the overwhelming U.S. military presence, any of the myriad proxy groups in the region might undertake such violence. Two categories of actors may use such "instrumental" violence because it has a political purpose: Iraqi substate groups and foreign states. In addition to the organized use of political violence for instrumental ends, violence between religious and ethnic groups (e.g., between Sunni and Shiite, between

---

[5]These comprise the "families, clans, long-standing associates and opportunists who have attached themselves to the regime" (Tripp, 2002–2003).

[6]Gareth Smyth, "US Will Oversee Return of Displaced Kurds," *Financial Times*, April 24, 2003.

rival Shiite groups, between Muslims and Christians or Assyrians) could well break out. At a low level, this can be treated as "simple" disorder; it would become a serious security threat if political and paramilitary movements orchestrated such violence for political ends.

Iraqi Groups. Depending on the success that the United States has in brokering an acceptable power-sharing arrangement between opposition groups, several groups with a claim to a share of power in Iraq have the military capability to make a power grab.

First, Shiite radical groups, including the Supreme Council for the Islamic Revolution in Iraq (SCIRI), al-Daawa, and loyalists of Muqtada al-Sadr may not have the wholehearted allegiance of a majority of the Iraqi Shiite population, but they appear to have extensive support networks in the country and the capability to mobilize lightly armed fighters and crowds. Their actions will depend in part on guidance from Tehran, but these groups could use violence to assert their authority and exploit popular feelings of insecurity to enhance their political position. In addition, the removal of the regime has allowed rivalries to surface within the Shiite political and religious hierarchy, the *hawza*.[7] Individuals close to the Sadr movement are already employing violence; some of these people were allegedly behind the killing of Abd al-Majid Khoei in Najaf. In general, leaders of Shiite radical activist groups are likely to exploit the anti-American sentiments that are likely to arise because of the U.S. occupation of the land in which the Shiite holy places, Najaf and Kerbala, are located.

Second, the capabilities of Kurdish groups, notably the Patriotic Union of Kurdistan (PUK) and the Kurdish Democratic Party (KDP), have been reinforced by the seizure of heavy weaponry from Iraqi army units. These parties might thus be tempted to use force in any of four ways:

- to make economic gains by seizing strategic territory or extending their control over oil assets or transportation facilities

---

[7] *Hawza al-ilmiyya'* [realm of knowledge].

- to resist future Turkish attempts to extend its military presence in northern Iraq and to consolidate a "buffer zone" inside Iraqi Kurdistan
- to improve their bargaining position or to make local geopolitical gains in northern Iraq, either against one another or against other groups, such as Arab nationalists or Turkomans
- to recover Kurdish property "Arabized" by the Saddam regime.

Third, other significant internal groups with access to arms include smaller movements with an "official" political or opposition status, such as the Turkoman parties, the Iraqi National Accord, or the Iraqi National Congress, and the wider set of "unofficial" regional "barons" who are exploiting the power vacuum to exercise local authority. Other, more disparate, internal groups could include military units and tribes with strong military links. These groups may use the cover of the conflict to stake out territorial or political bargaining positions. Any of these groups could seek to strengthen its postwar bargaining position over resources or a role in the new state through military action. All these groups are possible proxies for foreign powers.

Foreign Intervention. A period of weakness following the fall of the regime may tempt Iraq's neighbors—Turkey, Iran, and Syria—to intervene. Turkey's principal motive for intervention is to prevent Turkey's Kurdish insurgents, primarily the Kurdistan Workers Party, from using the conflict as an opportunity to consolidate their rear areas. Turkey fears that Iraqi Kurdish groups might funnel arms or other support to Turkish Kurds and that an extension of Kurdish influence in Iraq might embolden Turkey's Kurds to seek autonomy or independence. Turkey has both historic and economic motives for attempting to extend its influence over the northern oil fields and trade routes, but the U.S. statement that Iraq's oil belongs to the Iraqi people has probably served to dissuade any Turkish adventurism. Turkey has made clear its desire to promote the interests of Iraqi Turkomans, ostensibly out of concern for their fate. In reality, Turkey's intent is to exercise influence over the shape of the Iraqi polity through the Turkoman minority. This support could potentially spill over into support for Turkoman militias.[8]

---

[8]Such as the Turkoman Front, led by Mustafa Ziya.

Iran appears to have little interest at present in promoting wholesale Islamic revolution in Iraq, but it has extensive influence through its covert and paramilitary presence on the ground in the south and north of Iraq. The Iran-Iraq War taught Tehran that the majority of Iraq's Shiites were Iraqi nationalists first and coreligionists second. However, Iran retains a vital interest in influencing the future of Iraqi politics and security policy. More generally, it will remain intimately engaged in security, political, religious, and cultural developments in the Shiite religious heartland of southern Iraq.

In addition to normal diplomatic and economic measures, this influence is exercised through covert action, psychological appeals along religious lines, and infiltration of paramilitary forces and supplies (e.g., the Badr Brigade). While Iran will be wary of provoking U.S. retaliation, it will support elements favorable to it in the Iraqi polity and seek to weaken elements deemed hostile. Although reports are unclear, U.S. officials have expressed concern about the infiltration of Iranian agents into southern Iraq. If the Mujahideen-i Khalq Organization continues to operate from Iraqi territory into Iran after its cease-fire with U.S. forces, Iran will have an additional motive for intervening forcibly inside Iraq.[9]

Finally, Syria will suffer economically from the emergence of a new Iraqi regime, which will reduce Syrian gains from the illicit trade in oil and supplies that flourished in the last years of sanctions. More importantly, Syria will be worried that a new Iraqi government may support peace with Israel at the expense of Syrian strategic interests and may demonstrate the benefits of economic liberalization and political pluralism to Syria's populace. For all these reasons, Syria will be tempted to exploit its ties with Iraqi leftists, Arab nationalists, and Baathists, notably in the Iraqi military, to destabilize the new Iraqi regime. Nonetheless, Syria will be wary of provoking a U.S. response or fomenting serious unrest in Iraq that may spill over into Syria.

Force and Regime Protection. Physical threats to the U.S. and allied forces and the new Iraqi administration will come from three sources. First, expressive violence may threaten U.S. forces either from regime diehards or from elements of the Iraqi population if the

---

[9] *Middle East Online,* "US Strikes Accord with People's Mujahedeen," April 23, 2003.

U.S. presence is seen as a heavy-handed occupying force. Given the lack of reliable information about attitudes among the Iraqi population, it is impossible to reliably judge the medium-term attitudes of Iraqis to U.S. forces. The initial evidence is mixed. Many may be relieved by the removal of the previous regime, but this is tempered by dismay at civilian casualties, the failure to control looting, and wariness at foreign occupation. With memories of the resistance to British occupation relatively fresh, it would not be hard for "accidental atrocities" by U.S. or British forces to arouse popular ire, especially in crowd-control situations.[10]

The second set of risks to U.S. forces comes from Iraq's neighbors operating through proxies, as Iran and Syria did in Lebanon in the 1980s. Both Iran and Syria are adept at using terrorists. Iran might work through the Shiite community, including using groups such as al-Daawa and SCIRI, to attack the regime or occupation forces. Syria has extensive assets in Iraq, particularly in the Iraqi military. While not enough to overthrow Saddam, these assets could be used to launch attacks on the next regime or on U.S. forces.

Third, a final source of risks involves jihadist terrorism against U.S. forces. Sunni jihadists view the U.S. presence as another example of the war against Islam and see the future Iraqi regime as *jahiliya* (corrupt). Jihadist assets and networks in Iraq appear to be limited: Ansar al-Islam partisans have been removed by joint Kurdish-U.S. action; Arab volunteers who joined the Iraqi fight were ineffective; and Osama bin Laden's calls for action had little effect. Nonetheless, an extensive U.S. military and civil presence may present a target-rich environment for future jihadists.[11]

Law and Disorder. Aside from politically motivated violence, U.S. forces will face three law-and-order issues. The first is that of social chaos, allowing circumstances in which looting, revenge killing, and general malfeasance run unchecked. The extent of this challenge was borne out as the regime collapsed, with widespread looting and vigilantism in Iraq's major cities. The failure to curb this lawlessness

---

[10]Such as the fatalities during crowd-control incidents in Fallujah.

[11]The May 2003 terrorist bombings in Saudi Arabia underlined this continuing threat.

rapidly has already undermined the credibility of the U.S. and British forces' ability to provide security.

The second is that of banditry. It is endemic in most postwar environments and is fueled by military desertion, the breakdown of social structures, and demobilization. In Iraq, much of what is often presented as political insurgency can better be classed as banditry. This has been a particular problem in the south, where army deserters have turned to banditry. Deserters have also been something of a problem in the north.

The third is that of "normal" crime. This will be a challenge, since an important goal of a U.S.-supported Iraqi administration will be to create a climate of personal security for Iraqi citizens. The highly politicized Iraqi criminal justice system gives little real insight into the extent of crime in Iraq, but anecdotal evidence suggests that a combination of economic necessity, social breakdown, the focus of police forces on political and regime security, and the proliferation of weapons has led to relatively high levels of crime. It is already clear that organized crime is deeply entrenched in Iraqi society, as it was in the Balkans. Saddam's release of "ordinary" criminals in early 2003 will exacerbate the situation.

An additional problem has been the deliberate decision the Saddam regime made to encourage a return to tribal justice as part of its policy of retribalizing Iraq to fragment political opposition. This policy has meant that significant portions of the population have effectively been distanced from the state's criminal justice system, resorting instead to tribal elders and a range of traditional, sometimes summary, forms of justice. It is debatable whether this trend exacerbates or contains the level of violence. In any case, a new regime in Baghdad is likely to want to reextend the central state criminal justice system to the entire populace.

Instruments of Control. While U.S. and allied forces will dominate the macrosecurity environment, the new state will want to deploy indigenous security, intelligence, police, and military forces sooner rather than later. The following assets will be of most significance:

- Special Republican Guard and Republican Guard
- regular army, air force, and navy
- security and intelligence services

- police forces
- judiciary and criminal justice system
- assorted paramilitary groups formed by the state (tribal, Kurdish, etc.).

There are a number of important challenges. The first is dismantling the units most closely associated with the regime and agreeing on appropriate treatment of officers and men. The collapse of the Republican Guard and Special Republican Guard during the conflict has made this task much easier, since the organizations effectively ceased to exist as formed units. The regular army also disintegrated during the conflict, but it will be important to undertake a formal process of demobilization and a program to reintegrate enlisted personnel and junior officers into the civil economy. For more-senior officers and those suspected of human rights abuses, a thorough purge will be necessary to "de-Baathify" the officer corps. The extent of prosecution for crimes against humanity will have to be weighed against the need for "truth and reconciliation."

The future of the Iraqi army will be an important question to be addressed in the medium term. The United States is likely to retain some responsibility for Iraq's external security. However, a restructured and reoriented Iraqi military will have to find a new role that does not threaten its neighbors but that can preserve Iraq's interests and territorial integrity. Efforts to rebuild the Iraqi army will have to take into account the army's long tradition of involvement in both domestic politics and internal security.

Because of their intimate connection with the former regime and involvement in human rights abuses, the security and intelligence services may have to be dismantled and rebuilt from the ground up. However, functioning security services will be vital for preserving the security of the new regime.

It will also be important to establish an effective and credible new criminal justice system. The police forces should be purged, but a balance needs to be struck between deep reform and an effective police force. For instance, respect for human rights and the rule of law are not features of normal police behavior in Iraq; these will have to be inculcated into existing and newly recruited officers. It will be equally important to purge the judiciary while ensuring the application of transparent and objective justice. These reforms need to be accompanied by reform of the prison system and rehabilitation of political detainees.

Paramilitary forces loyal to opposition groups will also want to play a security role in a future Iraq. The significant forces include Islamist groups, notably SCIRI. SCIRI, whose military strength is concentrated in the Iranian-hosted Badr Brigade, could field forces in the south and has increased its presence in the north of Iraq. Since it has gained much of its reputation and leverage through military action against the Saddam regime, it will be reluctant to disband unless this leverage is translated into political gains in the Iraqi power structure. Other Islamist groups, such as al-Daawa, do not have formal militias, but they are likely to form such militias rapidly in postconflict Iraq, if given the opportunity.

The PUK and KDP field substantial militia forces in northern Iraq, which have been used to police the Kurdish zone and to pursue intergroup power and land grabs. Possession of these militias is part of the very identity of Kurdish political leaders. Nonetheless, a political settlement acceptable to both Kurdish leaders (within the north, between the north and Baghdad, and with the Turks) could encourage the PUK and KDP to draw down their standing forces.

Since armed force has been the currency of power and politics in Iraq, many political or political-religious groups have some form of armed wing. Some of these were built up before and during the conflict (Iraqi National Congress by the United States, Turkoman by the Turks). These groups may be easier to demobilize.

The challenges that will be faced in respect to these militias will include whether to seek full demobilization or partial incorporation into the reconstituted armed forces, police, or security services. It will also include the extent to which it is worth pursuing a program of disarmament. Iraq is likely to be awash in small arms. Voluntary disarmament is likely to be token; forceful disarmament by U.S. and allied forces could provoke popular unrest.

Weapons of Mass Destruction. The leakage of WMD to any of the internal Iraqi groups, foreign states, or bandits would greatly exacerbate the security challenge. We assume that the U.S. occupation forces will make it a priority to secure all Iraq's WMD and WMD-related infrastructure, including personnel. A thornier challenge will be dealing with Iraqi know-how in the long term. As with the former Soviet Union, solutions will have to be found for Iraqi scientific personnel who had been involved in WMD programs. The solutions could include detaining the most-senior researchers and ensuring productive work in Iraq or abroad for other staff. A longer-term program of international monitoring and verification and adherence to treaties, such as the Chemical Weapons Convention and Nuclear Non-Proliferation Treaty, will be essential.

Humanitarian

To date, the humanitarian situation in Iraq has been better than expected. This is fortunate because the United States and United Kingdom have been less well prepared than they might have been to tackle the foreseeable challenges.

The humanitarian challenges are primarily short term. In the medium term, once the Iraqi civil administration and economy are functioning, most humanitarian issues should be manageable. Outstanding problems, such as IDPs, should be solvable once security is achieved and economic reconstruction starts. Structural humanitarian issues, such as child mortality, the lack of supplies in the medical sector, and poor sanitation, should be soluble once sanctions are lifted and revenues are directed into economic and social reconstruction.

Fortunately, extensive damage to the oil sector, transportation, and electric power infrastructure was avoided. Nonetheless, the short-term humanitarian challenges are formidable. They are also of longer-term political significance in generating popular support for the U.S. presence.

There are a number of fundamental problems. To begin with, the Iraqi populace is much less resilient than it was in 1991. Declines in employment, income, nutrition, health, and household assets mean that Iraqis are much less able to fend for themselves than they were in 1991. They are more likely to suffer from disease and hunger. Since 1991, the majority of the population has become dependent on the state for the bulk of its food, in addition to other supplies and services. The World Food Program has estimated that 16 million Iraqis, approximately 60 percent of the total population, rely solely on food rations distributed through the Oil-for-Food Programme to meet household needs.[12] During the war, this supply network was dislocated because of the disruption of the civil administration in the wake of regime collapse. Finally, the level of resilience in the Iraqi physical infrastructures is relatively low. For instance, the power generation and distribution and water supply and sanitation infrastructures have been rebuilt since 1991 but suffer from inadequate maintenance and lack of spare parts.

Against this backdrop, the immediate humanitarian challenges include:

- **Refugees.** UNHCR is currently caring for 130,000 registered refugees inside Iraq.

- **Food supplies.** UN planning before the war assumed that 2.2 million people were highly dependent on the official distribution system and that there "would be a progressive run down and eventual cessation of distribution of commodities" in the rest of the country.[13] In the short term, it is important to reconstitute the ration distribution system, working with local agents and the UN. In addition to normal food distribution, the UN Children's Fund (UNICEF) estimates that some 3 million people, malnourished children and pregnant or lactating women, are in need of "therapeutic feeding."[14]

- **Health care and medical supplies.** The World Health Organization points to the following health care challenges:[15] (1) people requiring treatment for direct and indirect traumatic injuries from the conflict; (2) an increase in respiratory and diarrheal diseases as a result of disruptions of the potable water supply and possible air pollution; and (3) possible epidemics of infectious

---

[12]USAID, "Iraq Humanitarian and Reconstruction Assistance Fact Sheet," No. 24, May 1, 2003.

[13]According to a UN planning report to the Secretary General that had been widely leaked before the war (UN, "Likely Humanitarian Scenarios," New York, December 10, 2002). Also see James Harding and Frances Williams, "Over 4 Million Iraqis May Need Food Assistance in Long War," *Financial Times*, February 14, 2003, p. 7.

[14]UN (2002), p. 6.

[15]UN (2002), p. 6.

diseases, such as cholera, dysentery, and measles, as a result of poor sanitation and current low levels of vaccination.[16]

- **Electricity.** Because of disruptions to the electrical infrastructure during the conflict, the most immediate humanitarian effect has been on potable water supplies and sewage facilities. Iraq is an urban society, and over two-thirds of Iraqis live in cities. Baghdad has over 5 million people, and 12 other cities have populations of about 1 million people or more.[17] Urban residents depend on municipal sewage and water supplies. Any closure of water and sewage systems has dire consequences for public health.

- **Demining.** Minefields in the south and along the border with the Kurdish areas in the north, as well as unexploded ordnance expended during the conflict, will pose an ongoing hazard to Iraqi civilians and foreign personnel. There is currently no mine awareness program in the center and south; this will have to be developed and accompanied by a sustained effort to remove unexploded ordnance. With appropriate training and equipment, this could provide useful employment for some members of the former Iraqi army.

Before and during the conflict, U.S. and United Kingdom forces took major steps to lessen the postwar humanitarian burden. These steps included minimizing damage to key nodes in the civil infrastructure (e.g., bridges, the electricity distribution network), stockpiling humanitarian supplies in the region, and securing key entry routes (e.g., the Umm Qasr port and the land route from Jordan).

Led by USAID, significant planning took place to address humanitarian issues rapidly. USAID's Disaster Assistance Response Teams were deployed to the region, and tenders were issued for hundreds of millions of dollars of contracts for immediate and longer-term reconstruction of Iraq's infrastructure.[18] However, political tensions preceding the conflict reduced the desire and ability of U.S. agencies to

---

[16]UNICEF's vaccination program.

[17]Five million people have access to a sewage network that relies on pumping stations, perhaps 10 percent of which have backup generators (UN, 2002).

[18]Mark Fineman, "U.S. Agency Offers Blueprint for Rebuilding Iraq," *Los Angeles Times*, March 21, 2003.

work with the UN, the EU, and other allies on humanitarian relief and reconstruction plans, which may have reduced the responsiveness of these organizations. The U.S. military, through its civil affairs units, has become very proactive in humanitarian affairs, but its relationship with relief agencies remains unsettled.[19] In light of this tension, it appears to have taken some time for the Office of Reconstruction and Humanitarian Assistance (ORHA) to develop working relationships with the UN agencies already present in Iraq. It has also taken some time for the Oil-for-Food Programme to reconstitute existing critical infrastructures, such as the food distribution network, and to work with NGOs for the rapid delivery of humanitarian assistance.

As the immediate issues are dealt with, it will be important to ensure that humanitarian aid does not translate into dependency. In the medium term, there will be no benefit in replacing an interventionist and distributive Iraqi state with a similar aid infrastructure. Self-help, notably in agricultural areas, should be a priority. Moreover, the availability of financial resources to fund quick projects, such as clearing war rubble, making damaged buildings safe, and repairing combat damage, could provide jobs and promote a general feeling among Iraqis that progress is being made.

Civil Administration

Political and administrative transition in Iraq starts with one huge advantage: There is a relatively advanced and functioning civil administration covering large parts of the country. The corresponding disadvantages are the lack of real knowledge about the political forces and attitudes within Iraq and the lack of consensus on Iraq's future political structure.

The establishment of a civil administration and the road map for political transition will be treated separately here, but it is important to recognize that short-term pragmatic decisions made to establish a new administration will significantly affect the shape of the longer-term political transition. For instance, the individuals, institutions, and networks that held positions of formal or informal power and

---

[19]The UN and many NGOs argue that the direct delivery of assistance by the military has "more 'cons' than 'pros'" (UN, 2002).

influence in Iraq under the Saddam regime may be useful to the hard-pressed U.S. forces and CPA as they seek to deliver security, stability, and services in the short term.[20] The reconstitution of these power centers under the new regime may, however, undermine progress toward a new political settlement in the longer term.

Nature of the State. It is important to understand the nature and dynamics of Iraqi politics, yet our understanding of Iraqi political dynamics is woefully inadequate. While insightful analysis on Iraq's political and social dynamics in the pre-Saddam period exists, the closed nature of the former state means that there is little more than informed speculation to guide current policymaking.[21] Saddam's totalitarian system sought to destroy politics, and the external Iraqi opposition provides little real guide to forces and attitudes within the country.

Nonetheless, it is possible to make a number of contextual observations. While the British and the Hashemite monarchy sought to undertake state- *and* nation-building, both projects remain very much unfinished. State-building, in terms of the organizational and physical infrastructure of a modern, unitary state, made the most progress, until the 1990s. This is the basis on which a new civil administration can be structured. Nation-building, whether in a monarchist, Arab nationalist, communist, or revolutionary Baathist guise, has proceeded in fits and starts since the 1920s. The fact that few, if any, active Iraqi politicians now call for a breakup of the Iraqi polity or for secession is testimony to the relative success of the nation-building project. Nonetheless, despite the adherence of exiled opposition groups to the formula of a "united, federal Iraq," there is little evidence that basic questions of national identity are settled or that a transfer of loyalty to the Iraqi nation has taken place.[22]

Iraq has evolved into the most extreme example of what Nazih Ayubi has labeled the "fierce state."[23] This form of state features an authori-

---

[20]Examples include the army (more particularly, the Sunni officer corps) but also parts of the *mukhabarat*, certain tribal confederations and major business leaders.

[21]Hanna Batatu, *The Old Social Classes and the Revolutionary Movements of Iraq*, Princeton, N.J.: Princeton University Press, 1978.

[22]Ironically, the dependence of citizens on the state ration system under the Oil-for-Food Programme may have increased this sense of national identity.

[23]Nazih Ayubi, *Overstating the Arab State*, London: I. B. Tauris, 1994.

tarian power structure combining three elements. First, the *dimuqratiyyat al-khubz* (democracy of bread) is a tacit social contract in which the regime provides social and economic welfare in return for political loyalty.[24] Second, the fierce state employs a totalitarian coercive apparatus (the *mukhabarat* state). Third, it creates an ideology, which was Baathism in the case of Iraq. The central feature of the fierce state is that politics in this model is "largely deferential and nonparticipatory, conditional on the state's providential capacity."[25] In Iraq, this model has been overlaid with the characteristics of a rentier state. Oil revenues accruing directly to the regime have enabled the regime to implement a policy of *dimuqratiyyat al-khubz* to an extreme degree. It is important to note that Iraq went beyond the well-recognized model of the modern authoritarian-praetorian state.[26] While key military units buttressed the rule of Saddam Hussein, it was the intelligence services, or *mukhabarat*, that were the "keystone" in his rule.[27] These "bureaucracies of repression" shared in power at the highest levels.[28]

A real challenge for political transition in Iraq is that, while the emergence of the authoritarian state in the Arab world has been a topic of some interest to political scientists for a number of years, the real dynamics of the *mukhabarat* state and of "state violence has received . . . [limited] systematic attention in recent scholarship."[29] There is therefore a very poor understanding of what effects Saddam

---

[24]Larbi Sadiki, "Towards Arab Liberal Governance: From the Democracy of Bread to the Democracy of the Vote," *Third World Quarterly*, Vol. 18, No. 1, 1997, pp. 127–148.

[25]Sadiki (1997), p. 135; also see Jill Crystal, "Authoritarianism and Its Adversaries in the Arab World," *World Politics*, January 1994, pp. 262–289.

[26]Perlmutter defines *authoritarian praetorianism* as military-civilian fusionist rule in which the ruling elite of officers, bureaucrats, and technocrats "restrict political support and mobilization" and whose main "source of support . . . is the military establishment" (A. Perlmutter, *The Military and Politics in Modern Times: On Professionals, Praetorians and Revolutionary Soldiers*, New Haven, Conn.: Yale University Press, 1977, p. 95).

[27]Such as the Special Republican Guard and Republican Guard.

[28]The term is adapted from the title of a 1994 Middle East Watch report on Iraq's security services.

[29]Crystal (1994). Impressionistic and journalistic assessments of Arab police states, however, abound. On Iraq alone, see Samir al-Khalil, *Republic of Fear*, London: Hutchinson, 1989; Kanan Makiya, *Cruelty and Silence*, London: Jonathan Cape, 1993; and Hussein Sumaida, *Circle of Fear*, Toronto: Stoddart, 1991.

Hussein's regime has had on the Iraqi polity or the structures of power and authority in Iraqi society.[30]

Establishing a Civil Administration. This process will need to take account not just of the formal bureaucratic structures but of the "shadow state." Iraq has relatively well-established formal administrative structures. These cover all aspects of society, from central to local government, from education through public works to the oil industry. These structures are staffed by relatively well-educated and competent technocrats. Many of the most educated and skilled Iraqi technocratic elites are now in exile, but some will return home to assist in reconstruction.

There are six key challenges in revitalizing these administrative structures. First, although Iraqi ministries formally exercised competence under the Saddam regime, the totalitarian regime in fact deliberately undermined the authority of ministers and civil servants. The authority of the civil administration was essentially hollowed out. This authority needs to be rebuilt. At the same time, the senior civil service needs to be purged of discredited Baathists, and the worrying levels of corruption in the civil service need to be addressed. This will involve reforming recruitment and promotion systems to replace promotion on loyalty criteria with meritocratic criteria, and establishing a functioning system of ministerial responsibility.

Second, it will be important to balance expatriate expertise and influence with insider presence. There is a temptation for U.S. forces to fill senior positions with Westernized Iraqi technocrats who are not tainted with Baathism and who may have worked on transition plans.[31] This temptation needs to be balanced with the effects on

---

[30]Among the classic political science studies on the authoritarian state are Samuel Huntington, *Political Order in Changing Societies*, New Haven, Conn.: Yale University Press, 1968; Samuel Huntington and Clement H. Moore, eds., *Authoritarian Politics in Modern Society: The Dynamics of Established One-Party Systems*, New York: Basic Books, 1970; A. Perlmutter, *Egypt: The Praetorian State*, New Brunswick, N.J.: Transaction Books, 1974; and A. Perlmutter, *Modern Authoritarianism: A Comparative Institutional Analysis*, New Haven, Conn.: Yale University Press, 1981. Approaching the topic from a different angle, Stohl and Lopez have argued that social science has been too "antiseptic" and has ignored the real nature and political role of state repression and terrorism (Michael Stohl and George A. Lopez, eds., *The State as Terrorist: The Dynamics of Governmental Violence and Repression*, London: Aldwych Press, 1984).

[31]For example, in DOS's Future of Iraq project.

morale among Iraqi officials who feel they have stayed "inside" to keep the system running and who have nationalist memories of the British presence after independence.

Third, pay and morale will be an extremely pressing challenge. Civil servants have suffered heavily in terms of declining relative income and living standards since 1991. Anecdotal evidence suggests that most civil servants have difficulty surviving on their salaries and have been forced to draw down their assets and to take on additional work. To make the civil administration function effectively, salaries need to be paid immediately and regularly, and relative incomes need to be restored. These measures will also help to get a grip on rampant corruption.

Fourth, the role of the state administration in the Kurdish northern zone is also an issue. Since the mid-1990s, the Kurds have established effective administrative structures in the north of the country. Decisions will need to be taken on the relationship of these structures to the Baghdad-based apparatus, probably involving a degree of autonomy within a centralized framework.

Fifth, the role of the state administration among tribal communities will have to be settled. During the 1990s, the Saddam regime gave more authority to traditional tribal leaders and power structures at the expense of the civil government. It is likely that a new regime will want to reverse this retribalization, which goes against attempts to build a "modern" Iraqi state.

Finally, significant and far-reaching decisions will be required about the relationship between the state and the civil society. The redistributive and authoritarian nature of the Iraqi state has been reinforced by the countrywide ration system, which has made the bulk of the population dependent on state handouts and has reinforced the state's penetration, surveillance, and control of society.[32] Restructuring this relationship will require taking small steps, such as reenergizing private-sector pluralism and civil society, but also requires a more fundamental rethinking of the nature of the Iraqi state.

---

[32]Through some 43,000 food and flour agents.

In addition to these general issues, a medium- and long-term challenge will be to reform the educational, cultural, and media establishments, which were co-opted by Saddam's totalitarian system. Both the quality and the content of Iraqi education will require radical transformation, without, however, raising concerns over "educational imperialism." This will be particularly important, given the relative youth of Iraq's population.

In reforming the civil government administration, attention will have to be paid to the consequences of the postwar disappearance of the other major administrative structure covering the country: the Baath Party. The Baath Party, as an institution, was hollowed out by Saddam and had no political authority, but it did serve as an instrument of social monitoring and control. Like the Chinese Communist Party under Mao, its presence was felt on every street block. Although the party effectively disappeared with the fall of the regime and was subsequently banned by U.S authorities, it is not yet clear what the fragmentation of such a pervasive institution of social control will mean. In some cases, it has been replaced by vigilantism and local power grabs.

Informal power structures are common throughout the Arab world. *Wasta,* based on personal, family, or clan connections, both subverts formal bureaucracies and helps to soften the edges of the region's police states. Even after the removal of Saddam and his key lieutenants, the "shadow state" still exists. Thousands or tens of thousands of Iraqis exercise influence and deploy resources regardless of their formal bureaucratic positions. Understanding and engineering these power structures will be an important challenge for the transitional authorities.

A Road Map for Political Transition. A road map for political transition should be framed that takes account of the previous attempts to build a stable Iraqi nation. Such efforts date back to British rule after World War I, when British colonial personnel sought to create a new Iraqi identity and political structure. Since the 1920s, the major thrust in Iraqi politics has been to regard politics as "mainly . . . a way of disciplining the population to ensure conformity with the rulers' visions of social order."[33] The Bush administration's visions of a

---

[33]Tripp (2001), p. 2.

rapid transition to a pluralist democracy must be seen against this backdrop.[34]

The overarching requirement is for agreement on a new constitutional end-state for Iraq. Iraq has never had a constitutional and political structure that has engaged the interests of all its communities. As Kosovo has shown, failure to agree on the political end-state can perpetuate instability. Unfortunately, publicly touted political road maps to date have drawn on simplistic models of Iraqi politics. Options that have been touted include reliance on the Sunni officer corps to sustain an authoritarian, centralized system; a three-party federation, in which the Sunni, Shiites, and Kurds share power; and a pluralist "democracy," in which there is representation from multiple ethnic and religious communities, such as the Shiite, Sunni, Kurd, Turkoman, and Assyrian groups.

Any future Iraqi political settlement will have to address three critical questions. First, what is the nature of community politics in Iraq? Iraqi regimes have often deliberately reinforced communitarian identities (religious, ethnic, tribal). This has undermined attempts to build parties on horizontal, cross-community lines. It is unclear to what extent a future Iraqi polity will need to take account of vertical communal identities. Given the strength of the Kurdish movements and the relative success of the institutions in the north, there is no question that some form of Kurdish autonomy in a federal structure will be required. However, there is no demographic reality to the concept of a Shiite south and a Sunni center, so it is not clear what the units in a wider federation might be.

Second, how can the Shiites be enfranchised? While Shiites have been politically active in Iraqi politics since the 1920s, the Shiite lower classes and religious establishments have been disenfranchised politically and economically. There is, however, no such thing as a united Shiite polity. Iraq's Shiites are divided along geographic and tribal lines. Many Iraqi Shiites are secular; indeed, there is a long tradition for support of secular class-based movements. Since the 1920s, politicians from a Shiite sectarian background have often been very active in leftist or communist movements that sought to

---

[34]George W. Bush, speech on the future of Iraq, delivered to members of the American Enterprise Institute at the Washington Hilton Hotel, Washington, D.C., February 26, 2003.

empower the rural and urban working classes and often opposed Sunni Arab nationalists. Among more religious-minded Shiites, there are major differences between followers of different factions. Even in the short period since the fall of the regime, clear divisions have emerged between, for instance, Grand Ayatollah Ali Sistani of Najaf and the al-Sadr and al-Khalisi families.

Third, how can the need for demographic and democratic legitimacy be reconciled with existing centers of power? The formal power assets—military, security, and police services; civil technocracy; and business groups—are dominated by a Sunni elite. In addition to the Tikritis, the elite is often drawn from particular tribal confederations. Power in the Kurdish north is held by those close to the Barzani and Talabani clans. Therefore, even if a formal pluralistic system is established, this may not affect the real levers of power. Indeed, it is likely that the Sunni military and technocratic elite would vigorously oppose the ascendance to power of even a moderate Shiite leadership.

Given these challenges, any road map for political transition must balance the interests of different power brokers with the need to gain legitimacy and engagement from the disenfranchised populace. It needs to prevent politicians from exploiting community and religious politics for sectional ends, as happened in post-Tito Yugoslavia. Because of the lack of connection between the Iraqi opposition in exile and the Iraqi population, there is no clear process for legitimizing a new political dispensation in Iraq. The notion of "parachuting in" a government in exile was rightly rejected.

One factor that may help postwar transition is that Iraq has long had democratic structures, however nominal these have been in practice. Saddam's elections and the resultant party makeup in parliament were transparent frauds, but they at least preserved the form of pluralist institutions. On the other hand, Iraq's long experience with mock democracy, dating back to the British Mandate, will leave citizens justifiably skeptical of new democratic institutions that have form but no substance.

Rather than moving rapidly to national, party-based parliamentary elections, the transitional authorities would be advised to focus upon developing democratic building blocks, such as a free press, the rule of law, and local elected authorities. The Kurdish north now has some experience with these elements. At the same time, an all-encompassing constitutional convention could provide some legitimacy to any future political structure.

Reconstruction

Iraq faces a central economic problem familiar to its neighbors: how to generate growth to absorb its rapidly increasing and young population. Iraq is a particularly poignant case, since its people became accustomed to rapidly rising living standards in the 1970s. The Iraqi economy has long-term structural problems that will have to be addressed if a basis for sustainable growth is to be laid. These include dependence on an oil sector that requires heavy investment and modernization, a sclerotic set of nationalized industries, and an agricultural sector in need of reform. At the same time, the legal and financial frameworks have been distorted by the arbitrary and authoritarian nature of power. While these structural problems must be tackled, the immediate need will be to generate revenues from oil exports.

Initially, foreign aid is also likely to be important. In the longer term, foreign direct investment may also contribute to an acceleration of economic growth. Initially, revenues from oil exports and foreign aid will be needed for government salaries, humanitarian aid, and such vital services as health care. Iraq will also need to devote resources to critical short-term investments, such as in the oil industry.

Economic activity in Iraq plummeted after the 1990–1991 Gulf War. Three of the few semireliable indicators of the state of the economy indicate that output and living standards fell sharply. Oil production fell 85 percent in 1991, to just 305,000 barrels per day. Official imports fell from $9,899 million in 1989, the year before Iraq's invasion of Kuwait, to $423 million in 1991. The rate of infant mortality rose 50 percent in the year following the war, to 99.7 per 1,000 births. Since 1991, infant mortality rates have fallen slowly. Current estimates of Iraqi infant mortality, especially outside the Kurdish areas in the north, are still well in excess of the average of 43 per 1,000 in the Middle East and North Africa.

The decline in economic activity immediately following the 1990–1991 Gulf War had differential effects on income groups and regions. Iraq's large middle class suffered sharp declines in living standards and wealth as oil export revenues plummeted and as families drew down savings in an attempt to partially preserve former levels of consumption. Saddam Hussein's military campaign to put down the uprising in Shiite areas of southern Iraq had a devastating effect on the nonoil economy in that region. Kurdish areas in the north, partially protected by the U.S. and British governments, fared somewhat better. They benefited economically from smuggling oil out of Iraq and other goods in and from UN assistance. However, internecine conflict disrupted economic activity in the region through the mid-1990s.

Evaluations of the state of the Iraqi economy and of average living standards in 2003 are based largely on guesswork. A number of indicators suggest that the economic situation had become less dire by the end of the decade following the Gulf War. Oil production, one indicator of economic activity for which statistics are available, rose steadily through 2000, when it hit 2.571 million barrels a day (mbd). This was the highest level of output since 1989 and the third highest on record (1979 was the peak year, at 3.477 mbd). Valued in current dollars, oil output has risen from $1.8 billion in 1991 to $25.0 billion in 2000. Estimates of infant mortality show improvement since 1991. Imports are up sharply since the mid-1990s, providing further evidence that the economy rebounded from its low point in the immediate aftermath of the Gulf War. The apex of Iraq's post–Gulf War recovery probably came in 2000. Oil production fell by 139 thousand barrels per day in 2001 and an additional 481 thousand barrels per day in the first 10 months of 2002. In addition, world market prices for oil fell by about one-fifth in 2001, reducing export revenues even further. On the other hand, oil prices rose in 2002, probably by enough to compensate for the decline in production. The U.S. Central Intelligence Agency estimates that Iraqi GDP rose 15 percent in 2000 but then fell about 6 percent in 2001. The decline in oil production in 2002 suggests that the economy slipped again that year.

Iraq's basis for sustainable growth has severely deteriorated over the past decade. There has been little investment in public infrastructure. Maintenance has been deferred, and a number of utilities are in very poor condition. Some analysts trace the declines in oil output in 2001 and 2002 to a combination of depletion and deterioration in the oil field infrastructure. In addition, anecdotal evidence suggests that the health care and educational systems have also deteriorated.

Although Iraq has a substantial number of individuals trained at universities, the decline in oil wealth has curtailed the number of Iraqis able to study abroad. Illiteracy is relatively high, at 42 percent. In contrast to other Middle Eastern countries, illiteracy rates in Iraq do not appear to have declined over the last decade, suggesting that some children in poorer or rural families are being missed by the educational system.

In short, the Iraqi economy had less resilience going into the conflict in 2003 than it had at the start of the 1990–1991 Gulf War. As a consequence, Iraq has emerged from the recent conflict with a much-reduced stock of physical capital and probably less human capital than at the end of the Gulf War, making economic recovery to pre–Gulf War levels of GDP all that much more difficult.

BEST-PRACTICE INSTITUTIONAL AND POLICY RESPONSES

As outlined in the preceding section, the challenges the United States faces in Iraq are formidable. It is nonetheless possible to derive valuable lessons on how to deal with these challenges from the case studies examined in this report. There are four overarching grand strategic lessons to be drawn.

First, democratic nation-building is possible given a sufficient input of resources and a long-term commitment. However, these inputs could be very high. It is unlikely that Iraq would get the same per capita level of international troops, police presence, or foreign aid that Bosnia or Kosovo did. Nonetheless, lessons should also be drawn from the British experience in the 1920s and 1930s of seeking to secure Iraq on the cheap with aerial policing and from the consequences of the much-lower levels of security and economic assistance provided to Somalia, Haiti, and Afghanistan.[35]

Second, overly short departure deadlines are incompatible with the requirements of nation-building. The United States will only succeed in Iraq if it is willing to spend time establishing robust institutions and does not tie its departure to artificial deadlines. In this regard, setting dates for early national elections can be counterproductive.

---

[35]Michael Eisenstadt and Eric Mathewson, eds., *U.S. Policy in Post-Saddam Iraq: Lessons from the British Experience*, Washington, D.C.: Washington Institute for Middle East Policy, 2003.

At the same time, Iraqi memories of the British mandate are fresh. Any suggestion of a long-term U.S. or UN "neocolonial" presence will arouse opposition.

Third, political, ethnic, and sectarian fragmentation and lack of support from neighboring states are important hindrances to successful nation-building. Germany and Japan had homogeneous societies, while Bosnia and Kosovo's neighbors either supported transition or were powerless to disrupt the process actively. Iraq combines the worst of both cases.

Fourth, a balance between unity of command and international burden-sharing is critical to achieving successful political and economic transformation and long-term legitimacy. In Iraq, the United States is experimenting with a novel model that brings military and civilian efforts under one unitary command. While the current arrangement theoretically provides clear lines of authority, ORHA's early performance has shown the difficulties involved in securing wholehearted participation from other agencies, other nations, and international organizations, all of which have become more important than they were in 1945. The postwar uncertainty about a possible command role for NATO and the nature of the UN's "vital role" in managing transition indicate the importance of clear, early decisions on the role for international burden-sharing.

Security

Defeated or liberated populations are often more docile, cooperative, and malleable than usually anticipated. Nonetheless, the degree of success in establishing a secure environment depends on a number of variables. Of the six identified here, several are outside the control of the occupying power (e.g., social and ethnic unity), while others are under the control of the occupying power (e.g., troop and police levels).

First, social and ethnic unity of the society and the propensity of a society to internal violence as a result of political divisions or criminality have major consequences for internal security. An external intervention can reverse the relationship between the victims of oppression and their oppressors. Iraq has a tradition of political violence; criminality is rife; and arms are abundant. The society is also deeply divided along a number of lines. The looting that followed the

collapse of the regime in April 2003 indicated the potential for conflict between "haves" and "have nots."

Second, the nature of the political settlement is of great importance.
A comprehensive political settlement reduces the scope for violence
more than would one that is partial in geographic or political terms.
Iraq has never had a lasting political settlement that involves all
stakeholders in a peaceful and inclusive political process. The
prospect for such an all-inclusive settlement is reduced insofar as
there are fundamentally incompatible or zero-sum demands (e.g.,
for a Shiite theocracy, for elimination of class privileges).

Third, the nature and extent of demobilization can reduce the likeli-
hood of further conflict. A failure to demobilize and disarm fighters
and incumbent security forces can perpetuate violence and abuses.
Iraq suffers from banditry and lawlessness, which are rife among a
heavily armed populace. There are also numerous rival militias in the
country. The first step should be rapid demobilization of remaining
Special Republican Guard and Republican Guard personnel. Senior
officers and individuals suspected of crimes against humanity need
to be dealt with by an established justice and reconciliation system.
Other personnel need to be reintegrated into civilian life. The
remaining regular armed forces need to be gradually and systemati-
cally demobilized while the interim authority decides on the creation
of a new military and whether to retain conscription or form smaller,
volunteer armed forces. This decision must be taken in the context of
wider, Iraqi-led discussions about the role of the military in a future
Iraqi state. Meanwhile, political and tribal militias need to be
demobilized or integrated into the national forces.

In addition, significant restructuring, demobilization, and purging of
the security and intelligence agencies need to take place. Strong
security and intelligence agencies will be required to confront external and subversive threats, but these should not include senior officers from existing agencies or individuals guilty of serious crimes
against humanity.

Fourth, Iraq's neighbors can either improve or exacerbate the security climate in the country. A stable regional environment, in which
neighbors support the transition rather than seek to intervene,
makes it easier to promote security. Iraq is surrounded on three sides
by neighbors—Iran, Syria, and Turkey—that all have vital strategic

interests in the country, many of which are incompatible with U.S. interests. These neighbors have the ability to intervene to shape Iraqi politics and to destabilize the country. The United States therefore needs to take unequivocal responsibility to prevent them from becoming involved in significant overt or covert intervention in Iraqi affairs. At the same time, the United States must assert control over Iraq's borders to prevent infiltration by jihadists. The United States should also establish a consultative framework, which would give all Iraq's neighbors a forum in which to voice their legitimate concerns over the nation's future and to be kept abreast of U.S. plans and intentions.

Fifth, the size, deployment, posture, and command of the occupation forces will greatly influence the peace. The sizes of military forces deployed for postconflict security and nation-building have varied. Figure 10.1 projects these force sizes onto the Iraqi population. It indicates that, if Kosovo levels of troop commitment are used, some 526,000 foreign troops would need to be deployed through 2005. At Bosnian levels, this figure would be 258,000 by 2005; approximately 145,000 international troops would still be required to ensure security at Bosnia levels through 2008.

In addition to the overall force size, it is important to ensure an appropriate deployment of occupation forces that are configured for and attuned to constabulary duties. Large numbers of combat-ready forces confined to barracks will be of little use in promoting stability and security. Smaller numbers of forces trained for stability operations, including crowd control, will be much more effective. It will be important for these forces to be culturally sensitive and not to prioritize force protection at the expense of gaining local knowledge.

Furthermore, it is important to retain unitary command of occupation forces and the ability to act rapidly and decisively to prevent score-settling, attacks on minorities, and power grabs by local armed groups. The United States will initially hold command in Iraq—albeit with an ad hoc coalition of willing partners, such as the United Kingdom, Australia, Italy, and Poland—but can look to Kosovo for a good example of unitary command under NATO auspices that combines adequate U.S. leadership with very broad participation. Although

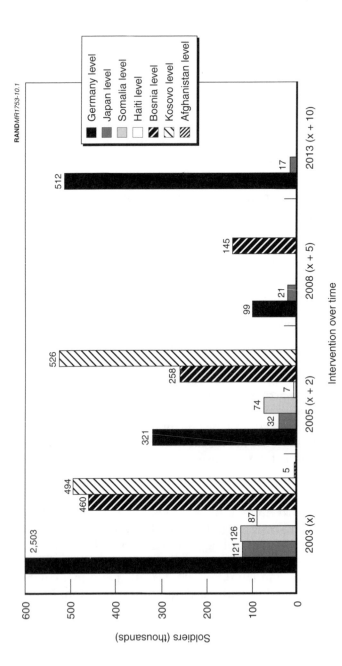

NOTE: Here, year x is the year of intervention, 2003.

Figure 10.1—Military Presence Projections for Iraq

some have argued for an Arab or Islamic force, there is no guarantee that such a force would be more welcome than U.S. forces—and good reason to believe otherwise. The presence of Jordanian, Saudi, Egyptian, Syrian, and certainly Turkish forces would raise additional fears of outside intervention in Iraqi politics.

Sixth, the extent of organized crime will influence the security climate. In the transition from authoritarian rule, organized crime can emerge as the greatest ally of rejectionist forces. If organized criminal groups make common cause with political rejectionists and armed militias, they can act as major spoilers in the process of transition. Therefore, the speed of deployment and the effectiveness of a reformed criminal justice system and civil police force are vital. A consistently weak aspect of such interventions as Kosovo has been the slow pace at which policing and criminal justice functions have been removed from discredited incumbents and the military and passed to international and reformed local civil police and courts.

International assistance with policing, economic reform, and anti-smuggling measures is vital for building the rule of law. Although Iraq has a functioning police and judicial system, it will need to be substantially purged and overhauled. This will involve the deployment of international civil police personnel and advisers. As Figure 10.2 illustrates, if countrywide deployment of international police officers were attempted on the same scale as in Kosovo, the numbers of international police personnel by 2005 could reach almost 53,000. This number is unlikely to be forthcoming. Instead, after order has been restored in the major Iraqi cities, priority should be given to deploying specialist units, such as organized crime investigation squads, to tackle serious crime and corruption and "third forces," such as Gendarmerie and Carabinieri units, to assist with public order.

Humanitarian

In almost all our post-1990 case studies, international institutions and NGOs have been the primary providers of humanitarian assistance. In Kosovo, KFOR initially provided humanitarian assistance as it moved into Kosovo. Within two months, KFOR transferred all these responsibilities to UNHCR, which coordinated deliveries of humani-

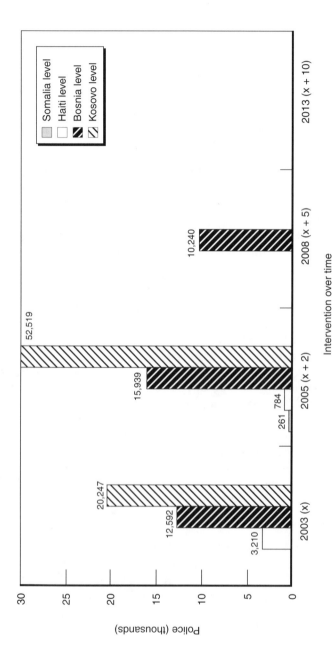

NOTE: Here, year x is the year of intervention, 2003.

Figure 10.2—International Police Projections for Iraq

tarian aid, primarily through NGOs, such as the Red Cross. The only exception to this pattern has been Afghanistan, where the U.S. military is taking a major role in providing humanitarian assistance.

In the immediate transition from combat to peace operations in Iraq, U.S. and United Kingdom military personnel have been the ones primarily responsible for the distribution of humanitarian relief. This approach has led to confusion over the role of USAID in the humanitarian aid process. More importantly, the U.S. and United Kingdom military face a number of challenges in pursuing this objective. For instance, military logistics systems were not designed and military personnel have not been trained for this role. NGOs and UN humanitarian agencies have already expressed discontent with the performance of the United Kingdom troops who distributed initial relief in southern Iraq.

Instead of relying heavily on the military, it makes sense to draw on international institutions and NGOs. The UN Office of the Humanitarian Coordinator in Iraq (UNOHCI) should serve as the primary coordinator for humanitarian assistance, working closely with other NGOs. Security in Iraq will probably be better than it was in Afghanistan, once coalition forces have deployed across the country effectively. This will make operating conditions for NGOs more secure. Some NGOs, such as the Red Crescent, have staff members who are native-language speakers and are familiar with local customs and problems. It could also be useful to request specific on-the-ground assistance from Arab countries. Although most Arab countries do not have extensive experience with disaster assistance, there is popular sympathy in the Arab world for the Iraqi people. The Gulf states will also have an economic and geopolitical interest in providing aid. An extra effort to involve Arab and Islamic institutions in humanitarian relief might stimulate the development of Arab NGOs, possibly setting up institutions that would compete with radical mosques that have taken the forefront in assisting the poor in most Muslim Middle Eastern countries. The Red Crescent will certainly be a valuable partner. At the same time, it will be important to guard against the use of Arab NGOs that may serve as conduits for terrorism and extremism.

The Oil-for-Food Programme provides a good institutional basis for distributing foodstuffs and other humanitarian assistance. Indeed, the World Food Program has expressed its determination to reinvigorate the distribution program. Distribution channels for importing and distributing food have been set up. The UN oversees the program, but Iraqis implement the distribution. The program should be able to expand to cover distribution of clothing and hygiene supplies, such as soap and water treatment tablets, without undue difficulty.

Civil Administration

As outlined above, the prospects for reconstruction of the civil administration in Iraq in the medium term are quite good. Revitalizing and reshaping the Iraqi economy will be crucial and feasible, drawing on the experience of international institutions, such as the IMF. Getting the civil administration back on its feet in the absence of the old regime's power structures and in light of the breakdown of law and order will be difficult but should not take too long, if adequate forces are provided. However, the most challenging questions that the United States faces in Iraq are over the broader program of political transition and democratization. Many lessons can be drawn from the case studies in this regard.

Leadership. Most international attention in the immediate postconflict period has focused on the question of who should lead reconstruction and nation-building in the interim before a stable and legitimate Iraqi administration emerges. At their summit meeting in Belfast on April 8, 2003, President Bush and Prime Minister Tony Blair proposed that the UN play a supporting role in providing humanitarian and financial aid and "advising" on political reform. This approach was confirmed in the draft U.S.-UK-Spanish UNSCR circulated in mid-May, which called for a "vital" UN role in "helping the formation of an Iraqi Interim Authority."[36] It is clear that prewar divisions affected this postwar debate, but it is useful to consider the longer-term lessons of the case studies. Recall that we concluded the following:

- Unilateral nation-building can be easier than multilateral efforts.
- Unilateral nation-building can be less effective than multilateral efforts at promoting regional reconciliation.

---

[36]10 Downing Street, "Draft Resolution Calls for Vital UN Role in Iraq," news release, May 12, 2003.

- The UN is an instrument through which national leadership can, with some difficulty, be exercised; it is not an alternative to such leadership.

- In peace operations, international military and civil functions should be closely coordinated and not rigidly divided.

In the short term, unilateral U.S. leadership in managing the civil and political transitions would likely lead to faster results and more rapid institutional change. However, a multilateral effort, particularly one conducted under UN auspices, may defuse popular resentment in Iraq and in the Arab world against U.S. "imperialism" and make it easier to ensure regional reconciliation and stability. The experiences of nation-building in the 1990s, however, demonstrate the importance of a careful balance. The UN Security Council, especially one as divided as it became in the run-up to the war, cannot exercise firm leadership. U.S. leadership will remain important, but the UN is a very important mechanism for legitimization and burden-sharing.

Whatever leadership mechanism is chosen, there are two important lessons to be drawn. First, it is vital to ensure close coordination between civil, economic, and military functions. In Afghanistan, these elements have been sadly fragmented. In Kosovo, they were better coordinated. Moreover, in Kosovo, the international authorities focused initially on macroeconomic stabilization and institution-building rather than on immediately trying to solve the underlying political problems of the disaffected province. Even if the United States or NATO retains the lead on military and security affairs, the chain of command needs to be closely engaged with the civil and economic chains of command, whether this is U.S.-led or international. It will also be important to transfer real administrative and civil authority to Iraqis as quickly as possible to avoid stoking resentment against either the United States or international agencies.

Is Democratization Feasible? Iraq has little history of democracy; most of its neighbors have fared no better, and there are clearly strong forces inside Iraq militating against democracy. Nonetheless, the case studies show that democracy is transferable and that democratic transformations can be aided by military occupation and can endure when the element of compulsion is removed. Moreover, democracy is transferable to non-Western, as well as to Western, societies.

Thus, there is no reason why Iraq cannot be democratized and establish democratic institutions and a pluralist polity. There are, however, a number of reasons why democratization will not be rapid or smooth in Iraq. The lack of a democratic experience and a tradition of authoritarian politics are complemented by the absence of agreement on power-sharing among the country's main ethnic, sectarian, and tribal groups. The hollowing out of the Iraqi middle class and a young population with little experience of the outside world do not provide a conducive environment for democratization. Existing power elites and the "shadow state" will resist transfer of power from their hands and may retain the economic and physical authority to undermine attempts to bring in new elites and power centers. Suspicion of the motives of the United States and United Kingdom, which many Iraqis will charge with having imperialist ambitions, may hamper progress.

Steps Toward Democratization. The initial approach toward democratization that the U.S. government championed envisaged a three-step process. First, authority would be vested in a U.S. military administration, with ORHA acting as the civil administrative arm. Second, an Iraqi Interim Authority would be created, to which civil authority would be gradually transferred. Third, an Iraqi constituent assembly would be convened, perhaps along the lines of the Afghan *loya jirga*, to elect a new Iraqi administration and possibly write a new Iraqi constitution. Under Lieutenant General Jay Garner, ORHA began the process of engaging Iraqi political groups and community leaders by holding "town hall" meetings across Iraq in mid-April.

As laid out in the discussion above, the construction of a democratic and pluralist Iraqi polity faces many challenges. Two of the most challenging issues will be drawing up a constitution able to meet Kurdish demands for autonomy, ensuring the construction of a democracy that will allow the disenfranchised majority to be represented, and protecting minority rights.

The case studies provide three lessons that may be of assistance in the Iraqi case:

- **The co-option of existing institutions can facilitate democratic transformation, but the results may sometimes be less thoroughgoing than starting anew.**

  Relying on existing Iraqi institutions, power networks, and notable figures after superficial "de-Baathification" will be the path of least resistance for the U.S. transition team. Co-opting these institutions will ensure that the civil administration is rapidly rebuilt and that stability is preserved. However, these institutions and individuals are likely to capture the political agenda and to ensure that resources remain centralized and that pluralism is undermined. A root-and-branch overhaul of state and political structures would involve the creation of wholly new organizations at the local and national levels and the recruitment, training, and management of new staff. This approach would be tremendously costly and would involve a long period of direct U.S. administration, akin to the early years of British administration of the Iraqi mandate or the Allied administration of Germany. It would, however, lay a sounder basis for long-term reform.

- **Elections are an important benchmark in progress toward democracy. Held too early at the national level, they can strengthen extremist and rejectionist forces rather than promote further transformation.**

  The case studies demonstrate that elections should start at the local level to allow the new balance of social and political forces to emerge and coalesce. While elections are an important tool to foster a spirit of pluralism, the lack of real party organizations in Iraq means that the electoral process will have to be gradual. Holding local elections around the 8- to 12-month mark seems to be reasonable. National elections around the two-year mark may then also be reasonable.

- **Imposed justice can contribute to transformation.**

  There is now extensive international experience with different models of postdictatorship and postconflict justice, ranging from efforts to draw a line under the past through a "truth and reconciliation" process, as in South Africa, to pursuing criminal prosecutions, as in the cases of Germany and Bosnia. Bringing senior figures accused of human rights abuses to justice is an important step and can assist in democratic transformation. As far as possible, the new Iraqi administration needs to determine the process and its extent, but the UN may be suited to provide judicial mechanisms. An important adjunct to this process will be the peaceful resolution of conflicts over property between victims of Saddam Hussein and his beneficiaries.

Reconstruction

A number of factors contribute to generating substantial sustained increases in economic output over long periods. Unfortunately, Iraq does not currently possess such key attributes as a highly educated population and well-developed transport and communications infrastructures. On the other hand, it does have a better-educated population and better infrastructures than many other countries in the world. It also has a well-developed petroleum industry and very large petroleum reserves. More importantly, Iraq should be able to create institutions and implement policies conducive to long-term growth. Below, we discuss "best practice" policies for fostering economic growth in postconflict Iraq.

The first order of business, as in any postconflict situation, will be establishing personal security for the Iraqi people and ensuring that they are fed and clothed. Next, the postconflict authority will need to create a framework for providing economic stability. Finally, the authority will need to create institutions and implement policies that are conducive to economic growth.

Just as unity of command is important for security and civil administration, so it is for economic reconstruction and development. Afghanistan has demonstrated the perils of allowing a "free-for-all" among international financial institutions and donors, while Kosovo provides a good example of centralized economic authority able to take decisive and rapid decisions. The United States would be advised to put in place a clear line of authority on economic matters, reporting to the head of the civil administration.

The following are the most pressing issues affecting the economic stabilization of Iraq:

1. controlling inflation and stabilizing the value of the currency
2. ensuring the solvency of the financial system

3. ensuring the security of property
4. rebuilding the oil sector
5. setting price, trade, and fiscal policies
6. beginning reconstruction
7. revitalizing the agricultural sector
8. resolving foreign-debt issues.

Controlling Inflation. Iraq is currently a multicurrency economy. A large share of the financial assets of both households and businesses is in foreign currencies. The dinar, the domestic currency, is used primarily for transactions. To create stable conditions for growth, the postconflict authority will have to restore confidence in the domestic currency. Iraq has a central bank and a cadre of nationals, at home and abroad, with experience in central banking or international financial markets. The IMF has a substantial amount of expertise in helping countries set up and operate central banks and the requisite statistical systems needed for a central bank to function effectively. The IMF has played a key role in setting up new monetary authorities in Afghanistan, Bosnia, and Kosovo and has provided assistance to Haiti. Asking the IMF to provide support for reviving Iraq's central bank and financial statistical system would be the best approach to creating an institutional framework for a new Iraqi financial system.

The IMF, if involved in postconflict Iraq, will have its own ideas on exchange-rate policy. However, the case studies analyzed in this report suggest that the best initial policy is a pegged exchange-rate regime. Germany, Japan, and Bosnia pegged their currencies to a foreign currency. Kosovo has adopted the euro. Because of Afghanistan's chaotic situation and limited financial resources, it is using a floating exchange rate.

Initially, pegs are preferable to free floats because they provide a nominal anchor for all economic actors—households, businesses, and the government. Because households and businesses already save in foreign currencies, the peg facilitates economic calculations, reduces uncertainty, and provides a medium-term guarantee for holders of the domestic currency. It also helps control inflation after a conflict, as import competition forestalls rapid increases in prices. Because of the potential size of Iraq's economy and its dependence on oil for export earnings, Iraq is likely to want to adopt a floating exchange-rate system in the medium or long term. As a consequence, the Bosnian currency board option would be inappropriate for Iraq because it would make the transition from a fixed exchange rate to a floating rate more difficult. For the same reasons, adopting a foreign currency as the national currency would not be in Iraq's long-term interests.

To operate a pegged exchange-rate system, the Iraqi central bank will need adequate reserves. The U.S. government or other parties will need to loan the Iraqi central bank sufficient reserves immediately in the postconflict phase to make a pegged regime credible. Although the IMF may eventually provide substitute or additional financing, it is unlikely that it will be able to act quickly enough to provide the necessary funds. Because the reserves needed to operate a pegged exchange-rate system for a country the size of Iraq are likely to be sizable, the U.S. government should be prepared to advance the necessary funds very quickly.

Financial System. We assume that Iraq's commercial and retail banks, Rafidian and Rasheed, are technically insolvent. The immediate task is to restore a national payment system. Such a system is highly important for facilitating money transfers, both within the country and from expatriate Iraqis abroad to family and friends within the country. A payment system will also quickly become important for relief efforts because it is needed to transfer funds for payment of local staff and for supplies. In Kosovo, branches of the central monetary authorities served as deposit-taking institutions and made money transfers. Although this is not a good long-term solution, it was very effective on a short-term basis.

The re-creation of a domestic financial system is fraught with hazards. Banking crises and panics have been a principal cause of recession throughout the world. In the case of Iraq, the postconflict authorities will probably inherit a series of bankrupt state-owned banks. In addition, Iraq, like all Middle Eastern countries, is home to a large number of private moneychangers, who transfer money among themselves through what are referred to as *hawala networks*.

The reconstitution of Iraq's financial system needs to proceed cautiously, on a market basis. In the more-successful cases we studied, the banking system grew in tandem with the recovery in economic activity. In many cases, the initial demand for financial services was primarily restricted to holding savings and making payments. Lending was not a precondition for jump-starting economic growth. It emerged naturally as the recovery became stronger.

To create a solid financial system after the reconstitution of the central bank, the postconflict authorities will need to set up clear bank licensing procedures, set high minimum capital requirements, and create a strong bank supervisory branch within the central bank. These are prerequisites for a solid private banking system. The IMF has successfully helped Bosnia and Kosovo set up these systems and should be tasked with helping in Iraq as well. The postconflict authorities should then open up a level playing field for domestic and foreign investors to create new banks or purchase state-owned banks in Iraq through open tendering procedures. Historically, Iraq has had a domestic banking system. A number of Iraqis at home and abroad have the financial experience to run banks profitably.

That said, most countries have found that purely domestic banking systems are more vulnerable to runs and fraud than those in which foreign banks have an appreciable market share. It is highly probable that a number of the banks in the Persian Gulf would be interested in investing in Iraq, although probably not in the immediate aftermath of the conflict. Western banks may eventually be interested as well. In the interim, the postconflict authorities will inherit the formerly state-owned banks. They will need to set up strong boards of directors and probably partner Iraqi staff with experienced foreign staff to clean up and run these institutions. Some assistance programs in other countries have focused on creating such financial institutions as cooperative banks, microlending facilities, and regular commercial banks, with mixed success. Some cooperative and commercial banks that have received assistance have gone bankrupt, and some microlending programs have had extraordinarily high transaction costs per dollar lent. In our view, at the early postconflict stage, energies would be better spent on expanding the payment system throughout the country and delaying assistance in creating financial institutions until the economy has stabilized and the postconflict authorities have a better sense of the remaining weaknesses of the financial system.

Property Ownership. An endemic problem of authoritarian regimes is the concentration of ownership in the hands of associates of the leaders of the former regime. Iraq is no exception. Adjudication of ownership disputes tends to be a lengthy, difficult process that usually has to involve an impartial arbitrator or judge and a system of property law. In the case of Iraq, we believe the postconflict authorities should take control of companies owned by the Iraqi government or associates of the current regime in the name of a future government of Iraq. The postconflict authorities will need to provide a legal promise to current owners that their claims will eventually be adjudicated through a transparent legal process but at an indeterminate time in the future. No promises concerning the extent of compensation, if any, should be made.

As with the banking system, teams of foreign managers should be sought to reorganize and operate each company in conjunction with Iraqi staff. Best practice in this regard consists of partnering each foreign manager in the team with an Iraqi counterpart who can expect to take over the responsibilities of the foreign manager gradually. Lower-level foreign staff members are usually the first to depart; the positions of chief executive officer, controller, and chief financial officer are usually the last to be turned over to local management. Strong boards of directors need to be created for each company that includes Iraqi and foreign directors. Partnering is probably essential because indigenous managers lack the expertise or incentives to reorganize state-owned companies in a way that will encourage enduring incentives to improve efficiency and controls to prevent the divergence of funds.

Despite the economic benefits of private ownership, it would be inadvisable in our view to embark on a privatization program until a national Iraqi government is set up. The postconflict authorities can encourage such a government to embark on a privatization program and explain the benefits of privatization. However, a number of countries, such as the United States, have state-owned companies, especially in the areas of transportation, electric power, natural gas, telecommunications, and energy extraction. The privatization of these entities is often very controversial. For example, proposals to privatize the Tennessee Valley Authority in the United States have been repeatedly blocked in Congress. In our view, it is more appropriate to have elected Iraqi authorities, not the postconflict authority, make these decisions. Uncontrolled privatization can also result in the wholesale transfer of state assets to well-placed individuals, as was often the case in post-Soviet Russia.

The Oil Sector. The future control of Iraq's state-owned oil companies is a particularly knotty instance of the disposal of state property. It is also a matter that cannot be decided on economic grounds alone. Although Saddam Hussein's Iraq, like many of its Gulf neighbors, was moving to give foreign oil companies a greater role in the development of Iraqi oil deposits, memories of the struggle against British control of Iraqi oil are very recent in Iraqi minds. Although Iraq's oil sector needs foreign expertise and capital, it is important not to allow opponents of an interim authority to make capital out of nationalist populism.

Nonetheless, on economic grounds, major reform will be required. State-owned energy companies around the world have tended to become enclaves unto themselves. Managers of these companies and their associates, political or otherwise, have been able to divert revenues into their own pockets or for their own political purposes. Overmanning and inefficient operations are often the norm.

Pairing foreign staff with Iraqi staff in state-owned firms, including in the oil sector, and establishing strong boards of directors will partially mitigate this problem. In addition, the postconflict authority should set up transparent royalty and tax systems to deal with the oil sector. These can eventually be applied uniformly to all future participants in the oil sector. Too often, state-owned oil companies are treated as treasuries from which revenues can be diverted at will. A clear, transparent energy tax code will ensure both that the Iraqi government can rely on a clearly defined set of tax revenues from the oil sector and that state-owned companies will be able to retain sufficient funds to conduct their own operations efficiently.

Under Saddam Hussein, the Iraqi oil industry consisted of a number of state-owned oil companies under the authority of the Ministry of Oil. However, the ministry acted more as a holding company than a regulatory agency. The Iraqi government exercised tight control over the industry, hiring and firing managers. Although the technical expertise of many of these managers has been rated highly by some observers, the industry still is inefficient. To improve the efficiency and transparency of the industry, the postconflict authority should break up the industry into production companies and independent refining and distribution companies. Oil production is capital intensive and politically sensitive. Refineries are also capital intensive. In the distribution business (filling stations), on the other hand, firms face limited barriers to entry. By removing all remaining barriers to entry into distribution, the postconflict authorities will provide opportunities for the Iraqi private sector and create competition for state-owned distributors. In the refining sector, the postconflict authorities can create competition by opening the economy to imports of refined oil products. Iraqi refineries are reportedly in disrepair. In light of the surfeit of refinery capacity in the Persian Gulf, it does not seem wise to divert limited Iraqi resources to rebuilding or expanding refinery capacity unless market forces indicate that this would be profitable. By placing Iraq's refinery operations in independent companies and forcing them to compete against imports, the managers of these companies will be better able to determine the extent to which investment in refinery operations is warranted.

An elected Iraqi government can impose additional disciplines on the state-owned oil companies by setting up clear, transparent procedures for tendering for exploration and development blocks. Blocks would be awarded on the basis of the highest bid. An elected Iraqi government might wish to provide more-favorable terms for domestic or state-owned oil companies, much as the U.S. government provides more-favorable contract opportunities for small businesses in the United States. However, these concessions need to be set ahead of time and made public. In addition, bids should be opened and judged by a board that initially includes representatives of the postconflict authorities. All bids should be published, and the criteria for choosing the winner should be explained.

Such a system assumes that royalties and corporate income taxes will be in line with international practices and will not be confiscatory. Some commentators appear to equate Iraqi oil revenues with potential Iraqi government revenues. This is not the case. Two well-regarded policy briefs argue that the oil industry has suffered from inadequate expenditures on maintenance and development of new fields.[37] Any new taxation system on oil companies needs to be structured so that companies can obtain an adequate rate of return.

---

[37]Edward P. Djerejian, Frank G. Wisner, Rachel Bronson, and Andrew S. Weiss, *Guiding Principles for U.S. Post-Conflict Policy in Iraq*, New York: Council on Foreign Relations Press, 2003, and Frederick D. Barton, and Bathsheba N. Crocker, *A Wiser Peace: An Action Strategy for a Post-Conflict Iraq*, Washington, D.C.: Center for Strategic and International Studies, January 2003.

This implies that tax revenues from oil will be constrained by the international oil market and Iraqi oil companies' financial performance. The postconflict authorities need to resist the temptation to treat the industry as a revenue source rather than a business.

Price, Trade, and Fiscal Policies. Monetary and exchange-rate policies should stabilize the Iraqi currency and quell inflation fairly quickly; humanitarian assistance should provide a minimum level of subsistence to all Iraqis. However, the policies the postconflict authorities pursue and the associated public expenditures will heavily influence reconstruction and economic growth.

Under Saddam Hussein, Iraq was cut off from the global economy. The country relied almost exclusively on oil for export revenues, and oil also provided the bulk of government revenues. The government used some of these revenues to support the population, in the forms of food deliveries and subsidized health care, education, and utilities. The government was also the largest employer.

Some have argued that oil is a curse rather than benefit for the economic development of nations. They point to Angola, Nigeria, Venezuela, and some North African and Middle Eastern countries as examples of states that have failed to develop economically despite their oil wealth or have become totally reliant on their energy sectors for economic growth. On the other hand, a number of countries, including Malaysia, Mexico, China, and Egypt, have benefited from tax and export revenues from oil even as other sectors of their economies have enjoyed rapid growth. The differences between the experiences of these two sets of countries tend to lie in their economic policies, especially those concerning trade, prices, and industry.

Given the seven case studies and the experience of the more-successful energy exporters, the postconflict authority in Iraq should immediately liberalize trade. In light of the availability of tax revenues from oil exports, the postconflict authorities would be well advised to eliminate all tariffs and thereby incentives for smuggling. Smuggling has been a key source of income for warlords and criminal bosses in Bosnia, Kosovo, and Afghanistan. Eliminating this potential source of revenue for similar individuals in Iraq would make it much more difficult for them to retain or gain power, as much of their authority is based on their ability to employ armed young men to terrorize their local communities.

Trade liberalization assumes price liberalization. The postconflict authorities should eschew any attempts to set prices, except for public monopolies that are also natural monopolies. For example, the state-owned oil company should be free to set prices at market-clearing levels but should also be subject to competition from imports. In the instance of natural monopolies, the postconflict authorities will have to make short-term decisions on pricing, basing them on comparable prices elsewhere or cost-recovery levels. Wherever possible, the authorities should introduce competition and remove themselves from price-setting activities. Eventually, an Iraqi government will need to create transparent systems for rate-setting and to appoint rate-setting authorities for the remaining national monopolies, but these activities are not a short-term priority.

The postconflict authorities will not have time to revamp the Iraqi legal system immediately. This is a long-term process that would be best for a representative government of Iraq to undertake. However, the postconflict authorities can simplify the system of registering and incorporating new businesses and ensure that licensing and regulatory systems are not set up to extort money from private businesses. Eliminating these barriers to entry will be key to restarting the economy.

The postconflict authorities should begin to introduce other types of taxes as soon as practical. Excise taxes on refined oil products are highly beneficial because they encourage more-efficient use of this national resource. They are also easier to collect than customs duties on consumer goods. The postconflict authorities should also plan for the gradual imposition of sales taxes, which would eventually be converted to a value-added tax. Payroll and income taxes can also be gradually introduced, as well as corporate profit taxes. Payroll taxes should be tied to pension and health-insurance systems because participation in these systems can be used as an incentive for compliance.

However, fiscal expenditures should not initially be constrained by tax collections. The experience of other postconflict countries shows that, in the immediate aftermath of conflict, tax revenues are minuscule. Initially, it is more important to restart the functions of the government, relying on external assistance to cover costs than to try to maximize tax revenues in the immediate aftermath of the war. The postconflict authorities need to ensure that effective systems are operating for paying government employees, especially teachers, health care workers, police, and firefighters. These payments help jump-start the economy because they ensure that, in every community, at least a few families are receiving a regular income. In addition, the postconflict authorities need to ensure that Iraqi pensioners are paid.

Reconstruction. The Kosovo case shows that government expenditures should be split between operating expenditures and capital expenditures. To reform government operations, as in state-owned companies, foreign staff should be recruited to work in tandem with Iraqi counterparts to revamp and help run Iraqi ministries. Government operations should be sized to correspond to likely future levels of tax revenues and then be constrained to these activities.

As in Kosovo, separate government entities should be established to supervise reconstruction. All domestic and foreign funds should be channeled through these entities. Again, foreign staff should be partnered with Iraqis to determine priorities for reconstruction, let and manage bids, conduct project audits, and release payments. All projects should be open to international tender, but stipulations concerning employment of Iraqi citizens and more-favorable treatment of Iraqi bidders may be in order.

The postconflict authorities need to confine their reconstruction activities to publicly owned infrastructure. Housing reconstruction is best stimulated by providing construction materials for households whose dwellings have sustained war damage. Otherwise, this sector can fend for itself. If tax systems are set up appropriately and if international oil companies are permitted to tender for blocks, the oil industry can also fend for itself. In a few instances involving capital-intensive industries, such as cement plants and oil refineries, the postconflict authorities could permit the reconstruction authority to authorize loans to the industries involved. However, the bulk of the reconstruction authority's activities should focus on reconstruction of transport infrastructure and public utilities, such as water and sewage. In these instances, grants may be in order. However, reconstruction of telecommunications and electric power grids should be financed by loans, repayable to the reconstruction agency.

A few brave souls have attempted to estimate the cost of reconstructing Iraq. We will not venture to do that here. Nonetheless, some observations are warranted concerning likely future government revenues and potential expenditures on reconstruction. As noted above, Iraq's oil production hit a post–Gulf War peak of 2.571 mbd in 2000, slipped to 2.432 mbd in 2001, then fell by an additional 20 percent in 2002, before rising in the first quarter of 2003. Oil industry observers argue that the recent decline is due to inadequate maintenance and depletion of existing wells and that substantial investment will be necessary to boost production to 3.5 mbd, the previous peak. The total value of Iraqi production in 2000 was about $25 billion, but this fell to an estimated $19.4 billion in 2001 and to roughly the same level in 2002. These are, of course, gross figures. Production costs, suitable depreciation allowances, and capital expenditures would greatly reduce the amount. If the Iraqi state-owned oil companies were to win exploration and production contracts, a substantial share of net revenues would be needed for development, at least until foreign financial institutions felt comfortable lending to such entities.

These figures suggest that, initially, Iraq will require substantial external funds for humanitarian assistance and budgetary support. Taxes on the oil sector are highly unlikely to be adequate to fund the reconstruction of the Iraqi economy in the immediate future. Judging by the experiences of Kosovo and Bosnia, which have higher per capita incomes than Iraq, budgetary support will be necessary for quite some time. In fact, in the case of operating expenditures, the postconflict authorities should first establish a reasonable level of expenditures, create a transparent tax system, and ask foreign donors to pick up the difference until Iraq gets on its feet. We believe this will be the most efficacious avenue to economic recovery.

While it is too early to predict the required levels of foreign aid accurately, we can draw comparisons from our other case studies. As Figure 10.3 demonstrates, supplying Iraq a level of foreign aid equivalent to that provided to Bosnia would require $36 billion over the next two years, which is equivalent to 16 percent of Iraq's GDP in 2001. Conversely, aid at the same level as Afghanistan would total $1 billion over the next two years and would constitute about 1 percent of GDP.

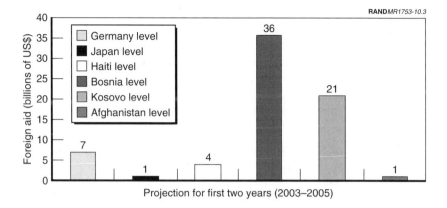

Projection for first two years (2003–2005)

Figure 10.3—Scenarios of External Assistance to Iraq

It would probably not be helpful for postconflict authorities to provide traditional development assistance to Iraq. Foreign assistance
programs are frequently criticized for trying to do too much with too
little. Providing foreign staff to help run government ministries in
conjunction with Iraqi partners and fully funding Iraqi government
operations, especially in education and health care, would be far
more effective uses of donor money than demonstration projects
would be. Only after a period of recovery and economic stabilization
would it be wise to consider starting more-traditional assistance programs, such as rural development and aid to small and medium
businesses, for which the track record is mixed. The postconflict
authority would be much better advised to focus first on making the
Iraqi government apparatus work well and only then turn to more
traditional, targeted development programs.

Agricultural Sector. In this regard, the postconflict authorities need
to be aware of the effects of assistance programs on various
economic sectors, especially agriculture. After an initial period, the
postconflict authorities should move from providing in-kind humanitarian assistance to alleviating poverty through targeted financial
assistance. Historically, Iraq has been an agricultural country. If food
is sold at market-clearing prices, farmers will have an incentive to
compete with imports. In this context, "dumping" U.S. or European
agricultural surpluses on Iraqi markets through Oil-for-Food or other

such programs should be discouraged and ended before the first planting because market prices have a heavy influence on farmer behavior. Because rural households tend to be the poorest, providing targeted financial assistance, as opposed to free agricultural commodities, will help them generate economic activity and income. In the medium and longer terms, the Iraqi government will have to address the structural challenges the Iraqi agricultural sector faces, including land reform and mechanization.

Iraqi Debt and Other Obligations. The Center for Strategic and International Studies estimates that total foreign claims on Iraq run $383 billion.[38] Of the total, claims remaining from the first Gulf War constitute about $199 billion (52 percent); foreign debt makes up about $127 billion (33 percent); and the remainder represents money Iraq is obligated to pay on various contracts, amounting to about $57.2 billion (15 percent).

Some of the pending contracts may be abrogated under *force majeure* provisions; others are being sorted out and honored through the Oil-for-Food Programme. It appears likely that contracts that provide needed, legitimate imports will be honored, while others, undertaken to provide goods to satisfy Saddam, probably will not.

The 1990–1991 Gulf War reparations are a stickier issue. The UN has recognized these obligations, and it created a system to adjudicate claims and sequester funds from Iraqi oil export revenues to pay them. Initially, Germany and Japan made some reparations. However, the U.S. occupying authorities quickly judged that the economic costs of transferring resources during the initial recovery period were so large that they were curtailing economic recovery. Reparations were scaled back and then halted, although after a period of economic growth, Japan and Germany provided substantial compensation or aid to a number of countries and individuals that suffered during World War II. In light of the costs of reconstruction that Iraq is likely to face, reparations would impose a considerable burden on the country that would slow economic recovery. The post–World War II experience suggests that forgiving reparations would greatly benefit Iraq's recovery. The U.S. government may have

---

[38]Barton and Crocker (2003), Supplement I.

to take the lead at the UN to argue for the reduction or elimination of reparations in the postconflict period.

According to the Center for Strategic and International Studies, Iraq's total foreign debt could run $127 billion, which includes an estimated $12 billion debt to Russia and a $47 billion debt to banks and governments from the Gulf Cooperation Council states. Iraq owes the rest to a variety of creditors, including a number of Eastern European and Middle Eastern states. In addition, unpaid interest is an estimated $47 billion.

Iraq's creditors do not have a strong hand. Iraq has not made payments on its foreign debts since the mid-1980s, when Iraq was entangled in the Iran-Iraq War. Iraqi paper is worthless on international financial markets. Notional debt levels are such that creditors have no prospect of Iraq fully servicing this debt. In such situations, creditors meet with the borrower and reduce the country's obligations to levels that can be serviced. The other option is continued nonpayment.

In our view, since Iraq is highly unlikely to be able to borrow on commercial terms for quite some time, debt renegotiations are not a pressing issue and can be postponed until an Iraqi government is formed. Iraq has no outstanding obligations to the IMF, so it is in a position to draw upon assistance from the IMF as soon as a new government is recognized. Moreover, debt negotiations almost invariably take years to conclude. Consequently, although useful, they are unlikely to be concluded in the near future and are not an overly pressing issue for the postconflict authorities or even a newly constituted Iraqi government. Russia and, to a lesser extent, France have rejected this view. Russian President Vladimir Putin, in particular, has stated that Russia has no intention of paying for the 2003 Iraqi war by forgiving debt owed it. However, having joined the Paris club of creditors, Russia is likely to find it most effective to pursue its claims within the club's negotiations. It is difficult to see how these negotiations will proceed quickly, leaving Russia and other Iraqi creditors cooling their heels.

As it embarks on its most ambitious program of nation-building since 1945, the United States can learn important lessons from the case studies we have examined. It has staked its credibility on a successful outcome in Iraq. This will require an extensive commitment of financial, personnel, and diplomatic resources over a long period. The United States cannot afford to contemplate early exit strategies and cannot afford to leave the job half completed. The real question for the United States should not be how soon it can leave, but rather how fast and how much to share power with Iraqis and the international community while retaining enough power to oversee an enduring transition to democracy and stability.

PROGRESS TO DATE

In its early months, the U.S.-led stabilization and reconstruction of Iraq has not gone as smoothly as might have been expected, given the abundant, recent, and relevant U.S. experience highlighted in this study. This is, after all, the sixth major nation-building enterprise the United States has mounted in 12 years and the fifth such in a Muslim nation. In many of the previous cases, the United States and its allies have faced similar challenges immediately after an intervention. Somalia, Haiti, Kosovo, and Afghanistan also experienced the rapid and utter collapse of central state authority. In each of these instances, local police, courts, penal services, and militaries were destroyed, disrupted, disbanded, or discredited and were consequently unavailable to fill the postconflict security gap. In Somalia, Bosnia, Kosovo, and Afghanistan, extremist elements emerged to fill the resultant vacuum of power. In most cases, organized crime quickly became a major challenge to the occupying authority. In Bosnia and Kosovo, the external stabilization forces ultimately proved adequate to surmount these security challenges; in Somalia and Afghanistan, they did not or have not yet.

Over the past decade, the United States has made major investments in the combat efficiency of its forces. The return on investment has been evident in the dramatic improvement in warfighting demonstrated from Desert Storm to the Kosovo air campaign to Operation Iraqi Freedom. There has been no comparable increase in the capacity of U.S. armed forces or of U.S. civilian agencies to conduct postcombat stabilization and reconstruction operations. Throughout the 1990s, the management of each major mission showed some limited advance over its predecessor, but in the current decade, even this modestly improved learning curve has not been sustained. The Afghan mission can certainly be considered an improvement over Somalia but cannot yet be assessed as being more successful than

Haiti. It is too early to evaluate the success of the postconflict mission in Iraq, but its first few months do not raise it above those in Bosnia and Kosovo at a similar stage.

Nation-building has been a controversial mission over the past decade, and the intensity of this debate has undoubtedly inhibited the investments that would be needed to do these tasks better. Institutional resistance in departments of State and Defense, neither of which regard nation-building among their core missions, has also been an obstacle. As a result, successive administrations have treated each new mission as if it were the first and, more importantly, as if it were the last.

This expectation is unlikely to be realized anytime soon. Since the end of the Cold War, the United States has become increasingly involved in nation-building operations. In the 1990s, the Clinton administration conducted a major nation-building intervention, on the average, every two years. The current administration, despite a strong disinclination to engage U.S. armed forces in such activities, has launched two major nation-building enterprises within 18 months. It now seems clear that nation-building is the inescapable responsibility of the world's only superpower. Once that recognition is more widely accepted, there is much the United States can do to better prepare itself to lead such missions.

NATION-BUILDING IN IRAQ:
IRAQ CONFERENCE PARTICIPANTS

Frederick Barton
Center for Strategic and
International Studies

Carl Bildt
RAND

Derek Boothby

Anthony Brenton
British Embassy

Richard Caplan
Oxford University

Frank Carlucci
RAND

Patrick Clawson
Washington Institute for
Near East Policy

Keith Crane
RAND

Graham Day
Office of the High
Representative

James Dobbins
RAND

Michael Doyle
Princeton University

Bill Durch
Stimson Center

Manfred Eisele

Scott Feil
Institute for Defense
Analyses

Robert Gelbard

David Harland
UN Department of
Peacekeeping Operations

Ray Jennings
United States Institute of
Peace

Seth Jones
RAND

Bernard Kouchner

Rollie Lal
RAND

Robert Malley
International Crisis Group

Gail McGinn
Office of the Secretary of
Defense

Jerry McGinn
RAND

Mark Medish
Akin, Gump, Strauss, Hauer
and Feld, LLP

Eric Morris
UNHCR

Kendall Myers
U.S. Department of State

Robert Oakley
National Defense University

Jim O'Brien
The Albright Group, LLC

Dick Owens
Office of Reconstruction and
Humanitarian Assistance

Kenneth Pollack
Brookings Institution

Andrew Rathmell
RAND

Kim Savit
Senate Committee on
Foreign Relations

Miriam Schafer
RAND

Jim Schear
National Defense University

Michael Schoenbaum
RAND

Eric Schwartz
Council on Foreign Relations

Steven Simon
RAND

Walter Slocombe
Caplin & Drysdale

Julia Taft
UN Bureau for Crisis
Prevention and Management

Dov Zakheim
U.S. Department of Defense

Fatemeh Ziai
UN Office of the Secretary
General

10 Downing Street, "Draft Resolution Calls for Vital UN Role in Iraq," news release, May 12, 2003. Online at http://www.pm.gov.uk/output/page3649.asp (as of June 12, 2003).

Addis Ababa Declaration—*see* Fourth Coordination Meeting on Humanitarian Assistance for Somalia.

Agreed Points on Russian Participation in KFOR (Helsinki Agreement), signed by the Secretary of Defense of the United States and the Minister of Defense of the Russian Federation at Helsinki, Finland, June 18, 1999. Online at http://www.nato.int/kfor/kfor/documents/helsinki.htm (as of June 25, 2003).

Alden, Jane M., "Occupation," in Hugh Borton, ed., *Japan*, Ithaca, N.Y.: Cornell University Press, 1950.

al-Khalil, Samir, *Republic of Fear*, London: Hutchinson, 1989.

Art, Robert J., and Patrick M. Cronin, eds., *The United States and Coercive Diplomacy*, Washington, D.C.: United States Institute of Peace Press, 2003.

Asahi Shimbun Staff, *The Pacific Rivals*, New York: Weatherhill, 1972.

Ayubi, Nazih, *Overstating the Arab State*, London: I. B. Tauris, 1994.

Baerwald, Hans, "The Purge of Japanese Leaders Under the Occupation," in Livingston, Oldfather, and Moore (1974), pp. 36–42.

Barton, Frederick D., and Bathsheba N. Crocker, *A Wiser Peace: An Action Strategy for a Post-Conflict Iraq*, Washington, D.C.: Center for Strategic and International Studies, January 2003.

Batatu, Hanna, *The Old Social Classes and the Revolutionary Movements of Iraq*, Princeton, N.J.: Princeton University Press, 1978.

Beeston, Richard, Michael Evans, and Ian Brodie, "Pentagon Refuses to Send Troops to Serb Area," *London Times*, February 29, 2000, p. 13.

Bensahel, Nora, *The Coalition Paradox: The Politics of Military Cooperation*, dissertation, Stanford, Calif.: Stanford University, 1999.

_____, "Humanitarian Relief and Nation Building in Somalia," in Art and Cronin (2003), pp. 20–56.

Bentley, David, "Operation Uphold Democracy: Military Support for Democracy in Haiti," *Strategic Forum*, No. 78, June 1996.

Bentley, David, and Robert Oakley, "Peace Operations: A Comparison of Somalia and Haiti," *Strategic Forum*, No. 30, May 1995.

Biddiscombe, Perry, *The Last Nazis*, Stroud, United Kingdom: Tempus Publishing, 2000.

Bildt, Carl, "Holbrooke's History," *Survival*, Vol. 40, No. 3, Autumn 1998a, pp. 187–191

_____, *Peace Journey: The Struggle for Peace in Bosnia*, London: Weidenfeld and Nicholson, 1998b.

Bonn Agreement—*see* United Nations (2001).

Bowden, Mark, *Black Hawk Down: A Story of Modern War*, New York: Atlantic Monthly Press, 1999.

Brooke, James, "U.S. Tasks in Afghan Desert: Hunt Taliban, Tote Plywood," *New York Times*, September 14, 2002, p. A1.

Burns, Robert, "US to Limit Kosovo Patrols," Associated Press, February 29, 2000.

Bush, George W., speech on the future of Iraq, delivered to members of the American Enterprise Institute at the Washington Hilton Hotel, Washington, D.C., February 26, 2003.

Byman, Daniel, Ian Lesser, Bruce Pirnie, Cheryl Benard, and Matthew Waxman, *Strengthening the Partnership: Improving Military Coordination with Relief Agencies and Allies in Humanitarian Operations*, Santa Monica, Calif.: RAND, MR-1185-AF, 2000.

Carafano, James J., "Swords into Plowshares: Postconflict Arms Management," *Military Review*, Vol. LXXVII, No. 6, November–December 1997.

_____, *Waltzing into the Cold War: The Struggle for Occupied Austria*, College Station, Tex.: Texas A&M University Press, 2002.

CARE International in Afghanistan, "A New Year's Resolution to Keep: Secure a Lasting Peace in Afghanistan," policy brief, January 2003.

_____, "Rebuilding Afghanistan: A Little Less Talk, a Lot More Action," policy brief, October 2002.

Center for Strategic and International Studies and the Association of the United States Army, "Post-Conflict Reconstruction Task Framework," May 2002. Online at http://www.pcrproject.org/framework.pdf (as of June 6, 2003).

_____, *Play to Win: Final Report of the Bi-Partisan Commission on Post-Conflict Reconstruction*, January 2003. Online at http://www.pcrproject.org/PCRFinalReport.pdf (as of June 3, 2003).

Charlier, L. M. Garry, "Review of the Impact and Effectiveness of Donor-Financed Emergency Poverty Alleviation Projects in Haiti Related to Basic Infrastructure Rehabilitation and Employment Generation," in The International Bank for Reconstruction and Development, *Haiti: The Challenges of Poverty Reduction*, Vol. 2, Washington, D.C., 17242-HA, August 1998.

Clark, Wesley K., *Waging Modern War: Bosnia, Kosovo, and the Future of Combat*, New York: PublicAffairs, 2002.

Clarke, Walter, "Failed Visions and Uncertain Mandates," in Clarke and Herbst (1997).

Clarke, Walter, and Jeffrey Herbst, eds., *Learning from Somalia*, Boulder, Colo.: Westview Press, 1997.

Cohen, Theodore, *Remaking Japan: The American Occupation as New Deal*, New York: The Free Press, 1987.

Collier, D., ed., *The New Authoritarianism in Latin America*, Princeton, N.J.: Princeton University Press, 1979.

Craig, Gordon A., *The Germans*, New York: Meridan, 1982.

Crane, Conrad C., *Landpower and Crises: Army Roles and Missions in Smaller-Scale Contingencies During the 1990s*, Carlisle, Pa.: U.S. Army War College, Strategic Studies Institute, January 2001.

Crane, Conrad C., and W. Andrew Terrill, *Reconstructing Iraq: Insights, Challenges, and Missions for Military Forces in a Post-Conflict Scenario*, Carlisle, Pa.: U.S. Army War College, Strategic Studies Institute, February 2003.

Crossette, Barbara, "UN Council Urged to Debate Political Future of Kosovo," *New York Times*, March 7, 2000, p. A6.

Crystal, Jill, "Authoritarianism and Its Adversaries in the Arab World," *World Politics*, January 1994, pp. 262–289.

Daalder, Ivo H., "Bosnia After SFOR: Options for Continued U.S. Engagement," *Survival*, Vol. 39, No. 4, Winter 1997–98, p. 6.

Daalder, Ivo H., and Michael E. O'Hanlon, *Winning Ugly: NATO's War to Save Kosovo*, Washington D.C.: The Brookings Institution, 2001.

Dahl, Fredrik, "First Kosovo Assembly Session Marred by Walkout," Reuters, December 10, 2001.

Dayton Accord—*see* Office of the High Representative.

Demekas, Dimitri G., Johannes Herderschee, and Davina F. Jacobs, *Kosovo: Progress in Institution Building and Economic Policy Chal-*

lenges, Washington, D.C.: International Monetary Fund, December 6, 2001.

_____, *Kosovo: Institutions and Policies for Reconstruction and Growth*, Washington, D.C.: International Monetary Fund, 2002.

Djerejian, Edward P., Frank G. Wisner, Rachel Bronson, and Andrew S. Weiss, *Guiding Principles for U.S. Post-Conflict Policy in Iraq*, New York: Council on Foreign Relations Press, 2003.

Dobbins, James, "Haiti: A Case Study on Post–Cold War Peacekeeping," remarks at the ISD Conference of Diplomacy and the Use of Force, Georgetown University, Washington, D.C., September 21, 1995.

DOS—*see* U.S. Department of State.

Dower, John W., *Embracing Defeat: Japan in the Wake of World War II*, New York: W. W. Norton & Company, 1999.

Duff, Ernest, and John McCamant, *Violence and Repression in Latin America: A Quantitative and Historical Analysis*, New York: The Free Press, 1976.

Duffield, John S., *Power Rules: The Evolution of NATO's Conventional Force Posture*, Stanford, Calif.: Stanford University Press, 1995.

Eisenstadt, Michael, and Eric Mathewson, eds., *U.S. Policy in Post-Saddam Iraq: Lessons from the British Experience*, Washington, D.C.: Washington Institute for Middle East Policy, 2003.

European Commission and World Bank, Office of South East Europe, Report on Progress Made in Committing, Contracting and Spending Donor Pledges to Kosovo, May 2002, p. 1. Online at http://www.seerecon.org/Kosovo/Reports/KosovoReportMarch2 001.htm (as of June 12, 2003).

Feil, Scott, "Building Better Foundations: Security in Postconflict Reconstruction," *The Washington Quarterly*, Vol. 25, No. 4, Autumn 2002, pp. 97–109.

Fineman, Mark, "U.S. Agency Offers Blueprint for Rebuilding Iraq," *Los Angeles Times*, March 21, 2003.

Fisk, Robert, "Return to Afghanistan: Americans Begin to Suffer Grim and Bloody Backlash," *The Independent*, August 14, 2002.

Flournoy, Michèle, "Interagency Strategy and Planning for Post-Conflict Reconstruction," draft white paper for the Post-Conflict Reconstruction Project, Center for Strategic and International Studies and the Association of the United States Army, March 27, 2002.

Flournoy, Michèle, and Michael Pan, "Dealing with Demons: Justice and Reconciliation," *The Washington Quarterly*, Vol. 25, No. 4, Autumn 2002, pp. 111–123.

Fourth Coordination Meeting on Humanitarian Assistance for Somalia, Addis Ababa Declaration, December 1, 1993. Published online by the Somalia Aid Coordination Body Secretariat, Nairobi, Kenya, at http://www.sacb.info/main_histdocs.htm (as of June 12, 2003).

Forman, Johanna Mendelson, "Achieving Socioeconomic Well-Being in Postconflict Settings," *The Washington Quarterly*, Vol. 25, No. 4, Autumn 2002, pp. 125–138.

French, Howard W., "A Nation Challenged: Donors," *New York Times*, January 22, 2002, p. A1.

Gaddis, John Lewis, *We Now Know: Rethinking Cold War History*, New York: Oxford University Press, 1997.

Gall, Carlotta, "Food and Hope Are Scarce for Returning Afghans," *New York Times*, September 17, 2002.

Ganzglass, Martin R., "The Restoration of the Somali Justice System," in Clarke and Herbst (1997), pp. 20–41.

Glasser, Susan, "Soldiers in Civilian Clothing," *Washington Post*, March 28, 2002.

Gray, Andrew, "Moderate Party Wins Plurality in Kosovo," *Washington Post*, November 20, 2001, p. 16.

Hamre, John J., and Gordon R. Sullivan, "Toward Postconflict Reconstruction," *The Washington Quarterly*, Vol. 25, No. 4, pp. 85–96.

Harding, James, and Frances Williams, "Over 4 Million Iraqis May Need Food Assistance in Long War," *Financial Times*, February 14, 2003, p. 7.

Harmon, Ernest N., *Combat Commander: Autobiography of a Soldier*, Englewood Cliffs, N.J.: Prentice-Hall, Inc., 1970.

Helsinki Agreement—*see* Agreed Points on Russian Participation in KFOR.

Hiltermann, Joost, *Bureaucracy of Repression: The Iraqi Government in Its Own Words*, New York: Human Rights Watch, February 1994.

Holbrooke, Richard, *To End a War*, New York: Random House, 1998.

Hosmer, Stephan T., *The Conflict over Kosovo: Why Milosevic Decided to Settle When He Did*, Santa Monica, Calif.: MR-1351-AF, RAND, 2001.

Huntington, Samuel, *Political Order in Changing Societies*, New Haven, Conn.: Yale University Press, 1968.

Huntington, Samuel, and Clement H. Moore, eds., *Authoritarian Politics in Modern Society: The Dynamics of Established One-Party Systems*, New York: Basic Books, 1970.

ICG—*see* International Crisis Group.

IMF—*see* International Monetary Fund.

InterAction, "Humanitarian Leaders Ask White House to Review Policy Allowing American Soldiers to Conduct Humanitarian Relief Programs in Civilian Clothes," news release, Washington, D.C., April 2, 2002.

International Committee of the Red Cross, *The Silent Menace: Landmines in Bosnia and Herzegovina*, Geneva, 1997.

International Crisis Group, *To Build a Peace: Recommendations for the Madrid Peace Implementation Council Meeting*, Washington, D.C., December 15, 1998. Available at http://www.crisisweb.org/ projects/showreport.cfm?reportid=173 (as of June 6, 2003).

_____, *Is Dayton Failing? Bosnia Four Years After the Peace Agreement*, Washington, D.C., October 28, 1999. Online at http://

www.crisisweb.org/projects/showreport.cfm?reportid=58 (as of June 6, 2003).

_____, *Kosovo Report Card*, No. 100, Pristina, Kosovo, and Brussels, Belgium, August 2000, pp. 42–46.

_____, *No Early Exit: NATO's Continuing Challenge in Bosnia*, Washington, D.C., ICG Balkans Report No. 110, May 22, 2001. Online at http://www.crisisweb.org/projects/showreport.cfm?reportid=297 (as of June 6, 2003).

_____, *A Kosovo Roadmap (I): Addressing Final Status*, Washington, D.C., ICG Balkans Report No. 124, March 1, 2002a. Online at http://www.crisisweb.org/projects/showreport.cfm?reportid=561 (as of June 6, 2003).

_____, *The Loya Jirga: One Small Step Forward?* Washington, D.C., May 16, 2002b. Online at http://www.crisisweb.org/projects/showreport.cfm?reportid=655 (as of June 12, 2003).

_____, *Return to Uncertainty: Kosovo's Internally Displaced and the Return Process*, Washington, D.C., ICG Balkans Report No. 139, December 13, 2002c. Online at http://www.crisisweb.org/projects/showreport.cfm?reportid=851 (as of June 6, 2003).

_____, *Afghanistan: Judicial Reform and Transitional Justice*, January 28, 2003a. Online at http://www.crisisweb.org/projects/showreport.cfm?reportid=879 (as of June 6, 2003).

_____, *War in Iraq: Political Challenges After the Conflict*, Washington, D.C., ICG Middle East Report No. 11, March 25, 2003b. Online at http://www.crisisweb.org/projects/showreport.cfm?reportid=927 (as of June 6, 2003).

International Institute for Strategic Studies, *The Military Balance 2000–2001*, Washington, D.C., 2001.

International Monetary Fund, *Bosnia and Herzegovina: Selected Issues*, Washington, D.C., IMF Staff Country Report No. 98/69, August 1998.

_____, *Islamic State of Afghanistan: Report on Recent Economic Developments and Prospects, and the Role of the Fund in the*

Reconstruction Process, Washington D.C., Country Report No. 02/219, October 2002.

_____, *Bosnia and Herzegovina: First Review of the Stand-By Arrangement and Request for Waiver of Performance Criteria*, Washington D.C., IMF Country Report No. 03/04, January 2003a.

_____, "IMF Concludes 2002 Article IV Consultation with Haiti," Washington D.C., Public Information Notice No. 03/23, March 3, 2003b.

International Security Force (KFOR) and the Governments of the Federal Republic of Yugoslavia and the Republic of Serbia, Military Technical Agreement, 2002. Online on the official Kosovo Force Web site: http://www.nato.int/kfor/kfor/documents/mta.htm (as June 12, 2003).

JCS—*see* U.S. Joint Chiefs of Staff.

Jesse, Jolene Kay, "Humanitarian Relief in the Midst of Conflict: The UN High Commissioner for Refugees in the Former Yugoslavia," Washington, D.C.: Georgetown University, Pew Case Studies in International Affairs, No. 471, 1996.

Kataoka, Tetsuya, *The Price of a Constitution: The Origin of Japan's Postwar Politics*, New York: Crane Russak, 1991.

Killick, John, *The United States and European Reconstruction: 1945–1960*, Edinburgh: Keele University Press, 1997.

Kim, Julie, *Bosnia: Civil Implementation of the Peace Agreement*, Washington, D.C.: Congressional Research Service, 1996.

Kraja, Garentina, "Kosovo Fails to Elect President," Associated Press, January 10, 2002.

Lakshmanan, Indira A. R., "Boredom Is Surgical Team's Ideal Battle-ground Scenario," *Boston Globe*, October 6, 2002, p. 16.

Lambeth, Benjamin S., *NATO's Air War for Kosovo: A Strategic and Operational Assessment*, Santa Monica, Calif.: RAND, MR-1365-AF, 2001.

Lampe, John R., *Yugoslavia as History: Twice There Was a Country*, New York: Cambridge University Press, 1996.

Leffler, Melvyn P., *A Preponderance of Power: National Security, the Truman Administration, and the Cold War*, Stanford, Calif.: Stanford University Press, 1992.

Livingston, Jon, Felicia Oldfather, and Joe Moore, eds., *Postwar Japan: 1945 to the Present*, New York: Pantheon Books, 1974.

Lovelock, Richard B., "The Evolution of Peace Operations Doctrine," *Joint Force Quarterly*, No. 30, Spring 2002, pp. 67–73.

MacArthur, Douglas, Reports of General MacArthur: The Campaigns of MacArthur in the Pacific, Vol. I, 1966a.

_____, Reports of General MacArthur: Japanese Operations in the Southwest Pacific Area, Volume II, Part II, 1966b.

Makiya, Kanan, *Cruelty and Silence*, London: Jonathan Cape, 1993.

Malcolm, Noel, *Kosovo: A Short History*, New York: HarperCollins, 1999.

Marrus, Michael R., *The Unwanted: European Refugees in the Twentieth Century*, New York: Oxford University Press, 1985.

Marten, Kimberly Zisk, "Defending Against Anarchy: From War to Peacekeeping in Afghanistan," *The Washington Quarterly*, Vol. 26, No. 1, Winter 2002–2003, pp. 35–52.

McGeehan, Robert, *The German Rearmament Question: American Diplomacy and European Defense After World War II*, Urbana, Ill.: University of Illinois Press, 1971.

McGinn, John G., "After the Explosion: International Action in the Aftermath of Nationalist War," *National Security Studies Quarterly*, Vol. 4, No. 1, Winter 1998, pp. 93–111.

_____, *Balancing Defense and Détente in NATO: The Harmel Report and the 1968 Crisis in Czechoslovakia*, dissertation, Washington, D.C.: Georgetown University, 2002.

Middle East Online, "US Strikes Accord with People's Mujahedeen," April 23, 2003. Online at http://www.middle-east-online.com/english/?id=5260 (as of June 12, 2003).

Natsios, Andrew S., "Humanitarian Relief Intervention in Somalia," in Clarke and Herbst (1997).

Oakley, Robert B., Michael J. Dziedzic, and Eliot M. Goldberg, eds., *Policing the New World Disorder: Peace Operations and Public Security*, Washington, D.C.: National Defense University Press, 1998.

Office of the High Representative, *The General Framework Agreement for Peace in Bosnia and Herzegovina* [the Dayton Accord], December 14, 1995. Online at http://www.ohr.int/dpa/default.asp?content_id=380 (as of June 6, 2003).

_____, OHR General Information Web site, ca. 2003. Online at http://www.ohr.int/ohr-info/gen-info/#4 (as of June 12, 2003).

_____, Peace Implementation Council Web page, 2003. Online at http://www.ohr.int/pic/archive.asp?sa=on (as of June 12, 2003).

The Organization for Security and Co-operation in Europe, *Kosovo/Kosova as Seen, as Told: The Human Rights Findings of the OSCE Kosovo Verification Mission*, Pts. I and II, Vienna: OSCE Secretariat, 1999.

Orr, Robert, "Governing When Chaos Rules: Enhancing Governance and Participation," *The Washington Quarterly*, Vol. 25, No. 4, Autumn 2002, pp. 139–152.

OSCE—*see* the Organization for Security and Co-operation in Europe.

Perito, Robert M., *The American Experience with Police in Peace Operations*, Clementsport, Nova Scotia: The Canadian Peacekeeping Press, 2002a.

_____, "'Odd Jobs': The Role of Special Police Units in Kosovo," draft paper, Washington, D.C.: United States Institute of Peace, July 25, 2002b.

Perlmutter, A., *Egypt: The Praetorian State*, New Brunswick, N.J.: Transaction Books, 1974.

_____, *The Military and Politics in Modern Times: On Professionals, Praetorians and Revolutionary Soldiers*, New Haven, Conn.: Yale University Press, 1977.

_____, *Modern Authoritarianism: A Comparative Institutional Analysis*, New Haven, Conn.: Yale University Press, 1981.

Peters, John E., Stuart Johnson, Nora Bensahel, Timothy Liston, and Traci Williams, *European Contributions to Operation Allied Force: Implications for Transatlantic Cooperation*, Santa Monica, Calif.: RAND, MR-1392-AF, 2001.

Peterson, Edward N., *The American Occupation of Germany: Retreat to Victory*, Detroit: Wayne State University Press, 1977.

Phillips, William R., "Civil-Military Cooperation: Vital to Peace Implementation in Bosnia," *NATO Review*, Vol. 46, No. 1, Spring 1998, pp. 22–25.

Pirnie, Bruce R., *Civilians and Soldiers: Achieving Better Coordination*, Santa Monica, Calif.: RAND, MR-1026-SRF, 1998.

Praso, Murat, "Demographic Consequences of the 1992–95 War," *Bosnia Report*, No. 16, July–October 1996.

Prusher, Ilene R., "Rich Donors Try to Finesse Flow of $4.5 Billion into Afghanistan," *Christian Science Monitor*, January 23, 2002.

Quinlivan, James T., "Force Requirements in Stability Operations," *Parameters: U.S. Army War College Quarterly*, Vol. XXV, No. 4, Winter 1995–1996, pp. 59–69.

Radio Free Europe/Radio Liberty, *RFE/RL Balkan Report*, Vol. 6, No. 47, December 20, 2002.

_____, *RFE/RL Balkan Report*, Vol. 5, No. 76, November 16, 2001.

Reuters, "NATO Eyes More Troop Cuts in Balkans," January 15, 2003.

Rose, Donald G., "FM 3-0 Operations: The Effect of Humanitarian Operations on US Army Doctrine," *Small Wars and Insurgencies*, Vol. 13, No. 1, Spring 2002, pp. 57–82.

Rose, Gideon, "The Exit Strategy Delusion," *Foreign Affairs*, Vol. 77, No. 1, January/February 1998, pp. 56–67.

Sadiki, Larbi, "Towards Arab Liberal Governance: From the Democracy of Bread to the Democracy of the Vote," *Third World Quarterly*, Vol. 18, No. 1, 1997, pp. 127–148.

Schaller, Michael, *The American Occupation of Japan,* New York: Oxford University Press, 1985.

Schmitt, Eric, "In Afghanistan: What's Past and What's Still to Come," *New York Times,* October 13, 2002.

Schonberger, Howard B., *Aftermath of War,* Kent, Ohio: The Kent State University Press, 1989.

Schulte, Gregory L., "Former Yugoslavia and the New NATO," *Survival,* Vol. 39, No. 1, Spring 1997, pp. 19–42.

Schwartz, Eric P., *Iraq: The Day After,* Report of an Independent Task Force on Post-Conflict Iraq Sponsored by the Council on Foreign Relations, New York: Council on Foreign Relations, 2003.

Schwartz, Thomas Alan, *America's Germany: John J. McCloy and the Federal Republic of Germany,* Cambridge, Mass.: Harvard University Press, 1991.

Scott, James, "Rebuilding a Country, One Village at a Time," *Charleston* [S.C.] *Post and Courier,* July 14, 2002, p. 9.

Seiple, Chris, *The U.S. Military/NGO Relationship in Humanitarian Interventions,* Carlisle, Pa.: U.S. Army War College Peacekeeping Institute, 1996.

Slevin, Peter, "U.S. Troops Working Relief to Modify Clothing," *Washington Post,* April 21, 2002.

Smyth, Gareth, "US Will Oversee Return of Displaced Kurds," *Financial Times,* April 24, 2003.

Snyder, James M., *The Establishment and Operations of the United States Constabulary, 3 October 1945–30 June 1947,* Historical subsection C-3, United States Constabulary, 1947.

State, War and Navy Coordinating Committee, "United States Initial Post-Surrender Policy Relating to Japan" (SWNCC 150/4).

Steiner, Kurt, "Occupation Reforms in Local Government," in Livingston, Oldfather, and Moore (1974), pp. 42–56.

Steiner, Michael, "Address to the [United Nations] Security Council," April 24, 2002.

Stohl, Michael, and George A. Lopez, eds., *The State as Terrorist: The Dynamics of Governmental Violence and Repression,* London: Aldwych Press, 1984.

Sumaida, Hussein, with Carole Jerome, *Circle of Fear,* Toronto: Stoddart, 1991.

SWNCC—*see* State, War and Navy Coordinating Committee.

Thagi, Hashim, and KFOR Commander Lieutenant General Mike Jackson, "Undertaking of Demilitarisation and Transformation by the KLA," Kosovo, June 21, 1999.

Trachtenberg, Marc, *A Constructed Peace: The Making of the European Settlement, 1945–1963,* Princeton, N.J.: Princeton University Press, 1999.

Tripp, Charles, *A History of Iraq,* 2nd ed., Cambridge, United Kingdom: Cambridge University Press, 2001.

_____, "After Saddam," *Survival,* Vol. 44, No. 4, Winter 2002–3, pp. 23–37.

UN—*see* United Nations.

UNHCR—*see* United Nations High Commissioner for Refugees.

UNMIK—*see* United Nations Interim Administration Mission in Kosovo.

United Nations, The Agreement on Provisional Arrangements in Afghanistan Pending the Re-Establishment of Permanent Government Institutions (The Bonn Agreement), December 2001. Online at http://www.uno.de/frieden/afghanistan/talks/agreement.htm (as of June 6, 2003).

_____, "Likely Humanitarian Scenarios," New York, December 10, 2002.

United Nations Assistance Mission in Afghanistan (UNAMA), homepage, 2003. Online at http://www.unama-afg.org/ (as of June 12, 2003).

United Nations Department of Public Information, *The Blue Helmets: A Review of United Nations Peace-Keeping Forces*, 3rd ed., New York, 1996.

United Nations General Assembly, "Assistance for Humanitarian Relief and the Economic and Social Rehabilitation of Somalia," 50th session, item 20(b) of the provisional agenda, A/50/447, September 19, 1995.

United Nations High Commissioner for Refugees, *The State of the World's Refugees 2000: Fifty Years of Humanitarian Action*, New York: Oxford University Press, 2000.

_____, "Assisted Voluntary Repatriation Summary Report," January 31, 2003a.

_____, *Return Statistics*, Sarajevo, February 28, 2003b.

United Nations Interim Administration Mission in Kosovo, UNMIK Police Annual Report 2000, 2000a. Online at http://www.unmikonline.org/civpol/reports/report2000.pdf (as of June 12, 2003).

_____, Bringing Peace to Kosovo Status Report, October 19, 2000b. Online at http://www.un.org/peace/kosovo/pages/kosovo_status.htm (as of June 12, 2003).

_____, *The New Kosovo Government: 2002 Budget*, Pristina, Kosovo, 2002.

_____, UNMIK Police Web site, 2003. Online at http://www.unmikonline.org/civpol/index.html (as of June 12, 2003).

United Nations Joint Logistics Center, Web Site, 2003. Online at http://www.unjlc.org/home/ (as of June 26, 2003).

United Nations Mission in Haiti, Web site, last modified September 19, 2000. Online at http://www.un.org/depts/dpko/dpko/co_mission/unmih.htm (as of June 26, 2003).

United Nations Office for the Coordination of Humanitarian Affairs, "Humanitarian Situation and Action 2003," December 31, 2002.

_____, ReliefWeb site, 2003. Online at http://www.reliefweb.int/w/rwb.nsf (as of June 18, 2003).

United Nations Security Council, Resolution 751, on Somalia, April 24, 1992. Online at http://www.un.org/documents/sc/res/1992/scres92.htm (as of June 12, 2003).

_____, Resolution 794, on Somalia, December 3, 1992.

_____, Resolution 814, on Somalia, March 26, 1993. Online at http://www.un.org/Docs/scres/1993/scres93.htm (as of June 12, 2003).

_____, Resolution 837, on Somalia, June 6, 1993. Online at http://www.un.org/Docs/scres/1993/scres93.htm (as of June 13, 2003).

_____, Resolution 1031 (1995), on implementation of the Peace Agreement for Bosnia and Herzegovina and transfer of authority from the UN Protection Force to the multinational Implementation Force (IFOR), December 15, 1995. Online at http://www.un.org/Docs/scres/1995/scres95.htm (as of June 12, 2003).

_____, Resolution 1244, on the situation relating to Kosovo, June 10, 1999. Online at http://www.un.org/Docs/scres/1999/sc99.htm (as of June 12, 2003).

_____, Resolution 1386, on the situation in Afghanistan, December 20, 2001. Online at http://www.un.org/Docs/scres/2001/sc2001.htm (as of June 13, 2003).

_____, Resolution 1401, on the situation in Afghanistan, March 28, 2002. Online at http://www.un.org/Docs/scres/2002/sc2002.htm (as of June 13, 2003).

_____, Resolution 1441, on the situation between Iraq and Kuwait, November 8, 2002. Online at http://www.un.org/Docs/scres/2002/sc2002.htm (as of June 13, 2003).

USAID—see U.S. Agency for International Development.

U.S. Agency for International Development, "Rebuilding Afghanistan: Our Current Efforts in a War-Torn Country," April 11, 2002. Online at http://www.usaid.gov/about/afghanistan/rebuilding_afghanistan.pdf (as of June 6, 2003).

_____, "Iraq Humanitarian and Reconstruction Assistance Fact Sheet," No. 24, May 1, 2003.

U.S. Bureau of the Census, International Data Base, October 10, 2002. Online at http://www.census.gov/ipc/www/idbacc.html (as of June 12, 2003).

U.S. Department of the Army, *Civil Affairs Operations*, Washington, D.C., Field Manual 41-10, January 11, 1993.

U.S. Department of State, *Occupation of Japan: Policy and Progress*, Far Eastern Series 17, Washington, D.C.: U.S. Government Printing Office, Pub. 267, 1946.

_____, *Occupation of Germany: Policy and Progress 1945–46*, Washington D.C.: U.S. Government Printing Office, Pub. 2783, 1947.

_____, "U.S. Humanitarian Demining Assistance to Bosnia-Herzegovina," media note, Office of the Spokesman, Washington, D.C., April 17, 2000.

_____, International Information Programs, "U.S. Congress OKs Another $14 Million for Demining in Balkans," press release, March 22, 2002.

U.S. Joint Chiefs of Staff, JCS Directive 1067, April 1945.

_____, JCS Directive 1380/15 (date unknown). See Supreme Commander for the Allied Powers, *Political Reorientation of Japan: September 1945 to September 1948*, Vol.. 2, Washington, D.C.: U.S. Government Printing Office, 1949, pp. 423–439.

_____, Joint Doctrine for Civil-Military Operations, Washington, D.C., Joint Publication (JP) 3-57, February 8, 2001.

U.S. War Department, Office of the Adjutant General, Machine Records Branch, *Strength of the Army*, Washington, D.C., December 1, 1945.

Vesilind, Priit J., "In Focus: Bosnia," *National Geographic*, Vol. 189, No. 6, June 1996, pp. 48–61.

The White House, Managing Complex Contingency Operations, Washington, D.C., Presidential Decision Directive 56, May 1997.

Online at http://www.fas.org/irp/offdocs/pdd56.htm (as of June 12, 2003).

World Bank, *Haiti-Emergency Economic Recovery Credit,* Washington, D.C., Report No. PIC1271, 1997.

World Bank and European Commission, *Bosnia and Herzegovina: 1996–1998 Lessons and Accomplishments,* Washington, D.C., 1999.

_____, *Report on Progress Made in Committing, Contracting and Spending Donor Pledges to Kosovo,* Washington, D.C., May 2002.

Ziemke, Earl F., *The U.S. Army in the Occupation of Germany 1944–1946,* Army Historical Series, Washington, D.C.: Center of Military History, 1975.

James Dobbins, lead author for this report, is Director of the International Security and Defense Policy Center at RAND. A career diplomat and veteran troubleshooter who has held senior White House and State Department positions under four Presidents, he most recently served as the Bush administration's special envoy for Afghanistan. Ambassador Dobbins served throughout the 1990s as a U.S. special envoy for Kosovo, Bosnia, Haiti, and Somalia, where he oversaw postconflict stabilization and reconstruction missions. His White House and State Department posts have included Assistant Secretary of State for Europe, Special Assistant to the President for the Western Hemisphere, Special Adviser to the President and Secretary of State for the Balkans, and Ambassador to the European Community. In the wake of the September 11, 2001, attacks, Dobbins was charged with putting together and installing a successor to the Taliban regime and reopening the American Embassy in Kabul.

John G. McGinn, colead author for this report, specialized in postconflict operations and defense strategy development during his tenure as a RAND political scientist. He is currently a Special Assistant in the Office of the Secretary of Defense. A former Army officer, he has a Ph.D. from Georgetown University and a B.S. from the United States Military Academy.

Keith Crane is a Senior Economist at RAND, where he works on transition issues in Eastern Europe, China, energy, transportation, and national security. He was also Chief Operating Officer and Director of Research at PlanEcon Inc., a Washington, D.C.–based research and consulting firm dealing with issues related to Central and Eastern Europe and the former Soviet republics. He holds a Ph.D. in economics from Indiana University.

Seth G. Jones is an Associate Political Scientist at RAND, where he specializes in counterterrorism, Middle East security, and European foreign and defense policy. He has also been Adjunct Professor at Georgetown University, Europe Editor at *The Christian Science Monitor*, and a fellow at the Carnegie Endowment for International Peace.

Rollie Lal is a Political Scientist at RAND, conducting research on international security policy in Asia. She is a South Asia specialist, focusing on U.S.-India strategic relations and the security implications of India's changing foreign relations and internal dynamics. She completed her Ph.D. in International Relations at Johns Hopkins School of Advanced International Studies.

Andrew Rathmell is a Research Leader at RAND Europe (United Kingdom). He leads research and analysis in counterterrorism, intelligence policy, Middle East security, and information assurance.

Rachel Swanger is manager for foundation and independent research at RAND. She focuses on issues related to Japanese history, politics, foreign policy, and defense.

Anga R. Timilsina is a doctoral fellow at the RAND Graduate School of Policy Analysis. He completed an M.A. in international development as an Asian Development Bank Scholar and with a Dean's Award of Academic excellence at the International University of Japan. He also earned a M.A. and B.A. from Tribhuvan University in Kathmandu.